good vibrations

COAST TO COAST BY HARLEY

good vibrations

COAST TO COAST BY HARLEY

Tom Cunliffe

SUMMERSDALE

Summersdale Publishers Ltd
46 West Street
Chichester
West Sussex
PO19 1RP
UK

www.summersdale.com

Printed and bound in Great Britain by Cox & Wyman Ltd, Reading.

ISBN 1 84024 113 6

Cover design by Blue Lemon

The motorcycle, black madonna, two-wheeled gypsy queen,
And her silver-studded phantom caused the grey-flannel dwarf to scream.
As he weeps two wicked birds of prey pick up on his breadcrumb sins,
And there are no sins inside the gates of Eden.

Bob Dylan 'Gates of Eden' 1965

contents

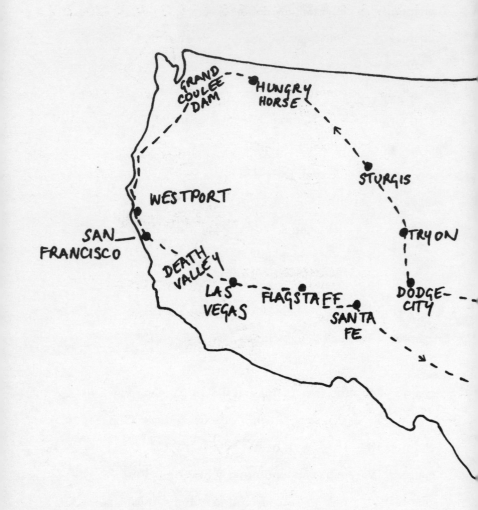

COAST TO COAST BY HARLEY

For many travellers, the mode of transport is arbitrary. To others, a charismatic vehicle such as a sailing vessel or a motorcycle can raise the mere function of running off the miles into an end in itself. Both demand a high degree of awareness and co-ordination, while abuse of either can lead directly to disaster. Despite the dangers, however, a diverse multitude of individuals undergo inconvenience, discomfort and sometimes penury just for the joy of making them go. On a major trip, boats and bikes have a way of opening doors that might otherwise remain shut, thus adding double value to the voyager's experience.

Most of my working life has been spent sailing; my preferred road machines have always had two wheels and a hefty engine. America has often been my destination and for two years its shoreline was home. This story is about how I struck out inland with Roz, my wife, to investigate the rest of the United States from the perspective of a pair of itinerant bikers. The ride alone was worth the fuel bill, while the people we met rounded out thirty years of intermittent familiarity with the coastal communities.

Conclusions about other nations are hazardous, and I have hesitated to draw any. Readers may find their own among the tyre tracks.

chapter one

searching the streets for betty

The day began with a hunt for a bike suitable for Roz. It didn't take long to exhaust the slim pickings off the Washington Beltway and move on to the hot-house streets of Baltimore. We were both jet-lagged after a classic departure from Britain – four hours' sleep, a delayed flight and aggravation in the luggage queue – so morale was easily eroded. Buying a motorcycle might not sound a major challenge for a woman in good shape who has battled gales off Greenland and fronted up to drunken dockers in Leningrad, but we'd found nothing in two sweltering days and I could tell that the latest used-bike joint shook her confidence.

From the outside, it was a squat, oblong box set ten yards from a shouting street corner where brakes squealed and vehicles poured out their heat at the traffic lights. Inside, the racket was hardly muted by the thin walls and there was no air-conditioning to ease our pain, but at least we were sheltered from the sun. Tossing the local newspaper advertisements page on to a pile of rubbish behind the door, I glanced around. Dead machines of indeterminate ancestry lay against the walls; rat-bikes still carried the dust of the plains in the spent oil beneath their crank cases; in a greasy corner a man with a nasty scar was ripping the skin off his knuckles trying to coax life into a Japanese no-hoper, while up front stood a 'full-dress' Harley-Davidson sporting the most tasteless, mock zebra seat cover ever devised. The motorcycles were demoralising, but it was the character slinking out of a door labelled 'Sales' that seemed to be creeping under Roz's skin.

She wore white stiletto slingbacks, a heavy chain on her right ankle and a long red dress slit to the knickers with a couple of buttons for modesty, which weren't done up. The higher reaches of the creation were equally revealing and a colourful tattoo of a murder weapon leered out from its left side just north of the cleavage.

'How can I help you?' Voice low and breathy. She ignored Roz and planted herself in front of me, looking directly up through the mascara.

At six and a half feet tall, I enjoy a splendid view of women in low-cut dresses who stand too close. I benefited from this now, but tore my gaze from the dripping dagger.

'My wife,' I said, 'wants a used Harley-Davidson that'll make it to the West Coast and back.'

She tossed her frizzed blonde mane and countered by asking if I was Australian. Lucky for her she wasn't accusing an Aussie of being a Brit, I thought. He might take offence. Not me though. I began to tell her that I was from Lancashire, but she had already clambered away through the heaps to an elderly blue Harley with an 8,000 dollar price tag. For an awful moment I feared she might throw a leg over it, but she invited Roz to give it a go instead. The seat had been fashionably lowered in some former life, so at least the bike was the right height from the ground. The first we'd seen.

Gingerly, Roz wormed her way into the sagging saddle to reassure herself that with the 'chopped' custom styling her feet easily reached the grimy floor. This was at least a beginning, because if a girl can't reach God's firm earth and has to support 600 pounds of iron from a standing start, she's backing a loser. Despite evidence on the tank and handlebars of a slide down some highway, this bike was the first to be chalked up for the trial squad, but it only took a couple of seconds to conclude that it wasn't going to make the final selection.

'Never mind the state of it,' Roz hissed in my ear, 'check out the starter button.'

There wasn't one. The bike was so ancient it had a kick-start.

A week earlier, on her forty-fifth birthday, Roz had passed her motorcycle test rather than risk sitting behind me for the entire trip. Paddling her own canoe has always been her style, but the sixth-hand, lightweight Suzuki that had satisfied the Minister of Transport's legal representative on the breezy heathlands of southern England, cut no ice with the massive reality of the all-American road-burner. The only similarities between 'Suzie' and this two-wheeled monster were a lack of electric starting and a readiness for the bone yard. Booting a tiny, worn down two-stroke into life might just be acceptable, Roz's look implied, but jumping up and down on an ill-tuned lump of rust more than ten times its mass was not on her list of 'things I must do'.

I didn't blame her. I remembered walking with a limp for weeks after spraining an ankle starting my Matchless, easy meat compared with this wild animal. That had been thirty years earlier back in Liverpool when I was a law student and founder member of the 'Ton-in-the-Tunnel Club'.

In those days, the two-mile Mersey Tunnel suffered from a provocative 30mph limit. The trick was to hit the entrance at 3a.m., dawdle casually past the security men, wind the bike up to 100 along the straight section under the river with your exhausts howling back from the walls and the lights flashing by like a lunatic fairground, then trundle out the other end after stopping for a minute or so before the last corner in case the cops were timing you through. I fancy I'm smarter now and didn't relish kicking the Harley either, so making lame excuses about blue being the wrong colour, we made for the door.

'What shade d'you want then?' The dragon came back fighting, armed with a closing question cunningly sheathed in compliance as her victims slipped the trap.

'It would have to be red,' replied Roz, marching on to sure ground. There wasn't a red Harley in the shop.

'Red's easy,' retorted the lady. I looked at her outfit and agreed. 'We can have it painted in a couple of days. You wanna take her for a blow down the road, Honey, while the big feller's sorting out the money?'

Having just been nailed by the hoariest selling trick in the book, we escaped by deploying the toughest chestnut in the unwilling buyer's manual.

'Great bike,' I lied. 'We'll think about it and let you know.'

Out on the street, the temperature was way up in the nineties with humidity high enough to soak our jeans. Watching the traffic, I thought about my own Harley, fresh off the boat from England and waiting to be bailed out of the customs pound down at the docks. Eighteen-wheeler trucks roared by shaking the ground, their engine covers the size of shipping containers, while tiny imported motor cars and self-conscious American lookalikes shuffled around their mighty tyres. Size has mattered for transport here ever since the first transcontinental railroad locomotives arose to dwarf their British forebears. The tradition has continued through rolling stock, the Flying Fortress of World War II, the battleship and, of course, the automobile. Building things large is the

American way. The trucks seemed an honest part of the scene. Not so the private transport.

Why, I wanted to know, has Detroit become embarrassed about its heritage, and whatever happened to those glories of the road that so recently proclaimed, 'Nobody else in the world can afford to be the size I am. I've got Style, Baby, with a capital S.'? The car manufacturers might have abandoned tradition, but nobody could accuse the only surviving motorcycle builder on the continent of capitulating to passing fashion. Heavy, chrome-embellished, noisy, with performance akin to a mad rhinoceros, Harley-Davidsons are Neanderthal by the standards of most modern motorcycles. Fast enough in a straight line, they offer no quarter when it comes to turning a corner and they are the very devil to stop, yet nothing on two wheels can approach them for charisma. Steel horses for the cowboys of today's concrete prairies, they remain as lonely survivors from the sunshine days when gas was cents for a gallon and Americans knew who they were.

'I think I need to chill out,' said Roz, as we slumped back into our rented Oldsmobile. The idea that discovering the right machine inside the US would be anything other than easy had never crossed our minds, yet here at the fountainhead, the bike we sought, if it existed outside our imaginations, was keeping itself securely hidden. Still reeling after Washington, Baltimore was now flogging us into retreat with its soul-sapping humidity. Desperation was eating at our composure, so we gave up on the newspaper small ads and headed south-east to Annapolis in search of a local dealership cooled by breezes from the Chesapeake Bay.

An hour later we swept into town past the soaring domes of the Naval Academy and on to where 'Harley-Davidson of

Annapolis' stood squarely at the opposite end of the 'Sales and Service' spectrum from the witch's cave. We parked under a huge Stars and Stripes floating on the afternoon breeze, dashed across ten yards of superheated reality and stepped into a climate-controlled fantasy world of self-confident tranquillity.

Gleaming bikes stood at ease on every side, modestly diverting attention from their colossal price tags. There were no brand-new ones because of a national two-year waiting list, with factory machines rarely making it as far as the showrooms. No such hold-ups trouble the buyer back in Britain, a situation that beggars understanding, but it was not for us to question the wisdom of one of America's most successful corporations. We had to leave that to millions of frustrated local bikers.

Glimpsed through the spotless chromium forest, a girl with eyes to go to jail for presided over racks of leathers and other flash gear. Out the back was the parts counter with an old-fashioned biker in charge. Tall and weather-beaten, the years whirling beneath his spokes had left him a grey ponytail and a pair of John Lennon glasses that stayed on if you were a straight operator, but looked as though they might still come off for an occasional showdown. Behind him and all around us, the cool, cream-painted walls were set off with giant posters proclaiming the true religion of the motorcycle.

Just inside the door of this air-conditioned temple, a jaunty, low-slung yellow bike sat coyly on her side stand perfuming the air with oil and polished leather. It was love at first sight. Roz hopped aboard before Scott, the dealer's son, had had time to check us out. She inspected the 'peanut' gas tank with its bold '883 Sportster' insignia; caressed the stylish saddlebags designed for Posers' Boulevard, made to hold a half of nothing; wrapped her long hands around the sexy buckhorn handlebars; then frisked the leather tassels hanging demurely from various strategic sites waiting to stream bravely on the wind. I noted the straight-through exhaust pipes that promised a clatter like an early machine gun and mused on noise emission laws.

Received wisdom is that nobody can push an 883 more than 100 miles, let alone across the continent. The engine just isn't hefty enough, it is said, and the diminutive fuel tank will never make it to triple figures. We deliberated this and Roz tried her luck with a 1200cc. Not a chance. It was far too heavy for someone whose last machine had been virtually a toy and besides, the seat seemed so ill-fitting for a lady that it could generate blisters without leaving the showroom. Clearly, there was only one choice. It had to be the sunshine Sportster and to hell with the pundits.

The bike was wheeled out into the furnace blast of the late afternoon while Roz kitted up. Proper motorbike boots, leather jacket, gauntlets and full-face helmet.

'You'll fry, Babe,' the man with the ponytail said kindly. 'Leave your helmet here. We'll look after your armour.'

I could see Roz was already sweating inside her gear, but I understood her concerns. For all she knew, she'd drop the Harley on her leg at the first junction. It generally takes a minute or so before someone reacts to help you, and as you lie there pinned down by the weight, the hot metal of the exhaust pipes soon burns through your jeans. Next it's your calves for the branding iron, and the cooking smell is depressing. There's also the skin ripped clean off your shoulders and the broken arm. With all this in mind, she was easing back on fashion and comfort to opt for some protection.

'I've left my leather pants in the car, you know,' Roz said, hoping to mollify her advisers, and I knew that even this had taken moral fibre. She had never been on a bike without full shielding before and I could sense her anxiety as she dug deep into her reserves of self-belief and let in the clutch. I was terrified the bike would stall, or she'd decide it was too much of a beast and the whole trip would be over, but the engine hesitated for a split second, then throbbed powerfully, pulling steadily away. After an initial, heart-stopping wobble, things seemed to stabilise as Roz changed up and opened the throttle. I almost cheered out loud as she rode off down the street.

To set the 883 in perspective for the lay person, it needs to be said that until the Japanese arrived on the scene in the 1960s with their 'rice-burners', few bikes of more than 650cc had been available in Europe. A motorcycle the size of the Sportster would have been beyond the dreams of the craziest pack leader at the Ace Café on London's North Circular Road in the monochrome days of rockers, Nortons, Bonnevilles and Marianne Faithfull, when 'good' was middle class, 'bad' misunderstood and the motorcycle offered stark hope to a generation of inarticulate searchers.

One look at Roz test-riding the primrose Harley reminded the boys in the workshop of the Betty Boop cartoon glamour girl who seems always to be hanging on in extraordinary circumstances; so 'Betty Boop' the bike became. Tim, the parts man, was still shaking his head over the choice of so 'small' a vehicle, but the question of whether Betty would arrive back on the East Coast smiling after 10,000 miles or be dumped, defeated, far out in the desert, could not be resolved in a shiny showroom. The answer would be found in the lands where talk is recognised for the jade it can be, and only the crankshaft bearings speak the truth.

We paid for Betty at six o'clock, long after the insurance underwriters had left their offices. There would be no riding her that evening, so we did a deal on a three and a half-gallon highway tank to be fitted the next day and used the phone to locate an old friend. Clark answered the call, and we hopped aboard the cool, white Oldsmobile and steered southwards into the woods.

Often to be found far from his native North Carolina, Clark has been a regular feature of our visits to the Eastern Seaboard. On this occasion, he was renting a neat wooden house nestling amid idyllic green woodland. White-painted, surrounded by screened porches and set on rising ground, the light summer breeze wafted through the building in a way that rendered air-conditioning redundant. A good thing, Clark later observed, because there wasn't any. We wandered around the back looking for him and discovered him flicking his battered Zippo under an orderly pile of boatyard scraps for a barbecue. I lobbed him the ritual six-pack of cold Beck's. He looked different, but I couldn't work out why.

'How's it goin', shipmates?' He opened a beer and up-ended its misted length to his lips in the sultry evening.

'Right enough if you don't mind melting. How about yourself?'

'Things are slow,' his easy Southern speech was like a homecoming. 'I'm not building boats commercially any more and it seems years since I earned a buck sailing.'

'Market not up to much?'

'Nothing wrong with that. But I'm working on a new project. No long-term point in making boats for rich people – "There you are, Sir. She floats. Ain't she pretty? Thank you, Ma'am, here's your bill. We don't take cheques." – I've set up a scheme for bringing kids from the city, giving them a workshop and something to do where they'll have to rely on one another. After they've built a boat or two, I'll teach them how to sail as well. They'll learn a trade and get some value into their lives.'

'So why are things not moving?'

'Everyone says the idea's fine. The town loves it, the government loves it, committees of wealthy people love it, I guess even the kids'd love it if they ever got a chisel in their hands. Trouble is nobody wants to put up any money, so I'm burnin' up my life tryin' to raise cash.'

'How's that work?'

'I have meetings with bankers, then well-intentioned guys and folks who want to see their names up in lights for doin' something good organise dinners for rich "maybes" and invite me along. One of them even wants to shove me sideways an' run the show. He sounds impressive to the trust-fund brigade, but he couldn't find a bottle of rum in a distillery. Whole thing's like beatin' against the current.'

As we talked, Mara, a house guest from out West returned. She kissed Clark on his shaven cheek, and I realised what was different about him. He had hacked off the most handsome El Greco beard on the North Atlantic so that businessmen in BMWs would trust him. Somehow, he looked diminished by it, but he was no fool, so clearly he'd done what he had to.

The day faded while we were eating our chicken, corn and potatoes, but its remains stayed jungle-hot. As the fire died, squadrons of whining, biting bugs zoomed in to the attack.

The locals whacked and smacked at them professionally for half an hour or so before admitting defeat and fleeing up the steps to safety inside the porch. In the darkness before moonrise, crickets kept up a non-stop buzzing and fireflies danced in the blackness beyond our screened haven as we drilled our way to the bottom of a quart of bourbon. In the deepening night, Mara talked of Flagstaff, Arizona, where she and her two young children were living in a small apartment with Fred, the father of neither of them. She told Roz about Hopi Indian villages high on mesas at the edge of Navajo country, and I fell to dreaming of the road stretching ever westward. It had always sounded a long way off. As the level in the bottle sank like water running through a meanly charged coffee filter, it began to seem even further, but progress on the bike front was promising and I could hardly wait to get cracking.

Shortly before midnight, Clark had soaked up enough whiskey to forget his troubles and blow the dust from his grandfather's copy of Uncle Remus. He perched himself high on a beat-up sideboard in the candlelight and read to the company in the full magnificence of his Southern drawl. Sadly, he lost interest just as Brer Rabbit hit the briar patch and we were on the edge of our seats, but as his eyes glazed over in the warmth of remembered companionship he sang us a sea shanty in a fine, strong tenor ringing from another life. Then he passed out, and reaching to help him I somehow contrived to fall down the stairs to the yard. The women now retired, leaving the men to live or die.

At the time, death seemed a soft option, but as I lay upside down I noticed the moon sailing out through the clouds from the east and remembered why I was there. Everything in the land seemed to be chasing the sunset westwards, and I thought for a moment about whether riding back towards this coast in a couple of months would feel unnatural. From my inverted perspective, the road to California spanned half the planet so, providing our resolve held firm and we kept the bikes upright, it was more than possible that the question would never arise.

In any case, the idea was too complicated to unravel, so I sagged off to sleep rather than try.

chapter two

bureaucracy baffles bikers

The modern port of Baltimore is so immense that it's hard for someone from a small country to get his head around it. Far from the oasis of Clark's house, our search for the shipping agent's office to rescue my bike led us through a melting noontime desert of wharves and warehouses to a group of colossal sheds surrounded by idling trucks and comatose truckers. We peered through a doorway into a hall the size of an aircraft hangar, echoing and empty. A thin, solitary man in a grey overall was sweeping dust into clouds in a far corner. We hiked across.

'Where's Wallenius Shipping?'

'Huh?'

'Wallenius Line.'

'Ladies' room? Out back and left down the row.'

'Thanks a lot . . .'

It was worrying that he didn't understand a word we said. Were our accents really so outrageous? But we followed his pointing finger to a rudimentary toilet facility which, like all sensible travellers, we used while we had the chance.

Hoping to improve on this failure, we tried the map instead. American road systems are generally logical and well sign-posted, but for some reason Brits of all classes have made an art form of getting lost on them. Still learning to fathom how the tarmac matched the clearly printed sheet, we blundered on down steadily deteriorating tracks until we finally lost our nerve on the edge of a pothole the size of a glacier crevasse.

The car rocked gently on its soft suspension as we stared in fascination at a vision of hell deserted.

Stark against the blue sky stood the colossal shell of an abandoned factory, which I fancied could once have been an outlet of the all-powerful Bethlehem steel works. Ridge after silent ridge, the roofs sagged and lurched in the still air. Smoke-blackened chimneys pointed to the vacuum of space like accusing fingers, ranks of blind windows gazed only inwards, while all around lay the general detritus of industrial America moving on.

Oh God of Bethel, by whose hand, thy people still are fed . . . The scene of dereliction stood light years apart from the images created by Dodd's 1755 hymn. What had arisen in the mind of the founding father who homesteaded here, to name the land he had wrestled glade by glade from forest Indians after the Judaean town? And what had gone wrong over the intervening three centuries? . . . *Who through this weary pilgrimage, hast all our fathers led.*

Fifty yards towards the sheds, a crow pecked apathetically at something unspeakable in the dirt. We paused for a while in respectful introspection as one does in a cathedral, then turned back towards the docks.

More by fortune than planning, a brief drive and a short walk brought us to the agents. We were relieved of eighty-five dollars in cash – no credit cards accepted – for the dockers' efforts and sent onwards across miles of sun-baked gravel to the customs shed for the next stage of what was starting to feel like springing my bike from prison.

Having dealt with stone-faced immigration officials on waterfronts from Rio to Russia, we felt confident that extracting Black Madonna from the US Customs shed would be pregnant with difficulty. It was not. The horrors slammed in a day later from an offside position. The Customs men were sweetness itself. We told them our plans and showed them our papers. They stamped everything, completed various forms in triplicate, handed me a 'release' to give to the jailer and wished us well.

Struggling to believe it was this easy, I decided to try the question that I had imagined would not dare to speak its name. The prices on used bikes in the showrooms suggested that Harleys like mine were actually worth more here than back in the UK. In case someone made me an offer I couldn't refuse, I had to know if there would be punishing import duties, or some other barrier to honest trade.

'Just suppose,' I asked casually, 'that, say, I felt inclined to sell this bike. What would be the position?'

'You can hawk it outside the dock gates for all we care,' said the boss. 'If it was an Eyetalian Ducati or one of them BMWs from Germany, that would be different,' then he continued with an almost straight face, 'but this is US made, is compliant with all US standards and is a credit to the American way of life. So it's OK.'

'It ain't no credit from where I'm sitting,' an officer who hitherto had said nothing spoke up as we were walking out the door, 'if I were you, I'd sell that flash heap of scrap first thing in the morning an' get yourself a Honda.'

I waited with indrawn breath for the avenging chain whirled by the all-American god, Harley, to crash through the ceiling and strike this heretic dead. But the cooling fans went on squeaking and nothing happened at all. In pragmatic Europe, people who ride Harley-Davidsons are sometimes suspected of suffering personality disorders for the logical reason that they could be operating faster, better-handling Japanese machines at half the price. There is far more to a Harley, however, than such naive considerations. I've known plenty of properly set-up madmen who have been proud proprietors, but there is something about the massively engineered brashness of these rolling icons that agitates unenlightened non-Americans. Particularly if they are bikers themselves. I'd have expected a remark like that back in Blighty, but never in a land where grown men strut around in Harley T-shirts that announce, 'If you have to ask why, you'll never understand.'

Fortunately for my sanity, one of this misguided commentator's colleagues took up the cudgel for national decency and waded into him on patriotic grounds. Roz and I slipped away, unable to believe our luck. Sadly, that was where it ran out.

To save us a further trip to the docks and a day of rental car charges, we had decided to whizz the bike straight out of its lock-up, and side-step the issue of insurance for the moment. We would buy that the following morning. Organising cover over in the US was necessary because, understandably, no firm back home was interested and also because Roz's bike had been an unknown quantity when we left. Since a minimum of third party liability cover is a legal requirement in Britain for motorcycles just as it is for any other motor vehicle, we assumed without question that the same would hold in the Land of the Free. We therefore decided to travel 'two-up' back to Annapolis as though there was a bottle of Bud balanced on my fuel tank, and avoid cops. A sound scheme, but it fell at the first hurdle.

Taking the release papers to Wallenius' shed at five minutes to four should have seen us away on the bike, dumping the car and grabbing Betty Boop from Annapolis. Through a dirty window I could discern the 'Heritage' behind a padlocked door. Apart from warehouse dust, Madonna looked none the worse for her ocean passage. Her wide, 'fat-boy' handlebars still set off the sleek, jet-black tank with its discreet, purple, coach stripes, the studded leather-work and the stark, black and chrome V-twin engine.

We had the paperwork, we'd paid the money, but the docker with the keys had sloped off work early. I complained at the office window, where a man in a moth-eaten vest and the obligatory baseball hat shrugged his shoulders.

'Your bike'll still be here tomorrow,' he advised philosophically.

There was nothing to be done, but the situation wasn't a dead loss. At least, we reasoned, we should be able to sort out the insurance in the morning and still be away before the weekend.

On our way out, we lined up the Oldsmobile behind four or five trucks at the dock gates, where the window on the security block was sited so high in order to accommodate the cabs that I couldn't reach the sill, even by stretching up. From somewhere above came the amplified command, 'Next!' I clambered on to the bonnet of the car to confront a checkout lady who looked like James Bond's ghastly adversary from *Smersh*, the nightmarish Rosa Klebb. She was looking for trouble, but couldn't find any. I handed her a release form I'd been given for the car and she nodded me through reluctantly. Roz was pulling away when suddenly the barrier slammed down. A heavy-duty cop appeared from nowhere and leaned into her window. His blue shirt was covered in badges like a

Boy Scout patrol leader, he had a broken nose and he smelt of yesterday's hot dog.

'Gimme your release.'

'I think we just did,' Roz replied.

'That one on the dashboard.'

'That's for our motorcycle. The bike's still in the pound. We'll need that form tomorrow.'

'Gimme the form, Lady.'

'If we do that,' I broke in, 'I'll have to go back to the customs for another, and I'm not taking the bike out now. There's only me and her and this car.'

At this point the cop, whose face had started out ugly, turned really unpleasant. I couldn't believe it.

'Don't mess with me,' he rasped, loosening the press stud over his sidearm. 'If I say I want the form, you give me the form.'

We gave him the form.

He screwed it into his trouser pocket and swaggered off back to his lair in the security block, where I supposed the lovely Rosa had the kettle on for a nice cup of tea. No suggestion of a 'Thank you', or the hint of human courtesy. I thought about some poor sod having his motorbike spirited out of the docks unmolested by Rosa or her deputies, and hoped to God it wouldn't be mine. There is a world of difference between asking a London Bobby the way to Mornington Crescent and arguing with a policeman weighed down with gun, ammo and night stick, sporting an extrovert pair of handcuffs at his waistband.

The Great Insurance Stress Binge began back at Clark's place the following morning. Four months previously, I had called

Harley-Davidson Insurance in the US to see how the land lay. A comprehensive policy for two bikes had been readily promised at reasonable rates.

'No problem,' the obliging chap had advised, exuding the brotherhood of the road. 'Just pick up the phone when you're ready.'

So I did, and was answered by a computer. I punched 'five' for 'new business' from the various electronic options and Harley propaganda came booming down the line instead of piped music. I enjoy this oddball mix of image mania and marketing gobbledegook. It beats garbled Mozart, and is an even better laugh than the Handel favoured by my accountant, which sounds like a Thai Temple dancer messing about with the cuckoo from a Swiss clock. Far better the roar of 'four 1200cc Sportsters flat out round the Daytona race track', or 'the local chapter ridin' out of town on a Saturday morning', especially when the rumble of the bikes is back-dropped with seriously funky blues music.

The underwriters of Carson City, Arizona, where the H-D office offers round-the-clock service, were obviously having an early hamburger, because the wait went on for a long time. I was grooving to John Lee Hooker and the obscure sound of 'a 1340cc Evolution engine cooling off after a fast ride' when the line cut them dead and a young lady called Tracy came on. Idly thinking about John Lee and his wayward baby, I told her I was calling to insure my bikes. That, she reassured me, would be no problem, so I groped for my papers and credit card.

First I gave her details of the machines themselves.

Fine.

Next, she asked me where they would be garaged.

I chewed my pencil. They wouldn't be garaged at all, of course, they would be on the road. But I doubted that this was what she wanted to hear.

Doing the right thing as it turned out, I was mean with the truth. She needed to believe the bikes would be kept locked away, so I gave her Clark's address and advised her that we would be doing some touring. That satisfied the form she was filling in, and we swam along merrily until the final question.

'What are the numbers of your Maryland driving licences?'

'We don't have any, but we have international driving permits that are recognised by the Federal Highways Authorities.'

A pause.

Then, 'Just one moment, Sir.'

I stood by to dish out a plastic number that would bill me for the promised 600 dollars.

'Sir, we cannot issue insurance to anyone domiciled in Maryland who does not hold a Maryland driving licence.' Tracy was back on the line and she was not carrying glad tidings.

'Yes you can,' I contradicted politely, imagining her a simple country girl who needed coaching in international matters. 'Your firm already quoted me. They knew I was from the UK and nobody said anything about Maryland licences.' Then I reminded her about the international driving permits.

'What is your quote number, Sir?'

With a sick feeling in my stomach, I had to admit I didn't have one. I had been optimistically content with the glib reassurance that H-D would deliver the goods. It had all seemed so simple at the time.

'I'm sorry, then, you must be mistaken.' Tracy was getting going.

'No, I'm damn well not. I've shipped my bike here on the strength of your company's promise.'

Tracy didn't want to hear about that. She held her stand and her composure without flinching.

'I'm sorry, Sir, I cannot issue insurance unless you have . . . '

'Yes. OK. You've made yourself clear. I'll try buying insurance locally.'

The receiver fell like a guillotine.

What now?

Clark was on the way out to meet a group of well-wishers with no funds. I told him my troubles.

'Jeez,' he shook his head. 'Nothing's ever easy, is it? We have our own problems getting insured for out-of-state vehicles. If we're living away, we just register the bike in the state where we have the licence. You aren't supposed to, but it generally does the trick.'

'But with my licence, it shouldn't make any difference what state the bikes are registered in.'

'Don't you believe it. Bureaucrats and stupid regulations breed in this country. Getting anything done that doesn't fit the boxes on their forms is so difficult that you sometimes feel like giving up. Try my agents here in town, and the best of luck.'

He handed me their business card, hopped into his huge pick-up and buzzed off through the trees.

Clark's agent gave me the same answer as Harley but was less polite about it. I began to feel a dark foreboding.

Roz tried next, with a company plucked from the Yellow Pages. She gave her man the cultivated, low voice on the phone line, all sweet reason. Not at all like me, now flat on the sofa with smoke coming out of my ears. It made no difference. Several calls later the message was crystal clear.

We had a serious problem: two motorcycles ready to go, a major investment in time and money, and no apparent way of making them legal. I have been in one uninsured accident in the US; it involved a boat, a man in New York City rich enough to take responsibility for his misjudgements but too proud to acknowledge them, and a lawsuit. It was not an experience to repeat.

'What happens with aliens who live and work here?' I asked the next agent in the book, but was handed a similar fistful of mould.

'If you're a diplomat or a student or are in the Armed Forces you can have insurance. Otherwise you have to get a local licence.'

'How do we do that?'

'That's easy. You just present your out-of-state licence to the Department of Highways and they'll give you one for a few bucks.'

'How does it work?'

'You take a four-hour course on drug and alcohol abuse, then you get asked questions about road safety. If you come out clean, you're issued with a temporary driving permit. Three weeks later you can take a driving test. Pass it, and you're entitled to a Maryland driving licence.'

I was delighted with the idea of the drug and alcohol abuse course. Perhaps we'd pick up a few useful tips, but further digging revealed the sad fact that as aliens we couldn't hold a Maryland driving licence anyway. You couldn't insure until you had a licence, but you couldn't have a licence whether you were insured or not. I'd been hearing for years that the United

States had become a haven for bureaucratic idiocy, but as a passer-by had never experienced it. Now here it was. Red in tooth and claw, and it had us by the throat.

I sat on the sofa in growing despair, cursing deeply and roundly. Already, I was scheming about selling the bikes to Clark for one dollar and letting him insure them, but I had a feeling it wouldn't be that simple. Roz ignored me and proposed a trip to town to rattle a few cages in person, to let these nameless faces hiding behind their telephones see with their own eyes that we weren't road-rage inspired serial killers. We could also grab a spot of lunch.

Down near waterfront Annapolis we discovered the Moon, 'a global café' where the sixties lived on without a hint of self-consciousness. I left Roz reading something inscribed in flowing script on the wall and strolled over to the gents. The men's room was decorated with planets, stars and optimistic visions of a distant future like images from Neil Young's 'After the Gold Rush'. I parked myself on the throne to wonder how, so soon after the hippy movement had promised sweet reason to all, mankind had arrived at such a bankrupt pass. Before I had an answer, an anxious fellow-sufferer started battering the door down, so I let him in and returned to the late 1990s. Roz had claimed a window table, where she was contemplating a menu of vegetarian marvels. Behind her, above the glass, was a quote from Oscar Wilde. It slotted in well with the images in the 'john'.

'Yes, I am a dreamer, for a dreamer is one who can find his way by moonlight, and see the dawn before the rest of the world.'

Our waitress skipped up wearing brief shorts of blue denim and a weenie bodice of the same material. I guessed she would be brown all over, but she wasn't born when I was picked up hitching on the Massachusetts Turnpike in 1967 by a girl who looked a lot like her. Marian had been all thick, dark hair, cheekbones and wandering brown eyes. The difference in my case was thirty years and a thickening around the waist; in hers, no flowers in her hair, no coloured beads cascading down her front, and of course, it wasn't really her.

The waitress started her ritual of reciting the day's specials, and my mind drifted away, past the insoluble problems of insurance, back through hazy decades to the sunshine summer when Marian had squealed to a halt in her full-sized convertible Buick. She had a couple of pals with her, but we all jammed into the inviting front bench and blasted off towards Cape Cod at seven-litre speed with the oversize radio speakers spilling out Country Joe and the Fish.

Now if you're tired and a bit run down,
Can't seem to get your feet on the ground,
Maybe you ought to try a little bit of LSD.
Only if you want to . . . [1]

Marian had married at eighteen and had loved her man. He had been drafted to Vietnam with the rest of his generation and had stayed there longer than even Uncle Sam had hoped; so long in fact that he would never be coming home.

Come on mothers, throughout the land,
Pack your boys off to Vietnam;
Come on fathers don't hesitate,
Send your sons off before it's too late;
You can be the first one on your block
To have your boy come home in a box. [2]

The Buick had been bought with money the government awarded her and she was driving out looking to forget and maybe start again. No more the straight life for her. She had rubbed herself off the voting register and signed on with the funsters of those days, when America was less worried about its health and more concerned with immediate issues, such as villagers being napalmed for what somebody else believed in, and the nuclear bomb. Arguing about whether or not you could become addicted to marijuana was irrelevant in times when annihilation seemed a day-to-day possibility.

Marian and her friends took me under their collective wing and together we cruised New England in a heady mix of freedom, serious conversation, insane ramblings and licence of a different kind altogether to that which was now making my adult life a misery. The Buick introduced me to the highways and the girls showed me how you could love a lot of people at once. We picked up strangers on the road, stacked up in desperate motels, ate very little and drank less, but we smoked grass in moonlit graveyards and made love on midnight tombstones while a brasher, mainstream America rushed by on either side.

My face must have betrayed my departure from the present, because our waitress had finished her long list of delights while I daydreamed and was now asking me for my selection.

'I don't think I'm up to any more decisions,' I said hopelessly. She sensed my mood.

'Choose your lunch,' she said with infinite gentleness, 'and be calm.'

It was impossible to imagine such an instruction being given under similar circumstances in Britain. The girl really wanted to be a hippy of the old school. For a moment I entertained unworthy thoughts along the lines of, 'Who are you to patronise me? You're young, white and American, and I'll bet you hold a Maryland driving licence!' but her sweetness probably did well up from the bottom of her privileged heart, so I ordered soup and a 'close-to-the-earth roll' with soya spread. I enjoyed it when it came.

Roz had the same, but instead of sliding off the rails like me, she was plotting her way past the abstract bastion that towered across our road west.

Her first plan involved a full-frontal attack on the State Insurance Investigator, a person whose existence had been hinted at by a number of our tormentors. This harassed official held court in a dusty office strewn with papers somewhere at the back-end of town. He thoughtfully introduced us to what he called the 'No-hopers Insurance Society', an outfit which specialised in covering the uninsurable. I don't recall their official title, but they wouldn't touch us with a long boathook. Gloomily, we trudged back to Harley-Davidson of Annapolis, where Betty Boop was straining at her locking chain and Gary, the dealer, was keen to see her away.

Scott was horrified at our tale. Like Clark and most of the younger generation, he had had a gutful of this sort of nonsense. He abandoned his coffee and almost cooked the phone wires trying to fix us up. Roz and I sat around drinking endless cold Cokes and reading bytes of wisdom framed in embossed letters on the manicured walls.

'God does not deduct from Man's allotted time those hours spent riding a motorcycle.'

The country seemed suddenly full of wise words emphatically not backed up with action. The chance to prove the complacent poster right would have seemed a fine thing. In the end, Scott succeeded, but only at 3,000 dollars per bike and that through Harley-Davidson, the people who were going to do the job for 600 dollars the pair.

The working day was now over. With our heads well down, we cruised back to Clark's in the pale Oldsmobile. There is nothing like denial for fanning desire, and our sole interest was now to climb on our bikes and get going. The idea of grabbing a fistful of throttle and squirting Black Madonna out across the Mojave Desert was all I wanted in the world. Even Roz had set aside her reservations and was itching to boot Betty into gear. The way things looked, however, it was going to be cheaper as well as a sight more comfortable to surf across to the far coast in the Oldsmobile, yet this was too bland a result to contemplate; an insult to the pioneers, the desperadoes, the gamblers and the ordinary, hardworking families emigrating west. For all the exposure to deepest America the rental car would give us, we might as well view the place on video. Out there, the land was only four generations away from plains Indians, virgin forests and driven men ploughing the deserts for gold. Beyond the far-distant Sierra Nevada, the fertile coastal regions had been more easily reached by clipper ship until the Irish Army built the first railroad across the wilderness. Marian's snorting Buick had been a car worthy of such a back-drop, but not our current smooth-running impostor. The following morning, our friend the State Insurance Investigator threw up his arms when he heard about the offer from Harley-Davidson and told us that if we paid that amount we were even more stupid than most bikers. Then he made his considered professional recommendation.

'Why do you want insurance, anyway?' he asked, leaning forward intimately across his cluttered desk. 'The easy answer is just to ride out of here.'

'You mean that's legal?' demanded an incredulous Roz.

'Well,' he picked his words carefully, 'it's not so much what's legal and what isn't. That may vary from state to state. The question's more concerning what happens if you hit somebody, or some guy steals your bikes.'

'Yes, but . . . that's the point, isn't it?'

'Not really. It only becomes the point after it happens. What you do is proceed with due caution, lock 'em up nights, and make damn sure you stay out of trouble.'

'Thanks for the advice,' I said, and the interview terminated.

That was Friday. Eased only slightly by some dedicated drinking, the weekend dragged by in a mixture of frustration, doubt about whether the trip was on at all, and embarrassment at infesting Clark's place for far too long. 'Fish and friends – off after three days' is a maxim only rarely wrong. In addition to these up-front agonies, there was also the hateful spectre of skulking back to Britain having failed at the first obstacle. Plenty had said we'd never make San Francisco and back. Either the deserts would fry us, or we'd be mugged, we'd crash, or the bikes would break down ('Hardly Ablesons', one engineer friend had brutally dubbed them), but not even the most cynical prophet had considered this angle for creating a non-event. The prospect of an ignominious retreat was too humiliating to face.

The new week dawned even hotter than its predecessor, but the sun rose on the decision to let optimism triumph over experience and to ride uninsured if that was what it was going to take, even though we couldn't afford to lose the 20,000 pounds tied up in the bikes to bandits or catastrophic accident. We had sailed the seas without a policy for twenty years and had mostly survived. Maybe we had to chance it again, now that the State Inspector himself had implied that getting caught didn't mean immediate consignment to the Tennessee State Penitentiary, or some other similarly dismal resting place. Buoyed up by the lighter hearts that came with a problem set aside, and resolved to 'underwrite our own insurance', we trundled down to the dealership to take delivery of Betty Boop. Because he offered, we gave the indefatigable Scott a last chance to work a miracle with his telephone manner.

Scott ignored the out-of-hours service at the Harley-Davidson insurance brokerage and sat out the long morning until the light grew over Carson City, Nevada. Then he gave it another hour for the power in that far land to have swallowed a second cup of Harley-Davidson coffee before he hit the lines and waded in. I shall never know what Scott said to the high-ranking lady who made it all happen, because he is a modest man who would quietly shrug off having moved Mount Washington half a mile to improve the view, but when he handed me the phone fifteen minutes later, a creamy voice said that it was sorry for my trouble and, of course, Harley-Davidson would not see two of the faithful stuck. She then sold us the promised policies at the right price as though nothing had happened. Shaking with relieved stress, I collapsed into Scott's chrome-and-leather executive chair. Roz ordered another round of Cokes to celebrate and Gary gave me a T-shirt.

Marking Scott down as the man to sign on if ever we found ourselves on a sinking boat out of sight of land, we rescued Black Madonna from the pound after explaining to the customs men why we needed a second release document. They exchanged glances, hesitated, then gave us one. I often speculated about the fate of the crooked cop, because in the UK the Revenue is mightier than the Law. I hope he got canned.

Dumping the crushing financial burden of the Oldsmobile was like being cold-chiselled out of a ball and chain. That night we revisited Uncle Remus and in the dewy sunshine morning we loaded up the bikes to follow the waning moon westwards into Virginia.

chapter three

wild beasts, camping and tourism

I settled back into my deep, studded saddle and watched as
Roz heaved Betty Boop gingerly off the side stand. She looked
far from secure as she folded the strut away with her left instep,
but she managed to hold the Sportster upright as the mass of
steel crackled into throaty life. All yellow enamel and black
leather, she accelerated away from a shaky start. I kicked
Madonna into first with the heel of my boot, enjoying the
deeper beat of her exhaust, then followed Roz into the trees
down Route 2. Before long the traffic and the woodland
thinned out, and suddenly we were throbbing across the green
open spaces of southern Maryland. Unbelievably, we were on
our way.

The weather was fine and not too hot as we cruised onwards
at the 55mph required by the speed limit. Our policy for the
early part of the trip was to avoid cities. This was less to steer
clear of the crime than to protect Roz until she had gained
enough self-assurance to tackle the frenetic traffic in the streets.
She was still very much a learner. On this first day, we swung
south and west through park-like farmland, admiring picture-
book wooden homesteads where the retired cut their modest
yards sitting on lawnmowers that would have done service as
small farm tractors in southern England.

Apart from the garden machinery, everything seemed on a
smaller scale than we had expected. In glades of cottonwoods,
black families sat on the porches of 'two-down, nothing-
upstairs and half-out-back' clapboard cottages. In contrast with

the prosperity down the road, the paint was thin and cracked. Elderly gents in crumpled trilby hats, cotton vests, and slacks held up by suspenders gossiped in the growing heat. One raised a hand, flashing by as the sun climbed high behind us. The bikes thumped their music into the quiet air; the gleam of their chrome appeared at odds with the softer cameos beside the route, yet they and the passing scene were equally at home in the American July morning.

By lunchtime, I was feeling a stiffness across my shoulders and Roz was more than ready for a break, so we parked up at the small town of Newburg just short of the bridge into Virginia, pulling in at the local 'strip' of restaurants and drive-in stores. We opted for fast food primarily because the air-conditioning in the likes of Taco Bell was as perfect as any on the planet. We also discovered at the outset that the two of us could refuel reliably and nutritiously for three dollars or even less, so long as we only drank tap water.

Noel Coward, that great philosopher and dietary expert, recommended his public, 'Never be tempted by water.' Under different circumstances, I would concur with this, but midday alcohol intake is not smart under these temperatures, even to mad dogs, and any alternatives mass-produced in the US are too sweet for our taste. Iced water is therefore a seductive option, especially as it is free. The Latino youth serving us observed that while it might be tasteless, a glass from the kitchen faucet was at least *mas economico*. The last time I had heard this natty phrase had been from a bum in a tatty poncho extolling the benefits of B&B under a Bolivian market stall in preference to facing the cockroaches in the local doss-house.

With lunch inside us, we crossed the wide Potomac into Virginia. The first useful chart of this waterway was drawn by

John Smith of Pocahontas fame in 1612, by which time it was carrying ships servicing the early colonial plantations, yet even in this most historic region of America, the paradox of its newness compared with my own land was always with me.

Bursting out over the dappled water from the noonday heat was bliss. The bridge was engineered from typical open girders, looking like the sort of structure every British schoolboy used to build with his 'Meccano' set. Beneath us, the navigable waterway was defined by buoys, the very business of my other life. An osprey nesting in the topmark of a navigation beacon far below peered up at me. Normally, he would have been part of my world. Now, I squinted at him like a tourist as I rode steadily by, pressed onwards by the flowing traffic.

The state line at the far side of the bridge heralded a surprising change in conditions. Straight away my bike started bouncing on rougher roads and soon my butt was feeling the strain. Every so often I had to swerve to dodge a pothole. Roz kept right on going ahead of me, but I was curious about how she was faring. Road surfaces can pass almost unnoticed in a car, but to a motorcyclist they are the beginning and, in the worst cases, the end of everything. Within a half-hour, I had stopped to remove my riding leathers as the afternoon temperature cranked a notch higher than even Washington had served up.

Opening the throttle to catch Roz, I enjoyed a few minutes of free riding, passing cars and trucks and letting my engine sing for a change instead of chugging. Soon I was back in her slipstream, following down an uncharacteristically twisty road through fifty miles of forest. She was taking her time, leaning gently, getting used to negotiating bends on the Harley that a modern sports bike wouldn't have noticed. I had a black moment when she lurched sideways to avoid a huge crack in the tarmac only to twitch back again double-quick to leave breathing space for a speeding truck coming the other way. The humidity must have been turning her to liquid inside her black jacket, until final meltdown came at around about the ninety-two degree mark.

'Take it off,' I suggested tactfully as we dismounted at our next drink stop, pointing out my own protective cowhide strapped across my pillion pack. Roz, of course, had been suffering this massive discomfort to give her some chance of escaping injury in case of an unscheduled meeting with the grit. Nonetheless, she was giving my proposition serious thought when two young lads wandered over from a car filling up at the adjacent fuel pump. They looked like adverts for 'what the well-dressed city kid is wearing' in their baseball caps and sloppy T-shirts. Or louts, depending on your perspective.

'Brilliant bikes,' observed the small one with frogs on his trainers.

I eyed him, wondering what was coming next.

'Of course,' this connoisseur of two-wheeled transport continued with a patronising leer, 'when I'm a little older I'll ride a Honda Fireblade.'

'And jolly good luck to you,' I congratulated him on the subtlety of his taste for the ultimate sports bike. You can't argue with a ten-year-old who knows his mind. You'll enjoy doing 150mph on these roads.'

The larger of the two exhibits was more down-to-earth.

'What happens if you blow a front tyre at seventy?' he demanded bluntly. I had a feeling I should be ignoring him, but I let him win.

'You're in trouble.'

Roz's mouth turned down at the corners. She'd been trying not to think about such unpalatable features of the motorbike.

'Yeah. But what happens?'

'The tyre goes flat, but you don't see much of that sort of thing these days with modern rubber.'

'OK Mister. But what happens to you when the tyre goes flat, even if it doesn't go flat often?'

'You fall off and slide down the road at high speed.'

'Great!'

The pair mooched off to a nearby soda machine to keep their weight up, while Roz turned her back on temptation. She zipped up her leather and never rode without it the whole summer, not even in Death Valley. The kid had a point, she decided, and she'd rather broil than bleed.

The inhabitants of the eastern states are well spread out compared with teeming Britain. A happy result of this was that we and anyone else who happened to be around rolled along at the speed limit. Occasionally we had to overtake, but the roads made the job so easy and safe that even a still-nervous Roz could manage without having to dig deep into her reserves of 'bottle'. This rendered travelling extremely restful compared with the standard European practice of tearing about the place at breakneck speed, eyes fixed in the mirrors to spot the police before they nick you. The key to the general quietude on country byways seemed to be that almost anybody below the unwritten cruising speed pulled hard over to allow faster vehicles to pass. It's intelligent, it's friendly and nobody suffers. Things can be very different on a busy interstate highway.

We worked steadily upward towards the easy foothills of the Appalachians through the remains of the afternoon. The traffic thinned out even more, farms came back to replace the forest and delicate blue flowers filled the roadside ditches. Lazy butterflies flitted around us like psychedelic autumn leaves as we lay beside the hot tarmac taking hourly breaks, then at about five o'clock we rounded a small bluff and right ahead lay the mountains. That blue ridge has been the first milestone on many a westbound trek out of Virginia, and already Annapolis and the insurance mania seemed a long way behind us. We gave our aching bones a rest and pulled off the highway near the attractive traditional town of Culpepper. There in the woods, we found the first of many campsites from the crypt.

Neither of us has ever liked tents, but with three months ahead of us and even the crummiest shelter charging twenty-five dollars per night, spending a proportion of our nights under canvas was a necessary option.

Roz's dislike of camping is entirely rational. Apart from a reasonable desire to sleep on something other than the cold, hard ground, there is always the question of the bugs and larger wildlife whose immediate motivations may not coincide with hers. Within minutes of pitching our 'Khyber Pass' double-walled, totally insulated masterpiece and lighting up the snappy little stove, mosquitoes were zooming in. 'Oh, God,' Roz blasphemed, smacking her neck and fastening up the net door screen, 'here they come!'

Mosquitoes are not my favourite creatures, but they drive my wife insane. They are pleased enough to take a meal off me but, offered the choice, they'll fill their tanks from her every time. How the early settlers coped with them I cannot imagine, and I've noticed they don't feature in any of the films about life in the developing US. Heroes of both sexes are depicted prevailing against Indian attacks, starvation and white men so evil that you fear for your sanity, yet Public Enemy Number One never gets a mention. To fight off the storm troops of human wickedness only to face a lifetime of defeat by an indefatigable insect assailant must have seemed cruelty in the extreme.

Survival is assured today because homes are fly-screened; bars, cars and Winnebagos air-conditioned, and the few souls brave enough to front up to the untouched wilderness with a backpack can lather up with bug repellents to make life tolerable. Leave the chemicals at base, though, and the hiker is in difficulties.

The situation was as serious here in Virginia as it had been in Maine where we had once arrived in our boat, looking forward to peaceful evenings in the cockpit enjoying the fabled sunsets. Not a bit of it. The only safe place to be from sundown minus thirty minutes until around plus two hours was battened down below. We never once saw the sun hit the pines, because the mozzies kept the show for themselves and woe betide any romantic who forgot who was boss.

Expecting no quarter therefore, we oiled up with 'Off', and Roz skulked behind her netting while I scrabbled together a snack. The bikes had clinked their way down to normal temperature as I cleared away under the rising silver moon. The conifers whispered in the light breeze, the heat had eased off, the bugs went home and we cuddled gratefully down into our lightweight sleeping bags craving the righteous sleep of the exhausted. The moon peeped in through the tent flaps and in the dying moments of the evening I relaxed at last, until Roz began ruminating about the possible presence of wild animals. I'd been trying not to think about this. All the statistics indicate that the chances of being eaten on a designated campground by anything heavier than a mosquito are far slimmer than the likelihood of running under a truck out on the highway, but statistics hold no water with me when it's dark and things start rustling.

All manner of major beasts run free in the wilds of the United States. Moose of a tonnage that would make a Hereford bull look lightweight toddle around the forests, while hungry bears with a taste for tourists are alleged to maraud through state campgrounds sizing up the inmates for a square meal. Add to this duo the mountain lion, plus an occasional snake snuggling up through the canvas to keep its blood warm enough to make an early start on the campers, and you will see that sleeping out is not for the faint-hearted. Nonetheless, because of its untamed nature, the wilderness holds great charm for many who are well-prepared. Emotionally, at least, we were not.

As the dark hours dragged by and the ground grew lumpier and harder, the breeze dropped and the frogs began croaking. They rasped and bellowed without stopping, with the foreman making a noise like a dying donkey. In a sense, the frogs were comforting because they couldn't hurt us and they kept their distance, so I drifted off to sleep until well after midnight, when loud snufflings around the tent convinced me that the bears had arrived. Roz awoke and we both lay frozen to the groundsheet by the wildest surmises, not daring to speak until what sounded like a large dog suddenly barked brazenly by Roz's ear.

Dogs Roz can cope with, so she started beating the canvas.

'Sod off!' she spat while I privately hoped the visitor was a family pooch and not a night-hunting Rottweiler. At this point, there came a snarling scuffle like a minor dogfight outside the back of the tent, after which all was silence save for the bullfrogs, which never stopped their chorus.

An hour or so later, the snuffling returned and I broke a lifetime's habit to peer out of my flap into the moonlight. Staring me boldly in the face was a racoon: bulbous eyes, striped tail, the whole works. Racoons don't bother you if you don't bother them, we'd been told, but I waved my fist at him anyway. He sneered at me and trotted off into the trees. I turned over on to a sharp stone to contemplate my own dislike of sleeping under canvas which stemmed, I concluded, from more sinister roots than Roz's.

Argue with my primitive self as I may, I never can entirely defuse a feeling of insecurity that creeps up with the twilight as I lie in my flimsy bivouac. I have heard many theories as to why strong men should be haunted by imagined horrors in the darkness. My favourite is that ancient peoples dreaming out the long nights of the ice ages walked in permanent terror of predators stalking the blackness. Outside the cave and the protection of the fire, sabre-toothed tigers prowled the gloom. The remains of anyone they caught were still there in the morning for all to consider. Thousands of years of living with this grim truth must have forged it on to the gene code of Palaeolithic man. Time has swept away the tigers, but the darkness remains and I seem to have more than my share of genetic leftovers.

Reclining on my personal brick after the racoon returned to his family, I recalled a night of prostrate dread when, aged eight, I had opted to sleep out in the suburban garden of my childhood home. All went well until my slumbers were shattered by what I later realised was a screech owl perched on the ridge of my little tent. I had no idea then what the noise was and could only assume that the Dark Angel himself had come for me. The idea of looking out to reconnoitre was stifled by fear of being seen by the demon, so I followed the policy of craven cowardice which has served me well ever since, pulling the covers over my head and hoping the predators would go away from the mouth of my cave.

Back in the USA of today, the welcome grey dawn and the scented air of night's departing finally crept in through the tent netting. Both of us were suffering from lumbar pain and contemplating the alternative comforts promised by the Great American Motel. Outside in the half-light, the bikes gleamed dimly, the morning smelled of pine and dry earth, the frogs had gone home for a good day's sleep and the only sound was the echoing song of the forest birds. Away through the woodland a fellow camper had lit a fire beside his motor home. I clambered stiffly into my jeans and sauntered over. He was at peace with the world.

Like most American travellers, my neighbour had sensibly tackled the outdoors from the beast-proof and bug-resistant security of a well-appointed 'RV', as recreational vehicles are universally known. This remarkable example had expanded in all directions once off the road, so that it now had two bedrooms hanging off its sides and a comfortable sitting area laid out behind a neat erection of fly screens.

'Pretty mornin',' our neighbour said companionably. He had the face of a pioneer, but probably worked in a Chicago office. 'You folks sleep good?'

'Like a pair of logs,' I fibbed.

'You from Australia?'

'Why should you think that?'

'It's your accent, I guess.'

'I'm English, actually.'

'Yeah. You guys from those parts all sound pretty much the same.'

For a moment this shook me, but I gathered my wits and politely pointed out that my accent has no more in common with an Australian's than an Alaskan fisherman and a Louisiana field worker. He handed me a cup of excellent black coffee and asked whether someone from London, England would be able to tell my pair of hypothetical Americans apart, should he come across one of them alone on a bus to Tower Bridge. I knew that he wouldn't, and began to understand the dangers of making snap judgements about other people's insularity. The fire sent a column of blue smoke into the trees above us and inside the wagon people were moving around, their footfalls hollow on the carpeted metal as they prepared for a new day on the road.

Down at the tent, Roz and I cleared our site, knocked back an aspirin apiece with a cup of Harrod's best tea and started up the Harleys. The din shattered the stillness of the dawn glade and I imagined chipmunks and the last of the lurking 'coons diving for cover.

We rode out past the RV man, whose wife was now perched on a lounger by the fire.

'Beautiful bikes', they called with a matey wave as we swung by up the rough track, creating a dust storm and noise pollution fallout that would have called down the curse of Cain in any European camping site.

good vibrations

Nice people, Americans, I thought, as we regained the blacktop gratefully and hauled away for the mountains.

chapter four

questions of time

Detailed route planning was deliberately not our strong point on this journey. Within certain rough parameters we preferred to let the road lead its own way towards the distant ocean. The first decision was to make our initial westing parallel to the coast down the Appalachian Mountains, then strike out across the continent from some point south of centre.

Early in the faraway summer that had led to Marian and the Buick, I had flagged and bussed my way across from New York City to California. I found no surf, failed to make out as a film star and soon limped back to the East Coast by 'Greyhound' bus. Many of the details of this jaunt have faded, but the fantasy factor in names like Deadwood, Santa Fe, Dakota and New Mexico have clung like snapshot memories. As the decades passed, the fire in them refused to die. The lure of the desert, said to burn somewhere inside every Englishman, has always called loudly to me. So has a fascination that the massive migration across heartland America, one of mankind's greatest, has taken place almost within living memory. History is so close here, it gets under your fingernails. At the outset of the journey, such vague notions provided motivation enough to press forward, searching for the essential romance that is the United States.

An hour after breaking camp on this second morning, we were at the 4,000-foot gateway to the 'Skyline Drive', being hit for six dollars each. After reflecting that the road was part of a national park, I dipped into my pocket on the assumption that since the scenic route along the ridge of the mountains served no commercial purpose, it must be paid for by those there for the spectacle. Serious travellers use Interstate 81 down in the Shenandoah Valley, but we imagined that our investment would buy us a look at an America unsullied by the roaring four-lane highway.

Once inside the barricades, we tried our luck in a visitor centre, but found nothing about hill people today, only brochures with pictures of folks long dead. Fearing that we had made a wrong turning across the often ill-defined line dividing travel from tourism, we swung away down an endlessly twisting route controlled by a nerve-jarring 30mph speed limit. In fairness, it must be said that the views were glorious and the surface excellent. The tragedy of the place was that even to the eye of one come to marvel at them, once you had seen one mountain vista of pine trees and receding blue ridges, you had seen them all.

We crept mesmerically along the escarpment, stopping only to goggle at more of the same from the official viewing points while craving for a cup of tea. I was leading by now and trying to discover a pull-in without a theme park sign in which to brew up, but failing wretchedly. In defeat, we finally climbed off and stretched ourselves at a manicured lay-by, deliberating how soon we could coast back to life as it is lived.

According to the map, this was going to be another couple of hours or so. After our sleepless night, the possibility of literally dropping off the bikes was lurchingly immediate, so we let the tea bags stand in the cups long after they had given their freshest in the hope of a serious belt of caffeine. We were just taking our first shuddering sips when four bikers buzzed smoothly into harbour, paired up aboard a Honda and a Suzuki. They stopped ten yards from us, all grey ponytails and lightweight leather jerkins, but they didn't say hello. The boys in Harley-Davidson of Annapolis had pointed out that considerable political tension exists in America between devotees of slick, fast, imported motorcycles and the faithful who have stuck to the only patriotic machine. In Harley circles, owners of rice-burners are often assumed to be the sort of moral derelicts who would allow the US flag to touch the ground when lowering it. Out West, there were rumours of Angel bars where Japanese bikes are hung from trees for small-arms target practice.

'Do you really think that "rice-burners" don't talk to Harley people at all?' Roz asked.

Since not knowing the answer to this question could conceivably prove injurious to our health, I sized up the opposition out of the corner of my eye. Like me, the men had been around long enough not to court trouble for its own sake, and the women had little of the hardcore 'biker's moll' image in their outfits, so I left Roz with her plastic mug and wandered across to ask how things really stood.

The two men pointed out that, as truckers on vacation from Ohio with their wives, they generally found little in common with the 'tattoo brigade' who, they thought, rumbled around incessantly on lumbering Harleys, but that it wasn't automatically a question of war. I offered them tea in throwaway cups, which they probably hated but nobly downed without flinching, while telling us fearsome tales of bikers decapitated by tyre treads coming adrift from trucks in the heat of the plains. I hoped the stories were apocryphal, because Roz was turning distinctly pale, showing that occasional capacity for self-doubt that the new world of motorcycling seemed to be bringing out. I changed the subject by asking what a man did to keep his mind off his troubles sitting in a fifty-ton eighteen-wheeler on a straight road for weeks on end.

'I listen to Agatha Christie books on tape,' said Bob promptly.

Another illusion shattered. But we didn't have to probe far to discover that he drove with a gun as well as his tape deck, so hope for red-blooded kings of the road remained alive.

Late that afternoon we coasted into the official park campground immediately above the first exit from the parkway. No sooner had the engines been killed than the sound of 1,000 light bombers presaged a mosquito blitz that would have been the envy of Hermann Goering. A visitors' book outside a ranger station advertising inflated prices for pitching a tent was full of jolly wildlife observations:

'Bear chasing deer through campground.'

'Rattlesnake run over on road (not by me).'

Roz had seen the flat snake and had already had a close encounter with a deer so tame it almost knocked her off her bike. The happy campers were locked safely behind the windows of their Winnebago wagons and the mountain air was loud with the roar of air-conditioners, so we pulled on our helmets and cleared out for the world beyond the park gates.

Crassly assuming that the bugs would back off nearer sea level, we stopped in the trees for a drink of water and to rest our seats. I rambled through the dusty pines to watch the chipmunks scurrying around while Roz sat on the ground for some refreshing yoga, but within fifteen minutes we were beating off a strafing so persistent that we had no choice but to take to the highway. We immediately blew our navigation and found ourselves on the interstate, where any speed less than 70mph spelt dire danger from overtaking trucks.

I'd been concerned about how Roz would cope with the higher velocities that sooner or later must come, so I encouraged her to lead on the divided road so as to make the pace. Speed feels like the proper thing on a motorbike. No sound and wind insulation shields the rider, who is almost literally flying through the air. There's no defence if the bike runs out of road either, which, I suppose, is why going like a banshee is such a blast.

In charge of a car, Roz is more than competent. I once sat in the passenger's seat as she drove a huge Pontiac at an average of almost 100mph through the winter forest night across the backwoods highway from Maine to New Brunswick. Fear at speed isn't normally part of her curriculum, yet the bike was definitely having some subliminal effect on her, because so far she had resisted all my attempts to crank our speed above 55. As we hit the interstate, she wound herself on an extra 10mph but it was not enough. At 65mph, Roz faced a dilemma. Either she cranked up to a strategically safe 75, which still felt faster to her than a motorbike ought to go, or she settled for her 'comfort zone' speed and risked being flattened by the traffic. Neither alternative appealed, because she turned off at the next exit and gave me a hard time for taking her on there in the first place.

Thoroughly rattled, we rode onwards in search of rest and quietness down one of the forgotten routes that often run parallel to the interstate system. Within ten minutes, the highway madness was far behind as we slipped into the country road again like a comfortable overcoat. On a site close to where, 130 years before us, Stonewall Jackson had crossed the ridge with 25,000 men on the way to his last fatal clash with the Yankees, we discovered a cameo from a bygone era.

The Greenwood Motel was a throwback to the 1950s. It sat on rising ground by the lazy highway that, in the heyday of them both, had carried much of the east-west traffic of the nation. Two single rows of rooms with metal-framed, plate glass windows, flanked a taller, shingled house. Back on the highway, a neon sign proclaimed 'vacancies', though no guests' cars were in evidence. We ventured in, curious as to what the price might be. The sixty dollars or more per night demanded by the average Days Inn was way over budget.

Still wearing my leather jacket, I propped Black Madonna and knocked on the door. There was a longish wait and we had just decided the place had closed down when a curtain twitched and a face peered out. I stepped back to minimise my intimidation factor as the door opened.

'Have you a room for the night?' I asked the shortish, middle-aged man who opened the door.

'You guys from England?'

I said we were and he nodded absent-mindedly, glancing at the shining Harleys.

'Nice bikes,' he said, rubbing an unshaven chin, 'come on in.'

The office desk stood under a high ceiling at the base of a heavy staircase, but it was hard to take in anything but the ticking. I once saw a movie whose central figure lived in a room surrounded by clocks, but the actuality of the ones in the Greenwood Motel outnumbered the fantasy of the script-writer by three to one. There were grandfathers with steady ticks like scythes shearing dry wheat, frantic cuckoos whirring up to their half-hourly flurry, elegant French carriage editions marked the minutes discreetly on a mantel shelf, and busy office clocks from a slower age strode through the hours in contempt of the wage slaves who had toiled in their thrall.

As we filled out the guest forms, something approximating to the hour came up. Carillons played tunes, Westminster chimes sang out, miniature soldiers banged cracked gongs then ducked back inside their sentry boxes, and from somewhere upstairs, the deep tolling of a large bell boomed out into the dusty air.

'Is this your own collection?' enquired Roz.

'Mother loves clocks,' responded our man absently, before moving back unexpectedly to the subject of our Englishness.

'Did you know,' he continued, 'that although the 1980 US census counted 50 million Americans of English descent, 49 million others were of German origin and the forebears of another 40 million had fled from the mess your people made of Ireland? Take me, for example, I'm a bit of most things, but I'm German and Irish mostly.' He looked at us mischievously, waiting for a reaction to the presence not only of the old enemy, but also of the one nation the Brits have always failed to understand, and they our closest neighbours too.

He didn't get one.

'I'm also at least 128th part Cherokee,' he said with a straight face, 'and a bit of English too, I'm afraid. So you see, I'm not anything. Nothing I can call a nationality. You guys, though, you know exactly who you are.'

'But you're 100 per cent American.' I was sure he was winding us up like one of his clocks.

'And what do you think that's about?' he retorted. 'Being American doesn't mean anything at all. Haven't you noticed that there are Irish Americans and Italian Americans and African Americans and Native Americans, but no English Americans? What do you make of that?'

I didn't know what to make of it, or of our host either, but he took us up to meet his mother anyway. This excellent woman was tall, thin and bore herself with a straight back. She led us into her clock-lined sitting-room and was soon discussing an antique specimen bearing the legend, *Beatus qui Partitere*. She had never met anybody with Latin in the fifty or so years she had owned the clock, so I gathered together the skills of a lost childhood and took a stab at the motto. 'Blessed is he who divides,' was the nearest I could approach to a translation, for although I could not in my life conjugate the third word, it surely had something to do with partition. It was good enough for Mother.

Many a Latin maxim is obscure taken out of context, but I couldn't help remarking that this one applied in perfection to the proprietor himself, a man with a truly advanced sense of the banality of nationalism, but we were now swimming in ever-deeper waters, so we pleaded the need for a shower and scuttled off to our room.

'Number 3' proved to be an apartment straight from a black-and-white movie. Outside was its own small porch equipped with traditional wooden chairs in which to whittle, spit and to enjoy the afternoon. The decent-sized bed chamber featured Venetian blinds and an antediluvian air-conditioning unit inserted as an afterthought into the rear window. The shower room was beautifully tiled throughout and boasted plumbing fittings of a quality that today's contractors would go broke trying to install. The fabric of the building might not have been exceptional, but the piping and the appurtenances would last a thousand years.

Roz took a shower that gushed forth like Niagara before collapsing on the bed complaining of a bad shoulder. She had torn something straining to hold the bike up when it had slipped beyond the balance point as she dismounted after her test spin, watched by the assembled troops.

'I'd rather have ripped my arm off than dropped Betty in front of that crowd,' she announced. I rubbed her upper back with 'Flexall', a sports muscle relaxant she'd discovered in a pharmacy and without which she had decided motorcycling could not be tolerated.

Leaving Betty Boop to take a well-earned rest, we rode Madonna through a wooded darkness singing with insect life to a nearby town in search of food. Here, Polly of Polly's Pizza' asked us what we were about. We chatted pleasantly of this and that, and she glided away to her kitchen, all soft white tennis shoes, soft voice, soft blonde hair and plump, welcoming body. A wholesome girl.

We were half-way through a huge 'Western Special' with extra cheese when she slid up to us quietly.

'I don't want I should alarm you, or anything,' she purred, 'but if you folks are ridin' out to the Midwest, y'all ought to be real careful out there.'

'What's the problem?'

'Thing is, once you're west of the mountains, you'll find some pretty strange people.'

'What about round here?' I asked her gently, and making sure not to offend, I glanced meaningfully at the assorted group gathered around the black Heritage out on the shadowy sidewalk.

'Those guys are OK,' she assured us. 'They're all from round here.' Which made it all right. 'Don't get me wrong, I ain't sayin' nothin', but in some of them states out West terrible things happen, and the folks is weird . . . '

We didn't tell Polly where we were staying when we paid the bill. I'm not suspicious by nature and she surely meant nothing but good, but she couldn't have checked out all those guys sizing up my motorcycle. One of them just might have been from out of state, and careless talk costs bikes, especially after dark away in Nowhere Land. So we roared off into the velvet night and returned to base by a roundabout route.

As I waited for sleep in the comfortable bed, I thought on Polly's remarks and recalled being warned by an otherwise perfectly sane lady back at the Annapolis dealership not to travel through Tennessee, our next state after the mountains.

'That place is full of hicks.'

As always, a chance remark made in daylight grew into horrors by the early hours, so I crept out to look around. All quiet, but just to be sure, I locked the bikes together with a large chain I'd lugged over from Britain and pondered on what folks out West must make of Easterners.

Roz slept late the following morning, still beaten up after her first two full days in the saddle. I slipped out of Room 3 without my boots hoping for breakfast with the clock man.

I was in luck.

The kitchen walls were as beset with timepieces as those of the rest of the house, but the coffee was far stronger than normal in the US and the waffles Olympian. Mine Host had obviously passed a disturbed night considering the enigmas of ethnic bonding and collective business responsibility.

'This country's full of fragmented national groups,' he said, taking a hefty draught of the thick, dark, un-American coffee. 'They're consumed by mutual suspicion and often they hate each other.'

'Surely all that went out seventy years ago – apart from colour down South?'

'Never believe it.' He wiped his mouth and poured maple syrup on a waffle.

'The other problem comes from big business. Taxes have multiplied in my lifetime, and big business is taking over everything worth having. People are so busy squabbling over the petty differences of their ex-nationalities that they don't see the genuine bandits coming. So they lose their freedom and the capacity to do things for themselves.'

'And who are the bandits?'

'Multinationals, and politicians on the make. The time's long gone when a little guy like Eli Terry can survive by building better clocks.'

'Who's he?'

'Eli was what you might call the last craftsman and the first industrialist. He set up in Connecticut back in 1807. Contracted with a major furniture maker to produce 4,000 grandfather clock movements at four dollars apiece in three years. Everyone said he was mad. A quality movement took two or three weeks to knock together in those days. Manufacturers charged fifty dollars apiece.

'Eli set up one of the first mass-production units. Fabricated the parts out of hardwood instead of brass. Like your man Harrison. Now there was a clock-maker!

'Eli used a water wheel for power and produced 3,000 movements in his first year. Made it possible for everyone to own a clock. But he never grew so big he got lost in his own outfit.'

'Lost in his own outfit . . . ?'

'Today's companies are so gigantic nobody's responsible for anything. The big shots hide behind "the times" when the company has to start screwing people. The man who throws you out of your home isn't to blame, you see. Oh no! Nothing personal. Things are changing and there isn't anything he can do. Think about it.'

I did.

That morning we worked our way back into the hills through the gap in the ridge at Waynesboro. Giving tourism the slip for the time being, we steered off the map so as to see the country, always making west-south-west along the grain of the land. With the bikes vibrating solidly under us we swept down green valleys flanked by soft, wooded hills. The slopes were partly cultivated by self-contained farms that cannot have changed much since the time of the settlements, except that pick-ups have replaced ox-drawn carts on the dusty driveways. Horses flicked their tails idly in shady corrals and small groups of dairy cattle grazed contentedly in the lush fields. When we climbed off to stretch our legs and ease our eardrums, there was ringing silence and birdsong. The heat was strong, but less so up here than down on the eastern low ground, and the bugs were taking a well-earned siesta. The valleys of the lower Appalachia are a rustic paradise.

Hardly a car appeared on the smooth, narrow road, no motorcycles and never a highway truck. Only farmers occasionally pulled out, gave us a wave, trundled a mile or two along the road, then turned back into the mystery of their lives down the side tracks, leaving us clear ahead for some of the world's finest riding. Long, fast straights punctuated by gradients, bends of all degrees of tightness, clear visibility, a decent surface and not a Volvo in the county. The best morale-builder Roz could have dreamed of. At one stop I definitely saw the familiar glint in her eye as she remounted and kicked Betty into gear.

'Come on then!'

The only thing to overtake us that day was the sun, starting its long dive towards the Rockies, but as it passed, it drew a blanket of high cloud in its wake.

'That'll be Bertha,' Roz observed as we stopped in a riverside campground by a main highway. All the talk in the towns had been of Hurricane Bertha, currently beating up the Atlantic beaches, and of whether her attendant wind and rain would reach so far inland. Bertha was out of time, because hurricanes don't officially become a threat until August, but here she was in early July, making a mockery of man's fine predictions. The cloud mass had a defined linear structure running athwart its progress, evidence that what we could see was the leading sector of the monstrous circulating system of the dreaded revolving storm. West of it was pure sky, now tinged with sunset pink, behind the line lay the possibility of motorcycle-stopping rain and high winds. Bertha was the first hurricane of the East Coast season. She wouldn't be the last.

You can, of course, use a bike in the rain, but I hate it. In days gone by, when two wheels represented my sole transport, I rode through everything that came. It taught me all about deep-tissue hypothermia, the horrors of sliding on wet, oily surfaces and blind riding with an opaque visor into the spray of a million trucks. In the learning process, I penetrated the deeper canyons of fear and misery, swearing that in a Utopian future, which to my surprise I now found myself almost living, I never would ride wet again. Some hope!

Hurricanes must have warm sea water to feed their atmospheric engine so, hoping that by morning Bertha would die of thirst from the drier air as she came ashore, we secured the tent in a seamanlike manner. To maintain a handle on her progress, I took a relative bearing on the cloud edge from a boulder by the river and we eased our backs by taking a stroll up the steep valley by the water's edge. Two hours later the storm front hadn't moved, so we unzipped the tent and gave sleep our best shot.

No wild animals tonight, only freight trains chattering and whining down the line across the river. The sound of a locomotive blowing its lonely siren into the darkness calls direct from the beating heart of America. That night I heard them from the bottom of a deep, deep sleep. I heard Johnny Cash at San Quentin prison, singing his song about a convict driven mad by the sound of the free railroad trains outside the walls, and roaring like the Orange Blossom Special.

Far from Folsom Prison, that's where I wanna be.

But that train jus' keeps on blowin', an' that's what's killing me.[3]

Twenty-five years after one of the century's most visionary concerts, the echo of the amplified bass still thuds out its alternate fifths to shake the throbbing sadness of a new audience.

At dawn, a grey mist was rising off the water. The river still flowed clean over its stony bed, the railroad was empty and Bertha covered the sky.

chapter five

running the storm

Back on the byroads of Virginia, it was half-way to lunchtime before the message sank in that we were unlikely to find breakfast in the tiny settlements that flashed by at fifteen-mile intervals. Many of these did not feature on our map at all and the ones that did had nothing to offer the hungry, so we gave up the search and motored up a deserted gravel track to heat up our last can of pork and beans.

Suddenly a sharp bang cracked the cloud-deadened stillness, followed by a single echo.

'Christ, what was that?' Roz jumped, although we both knew it was a gunshot. We gulped our beans faster as more shots followed and a man in a battered pick-up materialised to check out our victualling habits. Just to keep us on our toes, a steady series of vehicles followed. I suppose a couple of smart Harleys propped up in the forest beside a pair of Brits eating from the pan made an unusual diversion, but the words of wisdom we'd been offered so freely were taking a vigorous exercise gallop around my brain.

'Watch for weird people out West,' or, '. . . full of Hicks,' had just been samples. I recalled the fate of the two archetypal bikers in the film *Easy Rider*, blown to kingdom come by a redneck with a hunting gun, and grinned reassuringly at the passers-by. None of these guys had spruced up to peer at us and several of them carried rifles, but they nodded in a neighbourly way as they rattled slowly by. In the end, I concluded that their interest was mainly curiosity and asked myself who was afraid of whom in this country, and why.

The morning heated up in earnest soon after we had eaten, and we were not outrunning Hurricane Bertha. The cloud marched ahead of us down the road and always the blue sky was chasing away behind the rounded hills ahead. The Appalachian valleys stretched long, narrow and gentle as we hummed along, but the humidity climbed with the threat of rain and we stopped for relief by an antique Lutheran church on a wooded mound, immediately west of the tiny village of Sharon. Still in regular use, the white, weatherboard building dated from a different world. It was raised in 1817 when Indians roamed their ancestral woodlands in growing confusion and settlers from Europe began to clear the first fields.

Roz collapsed beside her motorbike to rest. I pushed open the chapel's heavy door and entered the calm twilight within. It was cool and so still that my ears buzzed with tinnitus from two hours of undiluted Harley. The air had the same odour of antiquity that one finds in a healthy vintage boat, and I remembered the vessel whose sale had made this journey possible. She had been over eighty at the end and I will recall the rich complexity of her smell to my grave. You can look at pictures of ancient buildings, but until you have breathed their air, you cannot hear them speak.

Two timber lecterns stood on either side of the shallow chancel, each bearing an ancient, guilded Bible in the 1611 King James version. No modern translation here to make light of the thunder of God's word. One was open at the book of Jeremiah, offering the casual reader a glimpse of a nation's future as the prophet tells that Judah will be carried away into Babylon. He concludes with a memorable cry of despair:

'Wherefore came I forth out of the womb to see labour and sorrow, that my days should be consumed with shame?'

Whoever had set these Bibles was in a dark mood, for the second offered little comfort after the gloom of the first. I found Isaiah in the blackest moments of his prophecy,

'We wait for light, but behold obscurity; for brightness, but we walk in darkness. We grope for the wall like the blind . . . we stumble at noonday as if in the night; we are in desolate places as dead men.'

Hoping I was committing no trespass, I turned the crackling, gold-edged page in search of something more positive and was richly rewarded.

'Arise, shine, for thy light is come, and the glory of the Lord is risen upon thee.'

I made myself comfortable in a front pew for half an hour and tried to extract some sense from what I had read. My brain filled with jumbled images of people in pilgrim costume sitting in these seats, deliberating on the meditations of a preacher whose mind probably knew no doubts and whose bones now rested in the adjacent graveyard.

It is the nature of mankind to daydream when sitting in church. God knows where the thoughts of the inaugural congregations had wandered. Perhaps they centred on the valley, the village and the steady striving to raise living standards for those whose journey west had stopped here. My own kept returning to my bike, the road, and my modern-world view. All we had in common, it seemed, was our language and the thin, unbroken thread of religion. Or so it would have been, except that decades of spiritual idleness have so worn down my capacity to pray that even here, where the past was plainly in evidence, it was hard to probe deeper. I left as peacefully as I could, unwilling to disturb the ghosts I had almost awakened, but my boots clumped heavily on the oak floor as I walked to the door.

In the shady graveyard, a tablet of stone reminded the passer-by that this settlement was once wiped out by dispossessed Indians. A solitary child had survived to tell the tale. It is said that the little girl hid behind a bush and escaped detection, somehow surmounting this unimaginable trauma to grow up a healthy woman. She went on to contribute her full share of offspring to the expanding white population who, by virtue of nothing more than numbers and industrial energy, would inevitably displace their antecedents. To the casual traveller at least, the Native Americans have vanished from these early-settled hills like the smoke of their fires, leaving only stone arrowheads buried deep in the leaf mould as evidence of their existence.

Meanwhile, a light drizzle had begun and Roz was clambering into her weatherproofs. At least there was no traffic to dash spray on to her visor or my shades. The only moisture would be falling out of the air or flying from our own wheels. Bertha rumbled and flashed around the hills but never really got going that afternoon. She managed a few heavy showers, yet unlike the situation in Britain where temperatures rarely rise above seventy-five degrees, showery weather in the American summer is of little consequence to the biker in no hurry, because the road steams dry within fifteen minutes of the day brightening up. All you have to do is find a handy tree under which to wait. There was still no proper rain by mid-afternoon, but the clouds were weeping and boiling above us.

Bertha was drawing back to gather her strength. Even at the death, a hurricane can deliver a spiteful blow.

The tarmac was beginning to glimmer in the sun's final half-hearted effort as we cruised a drawn-out dip labelled 'Fertile Valley'. Reflecting its name, the land looked as productive as a freshly ploughed Devon field. We stopped to fuel up at a general store run by a young woman with brown hair done in braids, the smoothest skin in the world and strong, unusual features. Two elderly gents drank beer at a dark corner of the wide, U-shaped mahogany counter. They peered through the window at our bikes and ignored the flickering images on a large television set where a man in jail was receiving a thinly-disguised blow-job from an enthusiastic young female on the right side of the bars. A pair of children were similarly unimpressed by the rhythmic action, as was the lady's assistant, a teenage girl.

Trying to divert my gaze from the huge screen, I paid for the gasoline while Roz struck up a conversation. Pots of spicy stews simmered on a hob on top of the counter. The women were discussing the contents, one of which was a chilli of some sort called 'Sloppy Joe'. In short order we were on first-name terms with Shannon and ordering an unscheduled meal which cost us next to nothing. The chilli was served promptly but we were certainly not eating 'fast food'. I could feel my system soaking up some serious benefit. Just as I was turning to leave, an energetic new arrival announced himself as Shannon's husband. Earl was older than his wife, and his accent was so deep in the hills that until I had tuned in to its music I had to try hard to follow his tale about a domestic electrical circuit he had patented. This was all set to transform the civilised world and make him a few bucks into the bargain.

He was installing one in the neighbour's store in the next hollow that very afternoon and would we care to swing by and expand our minds by checking it out?

'Sure.'

'Follow me then.'

Earl didn't bother to put on his shirt. He just swept Shannon into his well-used car - V-8 American, I was pleased to note – sank his foot into the carburettor and snarled away. We chased him at a gallop. I could see Roz in my mirrors, hanging on to Betty Boop reaching never-before-attempted angles on the curves as both of us watched for stray gravel. This lurked on hidden corners, either washed off the hillsides by the rain or thrown on to the road by the tyres of drunken, midnight home-runners. Gravel is the end of the line for a bike cranked over on a bend. On four wheels, you can always try opposite lock as you go into a slide. On a motorcycle, your only hope is that you land the right side of the bike and don't hit anything hard as you grind down the road. Tailgating a fast car on an unfamiliar, twisty trail can therefore have ugly consequences.

Tucking in behind another bike is better, because either the leader knows his stuff and will be watching for loose surfaces, leaves, horse-shit and anything else that induces a skid, or he doesn't and won't be. He'll also take the sting out of any tractor or boy racer that comes speeding around the next bend on the wrong side of the road. So long as he concentrates, you are in good shape. If not, you have two positive chances. Either you're both in luck and the road surface is smooth, or he loses it and hits the slitheries or the tractor. When it's the latter, your unhappy leader gets wiped out first, leaving you with a sporting chance of either stopping or dodging his remains. I contemplated these facts of life as we swung the bends, praying that Roz wouldn't lose her bottle and drop the bike, while feeling glad that I'd done the decent thing making sure I was the first to follow that car.

chapter six

banjos, moonshiners and the feds

The rain started in earnest as we arrived at Haggerd's store. With its rickety wooden sidings, sloping roof and porch propped up with rustic posts, it nestled in the West Virginian hollow like the sleeve image of a country music album. Haggerd was out back checking his oil tank, wearing blue dungarees that appeared to have grown on him. His powerful face looked out from a shock of white hair making him appear nearer fifty-five than his actual seventy years as he moved with purpose to greet us. Roz and Shannon splashed in through the door, but Earl and I hung out under the porch with him drinking bottled beer. Haggerd unloaded his grief concerning bureaucracy which, he said with Earl's full concurrence, would bring the country down.

'Fifteen different permits I needed to erect this here oil tank,' he grumbled, 'and 8,000 dollars in administrative fees. Not so long ago you could have built the thing for that money and had change.'

'Surely they have to have some sort of regulations so people don't spill the stuff all over the place,' I observed.

'Ain't nuthin' to the guys who make the rules if we do spill it,' grunted Earl. 'They're hundreds of miles away in the city. But these tanks today are so tight that there ain't no more spillage. All that paper serves no purpose . . . 'cept to breed more of the same useless crap.'

He lobbed his empty bottle expertly into a waste can fifteen feet away and opened the fly screen into the store. Inside, the place was out of time. Shelves lined the walls, forming the alleyways typical of a small supermarket anywhere in the Western world, but these were of well-worn wood, not some easy-clean composite, and many of the products on sale were 1950s and beyond. Hardware like Grandpa used peeped out from behind buckets of nails. The basics of handed-down cooking skills were prominent, including yeast for home bread-baking. Jostling the packets for space were cans of Stockholm tar, a vital unction for traditional boats and now almost unobtainable in coastal communities anywhere. Horses use it too, though I've never understood why. Baseball hats and other crucial items of gentlemen's outfitting drooped from the ceiling, while huge bags of potato chips were piled up near to the counter so that whoever was running the show could grab a snack.

The overall effect was one of a darkness where anything on earth could be found by an informed searcher. Save for the small front windows and the door, the only light came from an unshaded bulb dangling over a sagging, round table where the weeks' newspapers were open to be read by the customers. Coffee was available. A tattered sign announced that alcohol consumption on the premises was illegal, but the regulation group of 'good old boys' sat minding their own business, enjoying an 'Old Milwaukee' in the late-day humidity. The rain pelted down on the still-hot tin roof.

Haggerd picked a cardboard six-pack out of the tall cold-locker and tossed it on to the table. We pulled up shaky kitchen chairs, flipped the tops off our bottles and settled on to our seats. Shannon came and sat on Earl's lap. Roz was still over at the counter with Dolly, Haggerd's wife, who was confiding that Shannon, the lady we had marked down as in her early twenties, was actually thirty-nine and the mother of four. Her first grandchild was almost due. Perhaps her eternal youth was something to do with being part Indian.

I looked at Shannon sideways in the dimness. Her colouring was pure Anglo-Saxon settler, but the native blood showed in the outline of her face. I remembered the memorial to the victims of the Indian massacre back in the shade of Sharon churchyard and the terrified child who hid in the bushes to see her parents butchered and then went on to raise children of her own. Somewhere, as the wheel turned, one of her descendants or a compatriot had done better than call a truce with the red man.

Travelling in the young land of America, it is easy to see that when an energetic population pushes forward into new territory under pressure from behind, fate is on the march. Nobody can stop what must surely happen. Those caught at the frontier, whether advancing or retreating, are hurled about like rag dolls, their souls laid bare by the harsh searchlight of their times. Heroes arise on both sides, and cowards. The greedy, the hardworking, the rapacious, the cunning, people who will die sooner than give ground and those ready in the end to submit and change, all find their place. Some display the best in humanity, others the worst; many just keep their heads down and live their lives, but none will alter what must inevitably come.

Earl, meanwhile, was revealing himself as something of a Man of the Road.

'Used to be a gang of us with motorcycles,' he was saying, leaning forward, elbows on knees. 'We'd meet Friday nights down the valley, drink beer an' shoot the breeze. Sometimes we'd go off for a ride together. We had a sort of pres'dent who said where we'd go, an' that was the end of it. Either you went there with the rest or you was out. We took it in turns to be pres'dent.

'One time, we was down at Harry Harper's place late on, havin' a brew an' a barbecue. Harry was the pres'dent. He finishes his steak an he says, "I dunno 'bout you boys, but I'm headin' out to Nashville for breakfast."

'There was some grumblin', let me tell y'all, but we was all fuelled up, so away we went.

'We rode all through that summer night, through the Cumberland Gap and on down across Tennessee. The moon came up late as we was passing Knoxville an' we was in Nashville for bacon an' eggs like the man said.'

'So then did you all slug back home?' I enquired.

'No Sir,' Earl took a deep swig. 'We kick-started those bikes an' Harry headed straight on out West. We blasted clear across Arkansas and Oklahoma. It came on dark around Oklahoma City – which was 800 miles from the Grand ol' Opree. We stopped for gas and food and damn me if Harry didn't kick her over an' keep right on going. By now some of the guys had gone back an' a coupla ol' knucklehead Harleys had broke down, but the rest of us, that'd be half a dozen or so, we followed that crazy bastard on down into Texas.

'We ran the panhandle in the night time at ninety miles an hour. Never saw no cops. In the mornin' the sun came up behind us an' we was in New Mexico. We swung north and climbed off in Santa Fe.'

'So what did you do then?'

'We drank some whiskey an' turned for home.'

Whether or not this yarn was true, it was well-received. Earl's audience now began pumping him for details.

'Was you all ridin' Harleys?'

'Mostly. One British Triumph and a Honda 400.'

'A 400! How did that ever keep up?'

'She was quick enough,' Earl expanded. 'Feller ridin' her was nearly eighty. He never gave up, but on the second afternoon he starts askin' the guys to spell him cos that saddle was mean. I took her for an hour an' that was enough, let me tell y'all. How that ol' feller sat on that thing to Santa Fe I'll never understand. I didn't say nothin' when my hour was up because these were hard men. Your butt hurtin' wasn't somethin' you'd admit to, but I had to hand it to him. He had balls.'

The talk ran on until it was almost dark outside.

'Where you folks restin' up tonight?' asked Haggerd.

'We'll get back to the highway and find ourselves a room. Then on down towards the Cumberland Gap in the morning.'

Earl shook his head.

'You don't want to be goin' anywhere in that rain,' he said, and it was true. A wall of water was falling from the sky and the road outside the store had turned into a muddy stream. It was motorcycle mayhem out there.

'You could leave the bikes with Haggerd an' stay at our place,' offered Shannon, but Mrs Haggerd was a jump ahead in her hospitality.

'I think we'd all like to have you visit for a few days till the weather clears up,' she announced. 'The weatherman says this'll run the whole weekend. Haggerd's ma's house is empty now she's taken up with Fred. It's right up the back here. No one else needs it. You can even put your bikes under cover. Stay there till you're ready to move on out.'

And so Hurricane Bertha did us one of the great favours of the journey. She had led us into the arms of a family untouched in its structure by the TV dinner, the universal divorce and the video store. None of them were regular church-goers, though we were now firmly in the Bible Belt. Haggerd told me he'd never been inside a place of worship since the preacher stole his whiskey and his morning paper, but kindness to people on the road was as natural to them as sunshine after rain. Visiting was the main recreation, with yarns that were like the best tales of the sea and must have grown just as much with the telling. This was true oral tradition, a form of literature hard to find in Britain and in the cities of the US, but it flourished here in the hollow.

We unloaded the bikes in the clamouring darkness of the storm. The spare house was built on a slope opposite the store. It must have been just as his mother left it, walking out on her two strong legs to marry a childhood sweetheart. Fred had made good in a nearby town and, like Ma, was in his nineties. The photographs on the wooden walls could have been from folk history books, with tall, rangy, second-generation mountain farmers standing self-consciously for the camera, uncomfortable in Sunday-go-to-meeting outfits. The parents of those people had come here, many from England, Scotland and Ulster, in search of an improvement over impossibly hard times at home. They lived first by trapping, hunting and gathering what they could, only later planting crops near their simple cabins. On a sideboard under one of these images was Ma's television set, early 1960s with a tiny screen, mute witness to the changes she had seen. Creeping into the adjoining room, we found an ancient bed beneath a wondrous quilted counterpane. In the back kitchen the staple, dried food cupboards were full, but the wardrobe stood empty. Ma had gone for good.

We unpacked our gear then scurried through the downpour down to Haggerd's place for dinner. The men were sitting in the shelter of the porch enjoying the air, now cool and washed clean of bugs. Shannon and Dolly were inside cooking. Roz went to join them and Earl poured me a generous shot of what looked like whiskey, out of an unmarked bottle.

'This here is finest mountain dew,' he announced. 'Distilled right up in the woods.'

Haggerd offered me some lemonade to dilute the spirit, but I took a drop of water as I do with my scotch. The taste was much like a branded sour mash whiskey, but the illegal nature of its origin gave it a savour of its own.

'I didn't think people did their own distilling nowadays,' I said, and that was the trigger for a flood of moonshining stories.

Making whiskey ran in Haggerd's family but, as always, Earl led off by recalling his own father being hauled up before the judge by a new town deputy for being drunk in public. The judge fined Pa ten dollars and sent him out of court. An hour later, he was picked up again, even more drunk than before, and back to the courthouse he went. The judge now infuriated the lawman by handing out another ten buck fine and throwing him and his freed prisoner out. By this time of day the judge was well into his own cups, and as the deputy opened the door, the judge called out to him to quit bothering the court and to let the old man bring him in a couple of bottles. It was well-known by everyone in town except, it seemed, the sheriff's new representative, that the judge kept a supply of moonshine in a gallon jar that was painted white so it looked like milk.

Earl's pa gave the deputy a jaunty 'good day' and went home for the bottles. When he returned to the courthouse everyone had left except the judge, who had passed out on the bench.

The next arrival on Haggerd's porch was his son-in-law, Jim, who continued to work a still up the mountain as part of his own family tradition even though, as he observed, trade had quietened down as living standards had risen across the country. He opened a heavy banjo case and intermittently picked out tunes as the talk rambled around to building the simple apparatus needed for the job. Haggerd lamented declining standards in the automotive industry.

'Time was when you could take the radiator out of a 'Cat' tractor, clean her out, and set her up in the woods. They was pure copper and they made the dandiest little stills. That's all gone to hell now, though,' he sighed, 'them new radiators is all steel. You can never get all the rust out.'

I asked if people were ever caught in the act of distilling

'You still need to be careful,' he sipped his drink, 'but thirty years ago them revenuers was everywhere. Folks would always set their stills half-way up a hillside. If you heard the revenue men comin' through the woods you'd have to leave it to get busted up, but they'd never catch you on account of how you'd placed yourself.

'They'd have to be on foot,' he explained, 'because there weren't no four-track vehicles to get into the woods in them days. By the time they reached you, they'd already climbed a few hundred feet so they were pretty well washed up. You were fresh. So long as you ran uphill, you'd leave them standing.'

Earl had never been a prime mover in the distilling industry, but back in his extreme youth in the 1950s he had been a runner, carrying moonshine down to Georgia and North Carolina in souped-up automobiles. It had been a sort of deadly game, like motor racing with an honest profit for the winners. These were usually the moonshiners, but there were accidents and occasional convictions as state troopers with massive V-8 motors latched on to them. There were also shoot-outs, sometimes with tragic outcomes. The truth probably was that much of the trade had been far from homely fun, but in Earl's memory, the whole business had taken on a Robin Hood flavour.

Earl's favourite car had been a 1940 Ford with a three-speed on the column and a vacuum two-speed axle. This mighty motor was so hepped up that it would pull 125mph in second gear and Earl knew there wasn't a patrol man in three states who could catch him. Then a rumour began spreading about a 'hemi-head' Mercury with two four-barrel carburettors in the pay of a giant revenue man, but nobody in Earl's circle had ever seen this rocket ship. 'Feller who told me about it claimed it burned so much gas that you either had to switch off the engine to fuel up or find a fast pump, because even at idle it was using up the stuff quicker than you could fill that tank.' One night, Earl had unloaded down in Georgia and was driving home to the hollow through North Carolina. The absence of speed limits in the happy days before the 1970s oil crisis meant that you couldn't be pulled merely for driving fast, so long as you weren't killing people. Earl was cruising through the darkness at a modest 100 or so when a pair of headlamps appeared in his mirror.

'That car come up fast,' he said, 'and he drove in so close behind me that I couldn't see the lights no more 'cause they were under my trunk, just this bright glow. It had to be either a cop or a criminal and either way I didn't want him, so I booted the Ford on some. At 130 the lights were still under my fender, so I stamped the gas pedal hard down on the firewall. We was flat out through them pine woods. That road ran dead straight for fifty miles clear to the state line and I knew I'd out-run him. At 160, when I had no more to give, he just cruised up alongside me an' turned on his blue light.

'I stopped and he pulled in ahead of me. Wasn't nuthin' else I could do. I didn't want to end up in the ditch at that speed. I climbed out quick, 'cause you're always better looking 'em in the eye, and I checked their car. It was the Mercury all right. Fat bulge on the hood an' it was burble-burbling away on idle, the whole thing sort of shaking like there was a wild animal inside it just waitin' for the gas pedal to let her out.

'Well, let me tell y'all, one of the biggest men I ever saw climbed out of that car. The trooper who was drivin' got out too. He was a sizeable man, but he looked like a little kid alongside this revenue man. That guy weighed three-fifty pounds and then some more and he had tobaccer juice runnin' down from both sides of his mouth.'

Jim had lit a hurricane lamp and now he passed around the bottle. I had been so engrossed in Earl's tall story that I didn't even realise my glass was empty. I poured a stiff slug as Earl continued.

'The trooper kept me covered while the big guy checked through the car. All the jars had gone of course, but we used to keep a whiskey tank in the trunk. He opened her up an' she smelled to high heaven, but there wasn't even a puddle left inside.

'"OK," he says, "Where d'you drop the stuff off."

'"Not in this state anyway," I told him. I thought I'd get a pistol whippin' at least, but they just steps back an' the big feller says, "There's a diner open twenty miles up the road. Seems it'd be the neighbourly thing for me to buy y'all a coffee there, but your ol' Ford's so slow the coffee'd be cold by the time you dawdled in to drink her."

'It's three in the morning by this time and it's midsummer, but it's still dark. Away goes the Mercury. I heard him burn rubber as he changed into third an' he must have been doin' well over 100 by then, but I wasn't about to let him get away with his mouth. I was still tremblin', I'll tell you, but I give the Ford her head and ten minutes later I was walkin' into the diner. Like the man said, it was twenty miles. They'd bought me a coffee, an' it wasn't cold. I drank it and tried to get neighbourly, but they just stared me down, so I cleared out an' never used that road again.'

'Quit your jaw, boys. Supper's on the table.' Dolly called us through the open front door.

We ate braised steak and potatoes with macaroni cheese and the 'biscuits' of the South. These are more like large lightweight dumplings than anything else and are generally served with gravy, which they soak up with remarkable efficiency. As we filled our boots, Earl mentioned his plans for hunting over the weekend and Haggerd remarked that things had quietened down a lot since he was a kid.

'In them days, we'd only get beef steak once in a while, when times was good in the store. Mostly, Pa'd go up an' shoot squirrels. That squirrel gravy was often the bes' thing we could manage with our biscuits.'

'What about the 'coon hounds, Haggerd?' asked Dolly.

'My ol' Pa, he had the best pair of 'coon hounds in the hollow,' Haggerd rose to the cue. 'Specially bred they was, to 'tree' them suckers . . .'

'Which suckers?' asked Roz.

'Them racoons,' continued Haggerd, emphasising the first syllable. 'You can't get close enough for a shot often. They're quick when they know you're after 'em. But them 'coon hounds'll run 'em up the nearest tree. Mebbe there'd be two or three. Once you've got 'em cold you could shoot up there amongst 'em.'

'What did they taste like?'

Haggerd hesitated. 'Kinda like 'coons, I s'pose.'

'When I was bein' raised,' he continued, 'most families kept pigs. Hog butchering was a community activity. Folks'd bring their animals together in an open field down the way, then Pa and the other men'd slaughter up to twenty-five at a time. Nothing was wasted and sometimes me and the other kids'd be given a cup of that good, warm blood. Ma said it'd make us strong.'

'And did it?' Roz was hanging on to her steak gamely.

'Sweetest thing you ever did taste.' With his fork, Haggerd cut up another chunk of meat.

'Ma'd bring the carcass home, cut it up, scald it and shave it clean. She'd salt some down, but Pa'd come in and demand we ate a hunk fresh while it was there. We had some famous parties on hog-killin' night. But hard times aplenty came in between. Buttermilk and corn bread was all we saw some weeks.'

I remarked to Dolly that I had noticed no black people in the hollow, and she replied that when she and Haggerd were children there had been a fair sprinkling of dark faces. The Haggerds' neighbours were black; the children played together and often went into the kitchen of one another's homes looking for tit-bits. There, however, any fraternisation had to stop. Total segregation was enforced in school and Dolly remarked to my astonishment that intermarriage was illegal in Virginia until over a decade after World War II.

Black people had first arrived in the area one by one as runaway slaves. They were taken on by the local landowners, many of whom helped them out by giving them soil to till as well as a job. It was these workers who led the way clearing the fields, but as time progressed they moved to the industrial centres looking for regular wages. By the 1990s, not a single African American remained in the area. There had been no open racial strife. The migration appeared to have come about as a result of some mysterious economic process that did not apply itself to the whites.

Notwithstanding an open-handed attitude to the question of colour, Haggerd's father had maintained a tight grip on the way his children should live and who they should adopt as role models. When the white neighbours were visited by their relatives from the next valley there was always music and singing across the lane from the store. This is no surprise when you realise that the callers were Mabelle Carter with her family, who later recorded with Doc Watson and Earl Scruggs, and whose daughter June would grow up to marry Johnny Cash.

'Pa'd git madder 'n Lucifer if we went anywhere near them girls!' Haggerd chuckled to himself and poured a round of whiskey and lemonade.

'"Bunch o' damn gypsies! Always singing." Said they'd never come to no good. Wish he could see 'em now . . . '

Haggerd was interrupted by two of Jim's cronies arriving with guitar and fiddle. They settled in with the ritual drink, tuned up and away they went. It was a good night for music, with sweet songs and driving rhythm beating down the storm.

The rain stopped on Monday morning, but the sky said there was more to come. The weekend had resounded to the sound of incessant gunfire echoing around the hollow as the mountain men bagged their victuals. Now all was quiet. They had returned to their jobs, Haggerd was serving in the store and it was time for us to go. Sadly, we packed our saddlebags to haul out for Cumberland Gap and the widening countryside of Tennessee. As we cruised onwards, each locked inside our individual reflections, my own head still rang with the hard-driving lick of Jim and the boys ranting through 'Soldier's Joy'.

Following the route blazed by Daniel Boone towards the sunset, we passed a selection of motorcycles coming in the opposite direction. As they swung by, each rider stretched out the left hand of brotherhood offered by all-American bikers on the highway. The fingers never touch, but the gesture helps generate tribal feeling. A few were on giant Honda Gold Wing cruisers that made me think of armchairs on wheels. These guys always seemed to wear helmets. In contrast, the hard men and their girls on Harleys snatched off their headgear on principle every time they entered a state with no compulsory helmet law. Often they flouted enforcement where the regulation was nominally in force. The Honda Gold Wing is so sophisticated that it seems odd to me that anyone would choose one in preference to an automobile. Our noisy, inefficient, powerhouse Harleys embodied the spirit of Earl's mad dash to New Mexico and I was content with a bike which that symbol of American freedom might select if ever he travelled west again.

We stopped for the night in a motel run by a family from the Indian subcontinent. The cooking smells wafting into the office would have seemed to be more at home in the Indian quarter of Bradford, England, than in the Appalachians. Roz asked the sari-clad woman taking our money if there was any chance of a chicken tikka, but was given the thumbs down. Instead, we ate from the local store. The victuals didn't come near Shannon's standard and seemed a bad choice until we remembered the large bottle of mountain dew that Haggerd had stuffed into the top of my pack as we left. We drank some now, and felt a whole lot better.

Just before Roz fell asleep, she suddenly spoke from her side of the immense bed.

'If Daniel Boone had been offered a motorbike to break through into Kentucky, do you think he'd have ridden a Gold Wing or a Harley-Davidson?'

I turned on the light. The lines at the corners of her eyes were laughing at me and although the banjos were still marching through my own mind, I rejoiced, because I understood that she at least had returned to the road and was looking ahead. The visit with the mountain folk had settled her into this huge, wayward land, leading her thoughts from her immediate challenges and helping her shed the worst of her novice's nerves. She was beginning to feel a pride in her iron pony.

Roz had once given me a book about sailing the oceans and had written a quotation from John Masefield inside the flap. It was put there for me, but really it was her.

'Most roads lead men homeward,
My road leads me forth.'[4]

chapter seven

firetrucks and bibles

The following morning we traversed the Cumberland Gap near the tri-state border of Virginia, Kentucky and Tennessee. This crucial pass to the West was discovered in 1750 and named for some reason to immortalise the villainous 'Butcher Cumberland', the unlovely English Duke who had harried the Scots to their hearthstones after the defeat of Bonnie Prince Charlie, 4,000 miles from here on Drumossie Muir. The pass was not blazed as a settlers' route until twenty years later by Daniel Boone and a group of hard-nosed veterans of the French and Indian Wars. Using ancient Indian tracks, they constructed the 'Wilderness Trail', along which 100,000 settlers penetrated to the wide, undulating richness of Kentucky as far north as the Ohio River.

As we breezed down a broad valley from which the blue mountains seemed to have backed right off, Hurricane Bertha had dissipated into thin air, but the atmosphere was beginning to show signs of the constant threat of the summer storms of central USA. West of the Appalachians, a good day is just plain hot, but as one sunrise follows another the weather works itself into a series of steamy, humid climaxes until massive electric storms clear the sky.

From here to the Rockies, we saw these systems wind themselves up, drawing damp, tropical air masses into the heartlands from the remote Gulf of Mexico. Towards lunchtime on a typical storm day, the unsullied blue of the distant sky puffs up into fluffy white cumulus. An hour later, groups of these have crowded together into cumulonimbus giants full of evil potential. By 3:30 their undersides have turned grey and the tops are bubbling to impossible heights in undisciplined cauliflower confusion. Dismount to watch one and you can see it churning aloft to the very edge of space as the heat engine exhales in a colossal convection. Somewhere up there in the unbreatheable stratosphere, the cold becomes too much for the cloud to hold on to its moisture and it collapses into deluging rain, accompanied by a tumult of thunder and lightning whose capacity for heavy damage is made plain by shattered trees and occasional gravestone inscriptions.

American summer downpours bear absolutely no relation to the 'soft, refreshing rain' of England. They can drop their load in the form of devastating hail that flattens a crop and ruins a farmer in fifteen minutes, but even in the rain mode, they make driving an automobile extremely dangerous, so dense is the water in the air and on the ground. Anyone caught out is drenched in seconds, as thoroughly as if he had jumped into a river. Motorcycling while a summer storm cloud is venting its anger is unthinkable for all but the clinically insane.

Our first downpour trapped us immediately west of the Cumberland Gap in the town of Middlesboro. We had been searching the pitted streets for the *poste restante* and news from home when lightning split the afternoon and the initial spots of precipitation heralded an imminent insanity of falling water. The bikes were standing outside the large, square fire station and I was across the street returning from the mail drop when I saw Roz start up Betty Boop and cruise boldly through the huge open doors to worm her way into the cave between two red trucks. Fire stations in America are holy places into which

I could not imagine pushing even a dinky car without being consigned to the electric chair. The whole scene is decidedly macho and since it involves 'the safety of life', a subject in which America takes an even more morbid interest than Britain, it would be a foolish biker who risked getting in the way.

Worried, I dashed across, only to discover Roz chatting with a fireman who was urgently beckoning me to pull my monster under cover before the rain. I had almost made it back to my bike when the sprinkling drops suddenly turned into marble-sized projectiles. Black Madonna might as well have been under the fireman's hose by the time I squelched aboard, but she started up nonetheless and I threaded her gratefully into the echoing dryness of the garage. There she sat above a growing puddle, her engine and exhausts steaming, alive with the nostalgic pungency of the hot, wet de-greaser I used to clean her engine.

In their cultural impact, the fire trucks were like oversized six-wheeled Harleys; their paintwork a deep, scarlet gloss, their chunky chrome buffed to a markless finish and the externally visible machinery that gave them their butch character was heavy on shine and ready for action. Like our motorbikes and the enormous trucks out on the interstate, these were unashamed examples of US engineering at its best. Their mentor was proud of them, delighted that we appreciated them, and awarded us the freedom of the station.

We didn't take up the offer of a shower, but we did venture into the mess room where the 'watch on deck' were enjoying a raucous game of cards. It was clear from the dexterity of the dealing and the sharpness of the decisions to hold, draw or fold that these servants of the community spent weeks honing poker skills that would have been the envy of a riverboat operator in Maverick's day. Coffee and 'donuts' perched on the side, so we loaded up. The foreman sat out the next deal and after expressing surprise, came to terms with the fact that our accents were English and not from the northern outback of Queensland.

I spotted a large television in the corner, spewing out nothing of value.

'Why does everybody in this country think we are from Oz?' I asked him. 'I know the accents are similar to you, but there are so many more Brits than Aussies. Your chances of meeting one of us are far greater.' I glanced towards the screen. 'Do you watch a lot of Australian Soaps?'

'Ain't never seen no soaps from outside the US,' he confessed. 'I guess it must be that guy Crocodile Dundee. He was a major hit a few years back. You sound just like him.'

I reflected on Winston Churchill, the Beatles, Her Majesty the Queen and Benny Hill, to name but a few famous British voices. The awful truth was that each of them had been eclipsed in the American vernacular mind by a fictitious Australian with a large knife, a funny hat and endless resources of survival cunning. Thankfully, the fireman was the last person to put us through this particular interrogation. Perhaps Crocodile Dundee had been banned by the authorities beyond the Cumberland Gap on suspicion of not using a gun.

The land continued to open out after Middlesboro, although it remained largely wooded, keeping any distant views under some sort of control. Ever since the West Virginia hollow, evidence of heavy community involvement with Christianity had been building up. Churches and chapels were everywhere, and in greater profusion than bars, which comes as a surprise to an observer from heathen Britain. National churches such as Episcopalian, Lutheran and Roman Catholic were rarely seen, but sectarian meeting houses proliferated. People here said grace before every meal, and casual radio stations socked out Jesus as we surfed the dial for something worth hearing. Tub-thumping sermons from passionate orators were broadcast on television and they made compulsive viewing. We had rumbled into the Bible Belt, where peeling black letters on yellow plastic hoardings rivalled one another for the punchiest one-liner to lure sinners into the clinical insides of the missions.

'Jesus wants one Bride, not a Harem' blared a 'wayside pulpit' on a clapboard chapel whose preacher was clearly sick of his congregation's adulterous tendencies. I chugged by, recalling a Virginia mountain folk song.

They had a big meetin' on the Cumberland drag
An' the people gathered in.
The preacher preached till his tongue wouldn't wag
But he couldn't stop their sin . . .

It seemed that little had changed.

Along the road in the same town we discovered another man of God with similar problems, reminding the faithful that, 'The law of sowing and reaping has never been repealed.'

Still at the Lord's work, the Free Will Baptist warned readers in red letters two feet tall that, 'The worst company for a man is when he gets into a rage and is beside himself.'

The best tracts of the day, however, were nothing to do with hot gospel. These secular offerings came a couple of hours later on a street lined with knee-high hoardings encouraging those of voting capacity to take part in the democratic process:

'Elect Pam O'Grady for another great term in Municipal Cleaning',

and 'Vote D'Eath for Sheriff and keep crime underground'.

Ten miles out of town we were running a wide, straight road through scrubby pine woods when Roz slowed to a halt alongside a house parked on the back of a truck. Tired and sagging, it sat on the flatbed uneasily, looking as though it might fold down on either side. I wheeled my bike around and we parked in the dirt. Half a dozen men were guzzling sodas in the shade of the gable end.

'Is the house coming or going?' I asked a tall, rangy individual in brown overalls who stepped forward.

'She's coming,' he replied.

For a while, we talked of the pleasures and pitfalls of moving house with our man, who was the owner. Literally shifting your dwelling from one location to another is a realistic possibility in parts of North America where land is cheap, construction comparatively inexpensive and houses built of timber can be hoisted off their foundations and shunted around in one piece. Some builders specialise in movable homes. These are thrown together on spec., sold by house salesmen from lots like used cars, trucked to the site of your choice, with erection on the spot as part of the deal. They come fully wired and plumbed. You plant them, hook them up and it's 'home, sweet home'. Many are well put together, remarkably roomy and a sensible option where carting bricks across a distant field is going to be pricey. The building on this truck had nothing in common with one of these miracles of engineering.

Listening in to our conversation, the gang slowly gathered around to admire the bikes. One stepped forward. Pants dragging on the road, cream shirt work-weary and torn, unshaven for three days at least, and the most beaten-up straw hat this side of Arkansas. He looked like the hickest hillbilly in the West.

He held out his hand. 'Geoffrey Whitehead from London,' he announced in pure cockney.

This was bizarre in the extreme.

'How do you come to be here?'

'I was in the Army in Aldershot back in 1988 when I was called by God to Tennessee.'

His nearest mate chuckled. 'One of the Lord's saddest mistakes,' he remarked sagely.

I looked at the sign writing on the side of the truck.

'Maranatha House Moving Co.'

The only time I heard the word 'Maranatha,' it was the name of a nineteenth century pilot cutter from Bristol, owned by a Calathumpian lay preacher who brought ships to safety between bouts of dedicated God-bothering.

I told Geoffrey about this obscure connection. He'd never heard of a pilot cutter and had not been to Bristol, but he asked if I knew what the word meant. I had no idea.

'Even so, come Lord Jesus.'

Two brown and white puppies were panting quietly in the shade, being fed bologna sandwiches on white bread by one of the workmen. They belonged to the house owner. His bitch was lashed up in a makeshift kennel under a tree. Roz unzipped her leather jacket and bent down to fuss the pups.

'She had eight, but she lost six by leaving them out in the heat.'

I understood how the poor things must have felt. By now we were up to ninety-five degrees and the afternoon smelt distinctly Mediterranean. The clouds were starting to look as though they meant business and I knew from bitter experience that if we hung around I'd end up having a thrash-out with Geoffrey about either transubstantiation or the Holy Trinity, so I tore Roz from the doggies, wished the owner well and pressed my starter.

Twenty miles down the road we stopped at a dilapidated gas station to tank up the bikes and take on a swift pint of iced water apiece. The woman in charge was incongruously dressed in a tweed frock. She had a hunted expression and was clearly hiding from something in her air-conditioned comfort zone. Glancing sideways at the usual group of guys in baseball hats with their heads together at her coffee table, she advised us to stay inside after sunset.

'I don't go out after sunset at all now,' she said, her voice low.

'Why not?' asked Roz, for whom the dark is pretty much as the light.

''cause these crazies around here'll just run you off the road an' shoot you.'

'What for?'

'They're after your money, I guess, but some of them just do it for kicks. Years ago they'd never do nuthin' like that. Nowadays, they don't even ask you to hand over your pocket-book. They just shoot you.'

More talk of violence. Yet we still hadn't actually met anybody more threatening than the gentle-natured Christian house-mover. I considered the video stores in every town offering nightly entertainment in which nice people have their heads hacked off by maniacs armed with chainsaws, or muscular superheroes machine-gun the forces of darkness with graphically devastating effect. The toll of televised violent death is shocking. 'Only when you know how to die can you know how to live' had declared the Church of God earlier that afternoon. At the time, this had seemed like muddled thinking compared with the reassurance offered in lunchtime's burger joint that, 'We wash and sanitize our hands.' Now it didn't sound so soft. Somebody must believe all this stuff, I thought. But who? It certainly wasn't the mountain men, the clockmaker or my friends back on the coast. Nonetheless, I felt vulnerable on my bike as we started up again.

Later that afternoon we were again beaten by the rain. Storm clouds had been marching on either side of us since soon after lunch, and two major contenders had run parallel to our track for an hour or more. As we soared up the crest of a ridge, they altered course without warning and began converging. The air underneath them was opaque with precipitation and as I watched their relative motion with a sailor's eye, I knew that we were for it.

Thirty seconds before the deluge, a gust grabbed a pick-up driving along in front of us and hurled it to within a wheel's width of the ditch. I feared for Roz, gripped my own bike firmly between my knees and hung on. The downdraft hit like the sudden breath of a freezer. Surprisingly, it had less effect on the motorcycle than the truck, so that by leaning hard into the wind I kept Black Madonna on the road. As the first hammer blow passed, I glanced behind to see how Roz was faring. Betty Boop was taking it full on the beam, but Roz was reacting correctly and seemed in no particular trouble, although cranked well over. I remembered reading a discussion in the correspondence columns of *Motorcycle News* back in England, on whether or not one should lean into a cross-wind. In this wilder, wider land there was no question of scientific analysis. We responded like a pair of dinghy sailors scrabbling for the 'high side' as their unsteady craft is heeled to the point of capsizing by a sudden blow. As with most questions of balance on a motorbike, the answer is not to think but to feel, and to marvel at the magic taking place in the dark tunnels of the inner ear which were never designed to handle the additional quotient of 70mph.

I slithered up a side track into the trees as the first drops fell, but long before we found shelter, water was sloshing over us in a near-solid curtain. We jumped off the bikes under a thick, leafy oak and cowered behind a pair of retired tractors that had been there for a long time, judging from the foliage poking up through their vital organs. Our lightweight rain gear seemed almost superfluous, but we struggled into the useless things anyway. Roz's leaked.

'I've been drier on the foredeck in thirty-foot seas,' she remarked as we resigned ourselves to a soggy wait under a rusty engine.

After five minutes or so things calmed off to what the BBC Shipping Forecast would have described as 'Continuous Heavy Rain'. We huddled in our makeshift hide and listened as the popping of the rapidly cooling V-twin engines mingled with the steady drumming of the deluge on the tractors and our fuel tanks. Cleaning a Harley properly is half a day's work. Even tarting one up for the road can take the best part of an hour, so keeping the bikes dry had become a private obsession.

Despite our brush with Bertha, I was still living with an unrealistic horror of being caught in the wet, but now that there was no avoiding it, I recalled a favourite sailors' maxim: 'If you can't take a joke you shouldn't have signed on!'

Leaning back on the perished tractor tyre, I inspected Black Madonna. To my surprise, the rain was giving her a new dimension.

As the clear drops ran off her waxed tank to drip over the shining complexity of her power plant, each one carried an image, a tiny world that lasted only long enough to land on the smooth black gloss and run to the edge. Letting go its despairing hold on the underside to tumble on to the cylinder fins, its doom was sealed as surely as that of an iceberg sailing down from Labrador to meet the warm Gulf Stream by the corner of Newfoundland. The droplets hit the hot chrome and evaporated with a hiss, leaving nothing but invisible vapour, where a second earlier had been a fish-eye image of the tractor, me and the oak tree.

An hour later we were at the junction again, soaked through and desperate for a motel room, preferably with a veranda to hang out our kit in the last of the afternoon sun. This had now returned in splendour, the heat had been wound back up and, except for the still streaming road surface which for once had not instantly dried, the world had returned to normal. As we waited beneath the huge sky for an easy gap in traffic that the storm had bunched together, a procession of pick-ups, small trucks and modern cars swished by. Their windows were shut tight against efficient rubber seals and their inhabitants peered gloomily at their half-world through fogged-up glass. As we penetrated further from the East Coast, we had noted Japanese imports thinning out. This was a loud statement of heartland foreign policy, since, with the clear exception of the full-sized American cars, the only true difference we could finger between 'Tokyo trashers' and the home-grown puddle-jumpers was that Detroit cars were less efficient.

Suddenly, a pair of bright lights pierced the muddy spray that hung like a shroud over the tarmac. They were wider apart than the puddle-jumpers', but too low for a truck. As they approached, a motor car materialised behind them, long, wide and curvaceous; jacked up just high enough above its broad, chromed wheels to give it flair. Its mock radiator grill was divided in the centre and, as it swept closer, immaculate orange paintwork glowed through the filthy road-haze like a beacon of hope.

An early seventies Pontiac GTO.

I don't know when Detroit stopped making these sports saloons, but it was a sorry day for America. This one sailed by like a Wagnerian heroine riding the wings of the storm. Its exhaust pipes growled the discreet message that at sixty it wasn't working at even half-burn, and its pillarless side windows were wound into the doors so that we could see clear through to the woodlands on the other side. The driver turned to glance at the motorcycles through his shades, raised a hand in salute and rumbled on, lost after a few seconds into the mist of his wake. We kicked the bikes into gear and followed him with lightened hearts.

We had seen the Spirit of the Eagle.

chapter eight

old man river

Still soggy, but steaming dry in the comparative cool of the evening, we rode into the bustling tobacco town of Springfield, population 11,277. A feeling of run-down decay pervaded the untidy streets as we cruised along, aching all over, searching for lodgings. Tourism was not a factor hereabouts, so campgrounds were out of the question. Rough camping was also a non-starter because all land in America tends to be owned by somebody, and after the warnings from the lady in the gas station, we weren't interested in taking the chance of upsetting anyone.

Not long before, we'd stopped for an ice cream in a village and had felt a distinct hostility in the glare of a pair of farm hands who clearly didn't take to outsiders. At this stage of our journey, the phantom in the GTO represented my idea of one end of conservative American nationalism. These xenophobes placed themselves stolidly at the other. They were from the dark end of that street.

Entering from the east, the outskirts of Springfield held little charm. Straight road, dust, run-down business buildings and the occasional store burning up in the afternoon sun. No hotels. Past a square brick tobacco warehouse in dire need of pointing and identified by a huge leaf on one wall, we came abruptly upon a light-controlled junction with a main road. On the map, this throughway had looked nothing special, but in the flesh it was wide and busy as it swept around a long bend from the north and away out of town up a steady incline to the south-east. No high-rise buildings disturbed the skyline. Everything was on one, or at the most, two storeys.

To the left of the junction stood a motel that looked as cheap as it was. The room was filthy, the beds cripplingly soft and the television only worked if you hit it. The smart joints we could see in the distance down the north-south highway had 'Days Inn' and 'Holiday Inn' signs on tall stalks. Tempting, except that they were going to be sixty bucks and more. Such top-of-the-line accommodation would have set us back at least seventy pounds back in Britain. Here it could be had for a mere thirty pounds for two. Add the fact that we had just moved two heavy motorcycles 130 miles for a fuel bill of five pounds fifty, and you being to realise how cheap America is for travellers, even at the up-market end of town.

That night, our fleapit cost us fourteen pounds, plus five pounds 'all up' for a burger and salad apiece at a diner down the strip. We secured our budget but, as is often the case, we got what we paid for.

Outside the next room a young man was tinkering with a rusty, nondescript American car.

'Need any help?' I asked. I carried a useful tool kit in my saddlebag, but since most males from the US countryside can sort out an automotive problem any day of the week, the question was really more of an invitation to conversation.

'Nuthin' I can't handle,' he said slowly, adjusting an air screw. He looked me up and down. 'You guys bound for Sturgis?'

I'd never heard of Sturgis – with a soft 'G', or any other sort of 'G' for that matter.

'No, I don't think so,' I responded quizzically. 'Why would we?'

'Jus' wondered,' he drawled, 'you bein' bikers an' all. That's quite some event. Where you from anyway?'

Everyone on the road in America starts out by asking where you are from, and by now I'd given up handing out my life story. I set Sturgis on the back burner, skipped the 'Britain' bit and told him we were out of Baltimore, bound for San Francisco.

He whistled, and I returned the question.

'My buddy an' me are cruising down to South Carolina from St Louis. We do house carpentry. There's jobs to spare down on the shore since Hurricane Bertha hit.'

It was my turn to whistle.

'You mean you'll drive all that way – what is it, 1,500 miles? – to find work?'

'Sure . . . Besides, it's summer. Nice to be down on the beach. We'll find some girls. Have a ball.' He reached into a cold box in the back seat and tossed me a beer.

'So why aren't you on the interstate?' I asked. 'Why is everyone on this road when the highway's only ten miles away?'

'This here's Route 41,' he replied. 'Used to be the main drag from Chicago to Miami. Went by way of Nashville Tennessee, Chattanooga and Atlanta. You can't just shut down a road like this by building a bigger one. Me and my buddy, we run most of our distance on the interstate, but every so often, we come off and drive the back roads. We lose some time, but we see more action. It's gonna take above a few days to rebuild those houses. The work's not going away.'

Later that evening, I thought about America always rolling down the road. The average US citizen who fills in census forms will move seventeen times before he or she sinks back into the ground. Brits move eight. Perhaps these two guys would never return from Carolina. The beaches are a different world from St Louis, but they are still safe territory. Still the 'Good ol' USA'. It might be a thousand miles or more, but the change would not be remotely akin to waking up in New Zealand, or Ireland, or even Britain. They would find the same fast food, the same cars, the same essential tax structure from New Mexico to Maine, although not perhaps the same pre-set cultural data.

Tired after a long, hot day, we turned in early to the sound of constant traffic in and out of the space in front of the Crown Motel. I was fast asleep when a commotion started outside around midnight. Glad that I had double-locked the bikes and chained them to the rusty stanchion supporting the porch, I pulled on my jeans and stepped out.

The chippies had gone on down south, driving through the night to avoid the heat in their non-air-conditioned jalopy. In their place, a beat-up Chevvy van was discharging four men with overnight gear. All short in stature, they were calling loudly to one another in Spanish under the glim of the only exterior lamp that still worked. One was sitting on Black Madonna rolling himself a joint. I hated him for his arrogant invasion of my space, laying on me the clear onus to act. I groped round our door for my leather jacket, a proven psychological boost in a confrontation, then materialised over him from the shadows, feeling infinitely less menacing than I hoped I appeared. He stared me hard in the eyes and I could see he was lit up, but he was isolated by fifteen yards from his mates who were now piling into their room. To my relief he dropped his gaze after a few seconds, glanced around, then climbed to his feet. As he rose, two more of his chums tumbled out of the vehicle. This pair were gibbering from drink or drugs. My man wandered across and the three of them fell through the door into what must by now have been a crowded room. Two beds, six guys, at least half of them out of their minds. I was just wishing them as bad a sleep as they deserved when the sick-looking customer who'd parked his butt on my bike reappeared.

'You okay, Man? Got all you need? This is prime.' He produced a plastic bag of what looked like cocaine. 'Price is good . . .' he hissed, a hint of menace, despite the cartoon accent.

'I'm cool,' I mumbled, 'we got our stash together. You know how it is. Can't carry much on the bikes . . . '

He came on again, but before I had to turn him down flat, one of his more sober cronies flopped out and half-threw him into their room. Ignoring my existence he slammed shut the sliding door of the van and briskly followed his shot-away mate indoors. His attitude reeked of the confidence borne of a loaded hand gun.

I stepped back inside, locked the door and shoved a chair under the handle for good measure. The night passed sweating and sleepless, listening to the throb of large-capacity engines coming and going. I lay watching the shadows on the blinds. Twice I rose and peered out at the bikes, but there was no more mischief afoot than commercial travellers down the block pulling in hookers for one-hour sessions.

As I willed the van-men to stay away from our transport, the mystery of their existence, chasing round the country in their worn-out truck with their heads full of crack, homed in on my insomnia. I couldn't talk with them as I had the carpenters. I might as well have challenged deer in the woods, yet they had the same rights in this enormous republic as the two lads on their trip to the coast, or Clark, or the dude in the red Pontiac. Perhaps, on the other hand, they were among America's four million known illegal immigrants and had no rights at all, but whatever their electoral status, somewhere along the dark hours before dawn my brain shook them off and I dozed. In the morning, they too had slipped away.

The day after the wretched night in Springfield was to be our last before the Mississippi. I had the notion that things would change after we had crossed the United States' greatest natural artery, for while the riding was rarely tedious, we had already covered over a thousand miles and seemed hardly to have begun.

Pressing on harder now, we swung into Charlotte, Tennessee in the late morning, searching for shade and a cold Coke. The town had grown up around a small-scale colonial square with a two-storey brick courthouse in the middle complete with dome. By now we had realised that, in daylight at least, securing all our gear to the bikes then chaining them to the doors of the local bank was a superfluous precaution. Things might be different in the inner cities or sometimes by the high road, but in this divided land, the towns and villages away from the beaten track are remarkably free of petty crime. We therefore dumped our leathers on the saddles, hung the helmets on the handlebars and strolled on to the manicured lawns on course for the deep shadow of an ancient cottonwood.

Outside the courthouse doors a small group of people stood around in the powerful sunshine. One of these was a girl wearing slingback stilettos without stockings and a thin cotton dress. She leaned seductively against the wall smoking a cigarette, her dress pressed intermittently against her thighs by the light breeze. Occasionally she tossed a head of thick, dark hair. I couldn't hear her conversation with two young men, but with an act like hers she must have supported a voice straight from a Tennessee Williams play. Were they just clerks on lunch break or were they litigants who had walked out for air while an unseen jury reached its awesome verdict? I never found out, because the temperature was up in the nineties and the humidity climbing fast. We had to find a cool drink or perish there on the turf.

Roz spotted a Coca-Cola sign outside a small, antiquated pharmacy, but the place was padlocked. We were just turning to leave when the tall, elderly proprietor materialised and opened up. As we drank from traditional bottles – no cans here – Mr Elliot talked of his life in Charlotte.

The whole scene must have been already out of date by the 1950s. So, it must be said, was Mr Elliot today, in his cream linen suit and horn-rimmed spectacles, but he was none the worse for that. Profits had thinned out since the premature death of Mr Elliot's brother, the local doctor, but for those who still wanted the basics of medical chemistry, he maintained a supply of zinc sulphate, asafoetida and other reliable standbys. Beneath the counters he had buckets full of worked flints from pre-settlement times, and several shelves were stocked with wooden artefacts which he made himself and sold to boost business. He used only well-seasoned timber and would provide you with a honey dipper or a potato masher as easily as mix you up a bottle of cough linctus.

We bought a masher and were rewarded when Mr Elliot reverently lifted out a dog-eared photograph album from a deep drawer.

'You like history?' he said. 'Here's mine.'

As the faded pages turned, we saw the town as part of a linear progression of time from his own childhood, the black-and-white images tucked into the cartridge paper with corner 'stickies'. In the mid-sixties, the pictures changed to gaudy colour, now well past its prime, with the courthouse, 'the oldest in Tennessee', and the square thinly parked with '57 Chevrolets and other classics. Flicking back to the early pages of the 1930s, we saw a circus parading through town, elephants to the fore and tumblers manning the wings of the advance. Next to it was a sepia print of the pharmacist as a lad, standing on the stump of a twelve-foot diameter poplar tree.

'That tree was one of the last survivors of the primary growth of this country,' he said nostalgically. 'We nearly took the lot. I guess we knew no better. But our planet will not see such trees again.'

Beyond Charlotte, we passed through a nondescript succession of small green farms and woodland until late in the afternoon when we began to feel the unmistakable pull of the Mississippi. Imperceptibly, the undulating ridges of Tennessee gave way to flatter, longer lands where the pines were cut 100 yards back from the road, adding to the feeling of increasing space. At last, we were starting to see the tarmac in an undeviating line ahead of us, with traffic thinning out so that a converging vehicle became an event in the passing afternoon.

By now, certain patterns and practices were emerging in our teamwork. When Roz vanished from my mirrors, one of three things had generally happened. She sometimes saw things I didn't and elected to investigate, knowing that sooner or later I would retrace my tyre tracks. Or I might have made a wrong turning, leaving her waiting for me back at the offending junction. Many times, I was simply riding faster than she cared to, so she had elected to drop behind. There was, of course, a fourth possibility. She might have come off.

We were demolishing the last fifty miles to our next night stop at Dyersburg, itself twenty or so short of the river, when I missed Roz's headlight. There had been no junctions or possible places of interest for miles and I had been riding faster than I'd realised, so I stopped to wait. Things had been going well and I was beginning to ignore Roz's assertions that she was not yet ready for fast cruising.

No Roz appeared after four or five minutes, so I paddled Black Madonna around and set off in the opposite direction, going hard. No junctions had split the road for at least half an hour, so there was no wrong turning option to ease my mind. I dreaded what I might see. We had no intercom sets like the Gold Wing boys, preferring not to crash in on one another's privacy, but I wished to goodness that I could call her now.

My relief was almost painful when I came across the yellow Harley sitting demurely on her stand five miles back, with Roz crouched down by a small pond holding her right shoulder.

'You OK?'

'No, not really. We were doing nearly seventy when I hit that bump back there. My shoulder took a wrench. It felt as though someone had run a knitting needle through it.'

I propped my bike and walked around to hunker down beside her.

'I expect it'll all right,' she was saying, 'but I've had twinges across my back all afternoon. I think we're trying to do too much.'

I had been afraid something of this sort would happen. We were not, in fact, riding great distances, but neither of us were used to spending day after day in the saddle. I too had been feeling tight across my upper back, but we had to keep up at least the modest pace we were setting or we'd run out of time, or money, or probably both, before the trip was half completed.

Pointing this out to Roz, who knew it as well as I, would have been a bad idea, so I offered no comment.

'Have you noticed how dragonflies are on the increase?' she changed the subject.

I had, and we sat motionless in the reeds by the water for half an hour watching blue biplane insects of tropical proportions darting over its glassy surface. The weather was cloudless, washed clean by yesterday's storms. At length, a tiny frog swam by. Roz watched him disappear under a tuft by the bank.

'I think he's gone home for his tea,' she remarked. 'Let's see if I can make it to Dyersburg.'

We carried on at a modest sixty. It felt like a snail's pace on that road, but I thanked the gods of motorcycling that we were using Harleys and not the Japanese sports bikes we'd have been hugging ourselves on to back home – the same speed on a large capacity Kawasaki urges you in some mysterious way to go for much more and would have been maddening. Travelling anything other than fast aboard such a machine is barely tolerable on the twisting lanes of Britain, but on a ten-mile straight it would drive me silly. A Harley engine is happy in top gear at any speed from forty up to around ninety. Thereafter, the operator feels at risk from low-flying push rods. In some mysterious way that has nothing to do with speed limits, most of the US just doesn't encourage careering along at such velocity, so the bike suits the conditions to a tee. Sixty is extremely comfortable on a Harley-Davidson, so for the sake of Roz's shoulder and peace in the valley, we stuck with it for a few days more.

The combination of the previous night's threatening atmosphere and the hard-core rednecks of the day before had driven home the need to side-step the seedy side of life for a night or two. In Dyersburg, we splashed out on a privately run inn on Route 51 as it bypassed the town. The place was presided over by a handsome, ageless woman with a Scarlet O'Hara voice.

She was probably in her middle fifties, but she could have been anything from thirty-eight to sixty-five, depending on how you felt and the way she reacted. With her looks and rig, she might equally have been welcoming a congregation to morning worship or soliciting a sailor into a high-class bordello so, hoping she was presently in the former mode, I gave the British charm full power and tried for a cheap deal. It availed me nothing, but at least she had a room for us on the second floor fronting on to the highway, and a table for dinner. Funds did not extend to smart meals out on a regular basis, but we needed a treat so we signed up.

The room cost more than double those of the recent horror show, but it was comfortable and furnished with taste. In contrast to our last neighbours, the folks in the next apartment were a middle class couple travelling to visit their son in another state. While Roz was showering, I decided to pop into town to buy beer. As I passed through the check-in I noticed a polished wooden desk with an open Bible and a bowl of flowers flanked by a pair of tiny US flags. It was lit by an oil lamp. Artistically propped alongside the Good Book was a prominent pair of reading glasses, just in case the casual snooper had spent all day looking at the road half a mile ahead. I had done, so I put them on. It was Psalm 119: *'My soul cleaveth unto the dust'*. How had she known? I sidled back half an hour later with a cold six-pack concealed inside my shirt.

That night, we discovered the American salad bar. All you can eat; of such quality and variety that one and a half circuits makes for a full and satisfying meal. This is not to say that the locals, who were packing the dining room, did not give the main menu a thrashing. We were in fat-boy country here, with more large people to the week than a foreigner would expect to see in a year anywhere else. Perhaps predictably, the overweight index fell as we travelled on, dropping to almost zero in the deserts of the Wild West. If the source of the complaint is glandular, as some would like to believe, it is very area-specific. A man in a drugstore told me that while a few unfortunates simply couldn't help it, for most, it was to do with being basically unsatisfied with their insulated lives. Good food is cheap; bad food is almost given away on every street corner.

'Some people just eat their way from a vague unhappiness into total misery. They start out thinking they've a sharp appetite, but soon they get into the spiral and it's too late.' So he said, while ordering, 'Coffee, black, no sugar, to go.'

During dinner and even as we returned to our room, we heard the intermittent roar of motorcycles streaming north towards the next bridge over the Mississippi. I remembered the carpenter mentioning Sturgis and consulted my Harley-Davidson literature to find that it is a township in South Dakota in the shadow of the Black Hills. Once a year, it is awakened from its slumber when a quarter of a million bikers with a ragged army of hangers-on take over its one street for a week of racing, drinking, fornication and general mayhem. Sturgis seemed an event only the bankrupt of spirit would miss, but Roz wasn't enjoying her motorbike so much that she wanted to spend a week being deafened by thousands of others; especially as the night-riding gangs going early were joining with the pain in her shoulder to rob her once again of any worthwhile sleep.

Much later I awoke to hear the thunder of a big 'chapter' dying away. Roz was at last breathing evenly. Out in the moonlight, the headlights were snaking away towards the river and the Great Plains beyond. The undressed romance of it all bit me in the gut.

Across the yard a single lamp was burning in the hotel office. In the pool of light, our hostess was totting up her books. A complex woman to be sure. I couldn't imagine what voyages she had taken to arrive in Dyersburg. She was on the Lord's side now, but she'd been dancing to a different tune when she'd learned to size up a man the way she did. Memories of the paradoxically erotic hometown singer Emmylou Harris came crooning in my mind through the noise of the night highway, accompanied by a wailing pedal guitar and a cowboy vocalist who understood everything.

Now if I were a queen, and ruler of nations,
With diamonds and jewels profound,
Well I'd rather know that I had salvation,
Than to know my reward would be Satan's jewelled crown.[5]

By nine o'clock, the day was already shaping up into a scorcher. When we said goodbye to the Madam, she unpredictably relented her hard-line stand on discounts for nobodies. Flashing a glance that left me drained of all but lechery and holiness, she gave me ten bucks off the room and directions to the Walmart hypermarket, defusing my fantasy by declaring it the best place to buy hardware.

'You ride carefully, now,' she said strictly. 'Look after your wife. And the Lord be with you.'

I staggered out to join Roz in the sunshine as she watched us crank up and swing out to buy a pair of rain slickers that did not leak.

The motorcycles were still booming up Route 51 as we wended our way to the shopping plaza through suburban lanes called 'Hummingbird Road', 'Burger Alley' and the even more improbable 'Girl Scout Road'. The checkout lady in Walmart, a blousy brunette in her late thirties, noted our biker gear and our purchases.

'You guys headin' up for Sturgis?'

I glanced at Roz and responded.

'Probably not. Besides, it's half the country away.'

The lady glowered.

'Where are you going, then? You ain't from these parts.'

'San Francisco.'

'Listen up,' she was clearly not amused. 'If you're goin' to California, you might just as well hang a right an' take in Sturgis. If you're ridin' those two Hogs out there,' she gestured at the bikes outside the glass doors – 'Hogs' are Harleys in popular US parlance – 'you jus' can't come all this way an' not be there. Jeez, my ol' man an' me ride, but we ain't never got the time off work to go, and you cross our country like God Almighty an' don't even bother. It ain't right.'

It shouldn't have been difficult to put her straight with what appeared to me sound logic. Despite the signs we were seeing of early life, the event proper didn't start for another fortnight and, in any case, Sturgis was 1,000 miles from Dyersburg as the buzzard flew. How far it might be following our meanderings was anybody's guess.

The brunette wasn't hearing me. We had trespassed on her dreams in heavy boots.

'So what's bein' free all about? A mile here, a thousand there. What's the difference when you're ridin' out?'

Roz came to our rescue.

'A lot of people have said we should go,' she said. This bit was straight up. Our inquisitor was at least the tenth. Now Roz became tighter with the truth to avoid a scene and make a friend. 'I expect we'll end up taking your advice. But you know how it is when a man gets stuck on some road he's decided on . . .'

I almost choked, but this masterpiece of hypocrisy had the desired effect.

'Make sure you do, Honey. Get him up there. An' have one for me.' The lady patted Roz on the arm like a conspirator.

She took three dollars fifty for the leggings after breaking them out of the ten-dollar pack they shared with a waterproof top.

'Damaged stock . . . ' Then she charged us for one set of instant photo prints when we'd had two made.

As I walked out into the heat, I began to wish the lady who had told us to watch out in Tennessee could have travelled here with us. We had certainly seen one or two 'hicks' and had been warned yet again about others, but the state was emphatically not 'full' of them. We'd felt uneasy once or twice, but the only gratuitously dangerous characters we'd come across were as foreign to the area as we were.

The Mississippi was our second major milestone after the Cumberland Gap. At this point in our journey, we had made no decision about where to cross the Rockies, still 1,000 miles up the road. I was itching to head north-west to Sturgis, but was receiving scant encouragement from my partner. Beyond the wide, muddy stream lay Arkansas and Missouri, then Kansas, Oklahoma and the Great Plains. Further north, in its incarnation as the Missouri, the river penetrates deep into the Wild West, remaining at least partly navigable all the way into the last Indian territories. Custer took passage aboard a riverboat for a section of his catastrophic expedition to meet Crazy Horse under the huge skies of the Little Big Horn, and sharp-dressing gamblers from New Orleans plied their trade on stern-wheel showboats in the days when Oregon and Washington states were barely settled at all.

Until recently, there was no bridge across the river between Memphis and Cairo, 130 miles northwards in a straight line. Dyersburg lies about half-way. The distance is more like 200 miles on the winding water which, in a European perspective, is the length of the English Channel from the Dover Strait as far as Plymouth. On the eastern margin of the waterway, the semi-redundant US Route 51 runs south from the Great Lakes past Dyersburg to Memphis, then on to New Orleans. West of the river, Interstate 55 now carries the through traffic from Chicago to the central Gulf, taking in St Louis on its stressed-out way. For the inhabitants of west Tennessee and eastern Arkansas gazing across the water, never the twain did meet until a new bridge with interstate standing was constructed.

This system of soaring girders offers direct access to the west, but Roz and I had determined to avoid it. Crossing the Mississippi on a six-lane highway was not what we had left the New Forest to do, so we scrutinised our state map and discovered a remote ferry where a minor road disappeared into the river.

We set out from town after lunch, a bad mistake, because by the time we had dropped down on to the alluvial plain seven miles short of the water, the temperature must have been nudging 100 degrees. Riding a ten-foot high levee across fields as flat as a pool table, we could feel rather than see or smell the river. No wind stirred the air and the heat blurred everything more distant than half a mile. Beyond fields of melons, copses heaved and squirmed like faces in a Hall of Mirrors, while the few isolated farmhouses were surrounded by acres of mirage-generated ponds that shook into baked earth as we approached. Far away, a group of immense storage tanks grew slowly in stature as we crept up to them at thirty yards per second. From a couple of miles off they looked more like a spectral temple than a utilitarian necessity of rural life.

Not a single vehicle swam into view to break the spell. No friendly signpost encouraged us to press on; only the ever-narrowing levee pointed into the distance towards an acre or two of woodland, a few shacks and what looked like a bend in the road at last. The final farm before the end of the metalled track was abandoned and as we swung round the corner down to the river, the tarmac suddenly ran out and we careered too fast on to a rutted gravel trail. We braked gingerly as the bikes bucked and slid underneath us in a welter of loose stones, but we kept them on their feet as the river opened up through a gap in the trees. A derelict concrete slipway fifty yards wide sloped in crumbled ruin to the water's edge, so we parked the bikes at its upper margin by a wrecked Chevrolet, stripped off everything we wore except for modesty's demands and walked, sweating and dizzy with the heat, down to the brown swirling stream.

Old Man River was a mile wide as he poured steadily southwards under the sun, inexorably emptying the continent. The far bank was wooded and out in the middle a long, low barge was punching its way north to St Louis. Close to where we stood, a pair of tugs were worrying half-heartedly at a dumb barge that was fast aground, totally ignored by three or four men of assorted colours absorbed in their fishing. The foreshore was the dried mud and sand of half a continent, lapped by waters gliding relentlessly seawards.

One of the fishermen squinted at me from a stool pitched squarely not ten feet from a two-foot catfish, belly-up, in the medium stages of decay.

'Pretty day, Mister.' He seemed not to notice the humidity as his sweat dripped on to his large basket.

'We thought this was the ferry,' I said, although it was already obvious that the idea had been a hopeless pipe dream.

'Ain't been no ferry here since the bridge,' the fisherman replied, casting out into the current. 'Place has silted right on up in any case,' he finished, indicating the stranded barge and turning back to the water.

I kicked some sand and walked slowly away.

Just then, a pick-up skidded on to the ramp with five kids jostling in the open back. They poured out and ran noisily down to the water where they set about investigating the rotten fish. A handsome young couple hopped from the front drinking bottled Budweiser.

The man was tall and slim in Levis, a loose, checked shirt and the inevitable baseball hat advertising some unknown brand of cattle feed. The woman was lithe, with an uncompromisingly beautiful face. She reminded me of the actress Meryl Streep.

Meryl inspected the bikes in detail, then walked over to where Roz was leaning in the shade of a wilting tree.

'The yellow one yours?' she asked.

Roz said that it was.

'More women should ride their own,' Meryl continued, 'and that is one cute machine.'

They handed us a beer each from the bottomless depths of their cooler, tossing the caps into the undergrowth.

'You folks local?' I asked, getting the hang of things.

'Sure,' replied Randy, introducing himself. 'We live up the road, but I'm a trucker. Away more 'n I'm home.'

'Do you drive for yourself, or someone else?'

'Christ, I wouldn't drive my own truck in this country. Hauling's the most inefficient industry there is. It's OK if you just sit up behind the wheel like I do and collect your pay, but if you have to jack up the loads as well, you'd never get started; what with the insurance and the worries about lawsuits and some guy getting aggressive 'cause you're operating his favourite pitch, and all the rest.'

Another barge a quarter of a mile long steamed slowly by from left to right.

'Cotton goin' north,' Meryl remarked to nobody in particular, pushing the hair back off her sweat-damp face.

'Too early yet for cotton,' Randy contradicted gently, 'but if it ain't cotton, I dunno what it is, 'cause that barge is deep down in the water.'

So it was, but Randy had already lost interest. He threw his empty bottle into the trees as naturally as if it had been a stone, then pulled out another and one for me. He topped his and handed me the opener, keeping up the litter barrage with powerful dedication. Meryl lobbed her own bottle after her husband's then offered the same for Roz, but one beer on a hot day with an empty stomach and a motorbike to be ridden was enough for her.

As the kids paddled in the mud and the heavy, unhurried afternoon cooked up way past blood heat, Meryl was still anxious to learn. She wanted to know exactly why Britain continued to support a royal family when the rest of the world had opted for the republican persuasion. I took a life-saving swig of the ice-cold beer and began attempting to explain the inexplicable. The unelected constitutional monarch, universal and unquestioned allegiance to whom is a vital factor in individual freedom left her unimpressed, and after a minute she interrupted to demand that we dish the dirt on the Prince of Wales' sex life.

'You probably know more about that than we do,' I said. It was true. Every corner shop in the US carries a selection of pocket-sized 'human interest' newspapers such as *The National Enquirer*. These creative publications will give you the facts about men from Mars enjoying kinky sex with TV stars, massive ladies who lost 140 pounds in two weeks and, of course, up-to-the-minute data about sultry nights down at Buckingham Palace. They are a lively read in a lonely motel room, so long as you don't bend your head by making a habit of it. I've no doubt that Randy brought an occasional copy home from the road to keep Meryl abreast of developments.

Pouring clouds of half-burned fuel oil from the deep throats of their exhausts, the two tug boats now decided to buckle down to a full-power heave. They churned up the riverbed in a boiling stream of thick mud, their hawsers creaking and dripping as the water was squeezed out of them by their forty-ton bollard pulls. After a protracted float-or-bust equilibrium, the barge came off the mudbank and was towed out to safety in the main stream.

Turning to Meryl, I observed that it was difficult to imagine how a professional barge skipper could strand his vessel so comprehensively in what must be one of the world's better charted rivers.

'The channels shift all the time,' she said, screwing up her eyes against the glare, 'I've been coming down here to swim ever since I was fifteen. Sometimes I'll work out towards the middle in the full current, then suddenly I'm standing in two feet of water. The next week, the bank'll have gone again. The pilots out there have a tough job.'

An hour later we crossed the river into Arkansas on the interstate, slumped off the bikes and tottered into a diner, more for the air-conditioning than the prospect of an afternoon snack. The Harleys were so hot that it hurt to sit on them. After a round of double iced waters, Roz spread out the map on the formica. There were numerous routes from here to Kansas. They all looked the same and they all looked like a long way on a burning saddle.

chapter nine

music of the ozarks

A traveller's state of mind when riding a motorcycle depends entirely on the road. If this is challenging, as it invariably is in Britain, it fills your head. Either you are setting the bike up for the next bend and moulding your body into the machine to hit the power and the shift of balance just right, or you are concentrating so hard looking out for flashing blue lights or the gravel slurry that you have no time for anything else. In the States, however, particularly in the vast tracts between the Rockies and the Appalachians, it is normal for the straight roads to demand less of you than walking down a country lane. The all-important surface quality varies, but any bike-slaying cracks are generally visible well before you arrive. In a car you click up the air-conditioning and the cruise control, turn on the radio, play your favourite tape until you are sick of it, or talk the sanity out of your companion. The bike offers none of these options for evading the main issue. You are alone, surrounded by nature with time defined by the scrolling highway. Your consciousness is in freewheel to follow what track it will.

One thing I never ask Roz is, 'What are you thinking?' This includes what was in her mind when riding. We both lived inside our own heads. For me, this often meant speeding along with my ears full of phantom music. Much of this took the form of 'country' numbers, some was rock-'n'-roll from the simplistic world before Sergeant Pepper, but right now and all the way through the Appalachians, my personal bubble resounded with traditional mountain music. At Haggerd's place, I felt I could reach out and touch the Carter Family with their ageless values and Mother Mabelle's spine-crawling accent. Thinking of the Virginia clan as I rode down the road, the droning nostalgic truths of 'Will the Circle be Unbroken?' sang intermittently. Later, contemplating the awful realities of a smashed automobile with freshly mangled bodies spilling out of it, the cracked tones of a pensioner I had heard somewhere came droning back,

There was whiskey and blood run together,
All on the road where they lay.
I saw the wreck on the highway,
But I didn't hear nobody pray . . . '

Running across Arkansas towards the Ozark mountains, I recalled an album on tape that I had been given in the mid-seventies by a man called Ambrosio. The cassette looked as though someone had been sleeping on it and it must have been at least the fifth re-record from the original, but it became a part of life aboard the boat I had then.

Roz and I had run out of luck in Charleston, South Carolina, but found a snug haven up a muddy creek alongside the shrimp boats. Here, we fell in with a mixed community of fishermen and freelance engineers with a sprinkling of out-of-work hippies who styled themselves 'The Hungry Neck Yacht Club'. The fishermen were hard, but they gave us a crab pot that fed us night after night. The engineers sorted our mechanical problems which had defied the best brains in the North Atlantic basin. The hippies gave us a music tape.

Ambrosio wore the classic 'freak' outfit of ragged jeans, flower shirt, beads and a beard that would have been the envy of Moses as he turned the Nile to blood. This not-so-young

good vibrations

American lived aboard a no-hope yacht of around thirty-five feet overall length. His partner in the enterprise was a girl of fiery temper and hair so carroty that if it hadn't been genuine it would have been unbelievable. She was said to be the owner of the vessel. Then there was Ricky, who squatted with an extensive stash of grass in a rusted-out Cadillac Eldorado that had once been pink, a mad Irish farmer busted out from Oklahoma and a lawyer called Suzie who was right on the edge. Suzie lent us a fifty-dollar Plymouth in which you shifted gear by pressing buttons. It was a wild car that was even nearer falling over the cliff of polite society's bitter end than its owner.

One day, Roz and I had taken the Plymouth into Charleston to buy a part for the boat. Homeward bound across the narrow river bridge one of the tyres blew, so we stopped to change the wheel. This blocked up one lane. The more athletic traffic managed to squeeze by outside us, but we had soon created a tailback. I opened the trunk to grab the spare and discovered it was flat. Help was needed, so I left Roz in charge and flagged a lift to the creek a mile or two further on. Ricky mustered the troops and we found a wheel that looked as though it might do. Then we all piled into the massively illegal Cadillac; Ambrosio, the carrot-haired girl, Ricky, myself, a mechanic named Andy, his girl who was memorable for the legend on the bulkhead of her boat, 'Isn't this a lovely day? Just watch some bastard louse it up!' and a shady fellow said to have murdered several people.

The pink monster careered out on to the bridge in fine style. Its offside front panel flapped like a broken wing and its non-existent shocks had it pitching like a ship in a heavy sea. On we went in a blue haze of marijuana smoke with Andy sitting on the trunk hanging on to the spare wheel and Ambrosio serenading us on a beat-up guitar. Breasting the summit under the criss-crossed girder structure, we could see a mile-long queue ahead on the other side of the road.

'I think,' said Andy, leaning into the accommodation space, raising his voice against the slipstream and the roar of the lace exhaust, 'we'd better keep right on going.'

'Waddayamean?' shouted Ricky, a joint the size of an empty toilet roll clamped firmly in the side of his mouth against the buffeting wind.

'Jus' take a look at the car behind the Plymouth,' drawled the mechanic with laconic deliberation.

We did. It was a state trooper.

'Oh shit!' Ricky hit the gas. As we swept by on the other side, Roz was being slowly pushed, fender to fender, by an angry-looking cop. The Plymouth was limping badly and the only place for our car-load of crime to be was anywhere but here.

By the time we returned to the creek, Roz had managed to chat up the trooper who had seen to the tyre and had even bought her a burger. By the mercy of God, he left just before the Cadillac lurched into the yard.

We heaved up the wriggling crab pot, Suzie arrived with a crate of beer and life kicked in once more.

That night, Ambrosio gave me the album, *Music of the Ozarks*.

'This is the very best music ever made, Man,' he confided, his eyes bloody with booze and bonhomie. 'And you can't buy the tape.'

Ambrosio was right.

The last we saw of him was some weeks later. He was motoring the battered yacht northwards out of the creek, with

Carrot giving him major earache, just as the murderer was driving into the yard, tanked up on rum.

'That bastard's got my money,' raved the enemy, dashing around the boats looking for one he could steal to give chase. 'He did a job on my yacht an' it's all turned to horse-crap. The thing's sunk an' now he's away out of it. I'll kill him. Just gimme a boat!'

The assassin made off with a small, tatty speed-boat and tore out into the harbour heading south. I hope they never met, though Andy had suggested we tip off the cops anonymously to look out for the sport boat, near to which there could well be a 'homicide in progress'.

I still have Ambrosio's original tape. *Music of the Ozarks* is a collection of folk songs and instrumentals from amateur players in the mountains that now lay ahead of us, twenty years after Ambrosio puttered out from Shem Creek. There are tales of faithful horses, 'The Tennessee Stud'; gospel songs from a cleaner, simpler time; obscure ballads about people dismembering their lovers for no apparent reason while the river flows on to Knoxville Town. Moonshiners fool the Revenue Men, and Old Bill Jones slips his reluctant mistress an anaesthetic dose of hooch then marries her while she is still unconscious. Pounding all through like the weft of a woven cloth, run wild fiddle and banjo rhythms, lifting the spirits of any but the dead of soul.

I have listened so often to Ambrosio's music that I know every lilt and slide as well as I know the tides of the Solent. Riding across that fertile plain west of the Mississippi, it took over my mind while the Harley churned ahead through the sultry afternoon, vibrating all through my body, urging onwards to the subliminal rippling of the long-dead hillmen's reels. The small farms of eastern Arkansas flashed by on the board-flat land as we turned off the main highway of Route 412 to jink our way via an unprecedented eight turnings between lunchtime and the storm-determined end of the day.

The threat of storms stalked us all the way from the Appalachians to the high plains of eastern Montana. Back in the hill country, or along the border of Tennessee and Kentucky, it had been tough to get a fix on cloud movements and impossible to organise any avoiding action, so we took what came on our chin straps. As the country opened out into wider spaces and large-scale chequer-board road patterns, storm dodging developed a remarkable similarity to operating at sea in squally conditions. We made radical course alterations using the ninety-degree road junctions to enable the storm clouds to shift their relative bearings in the changing apparent wind. Half a lifetime of subconsciously analysing airflow patterns must have helped, and so long as we could keep the nearest edge of the rain moving backwards against the horizon, we stood a fair chance.

In the afternoon, we were passing though the town of Sedgewick when rapidly darkening clouds suddenly stopped cruising around aimlessly and gathered with ominous intent. Sedgewick didn't grab our fancy, and as it was only four o'clock we decided to chance our luck and blast up the main road towards the imaginatively named settlement of Pocahontas. For me, at least, romantic names formed the mainspring of parts of this trip, and Pocahontas was surely a queen in this department. Nearby was a smaller village called Powhatan. We had no special interest in this father-and-daughter team and their English chum John Smith the chart maker, but the name alone was pulling us in when we felt the now-familiar blast of cold air from the heavens. The bike was blown sideways by the gust, while away to the north-east a black wall of rain was establishing itself and advancing athwart our course with the speed of a modern mechanised division. The anvil cloud above it was striding straight towards where we would be in five minutes time and all seemed lost when we came upon a road junction offering a way out to the south-west. 'Hoxie', read the signpost. In the intermediate distance we could actually see the buildings rising above the plain. Two miles, maybe three.

I decided unilaterally to swing the corner and together we opened up wide and let the rubber rip the road. For a few heady moments, Roz lost all speed-shyness as we cracked on up to the railroad crossing that stood between us and the single main street of town. The bells were ringing to announce a train, but the barriers were still up so I dropped the clutch and lurched across a rough set of rails. Turning to check Roz, hard on my back wheel, I saw her glance towards the storm. Shining out of the roaring blackness like a warning beacon, the powerful headlight of a locomotive was in plain view up the track, growing fast. Roz watched it coming, stopped and appeared mesmerised. Just as the barrier started to drop, condemning her and Betty Boop to an unavoidable soaking, the train whistle blew. 'Whaaaa, Whaaaa!'

The American train siren has the psychological effect of a gigantic invisible hand sweeping anyone near the tracks clear of the approaching judgement day. The car-count on the freight trains pounding through Hoxie ran well into three figures, pulled by four locomotives strapped together weighing in at hundreds of tons apiece. Squealing to a sudden halt to avoid crushing a yellow motorcycle would not be an option for the engineer, even had the timetable permitted its consideration. To my astonishment, therefore, having apparently committed herself to the discomfort of the safe option, Roz scrutinised the storm cloud, glanced at the locomotive, then flicked the Sportster into gear with her left boot and shot across the iron road, arriving on the dry side just as the barrier slammed shut behind her. The rain was cutting towards us like a scythe with the train hot on its heels. I could hear the falling water hissing on the melting tarmac as we turned to flee before it, racing along a one-sided street with buildings to our right and railroad to the left. We wheeled into the shelter of the portico outside the 'Ol' Hickory Motel' with not ten seconds to spare.

Thirty yards across the road, the giant diesel rumbled by shaking the ground, dirty yellow, with 'Union Pacific' proudly painted down its flanks, the tail-end of its train fuzzing out of vision in the heat haze beyond the storm. The tan-vested engineer peered through the rain-lashed window of his cab and raised a hairy arm in ironic salute to Roz. It took two full minutes before the guard's van clanked by, leaving the scene oddly quiet and bare, with only the Mack truck drivers heading down to Little Rock, Arkansas behind their slapping windscreen wipers, and the brown swooshing sound of the rain on the shingle roof.

A little later, I strolled across the street to examine a stationary freight train. The wheels of the first box-car I came to were chest-high from where I was standing and the whole unit was as tall as my cottage back in England, and considerably longer. I paced out the length of the carriage, added a few feet for the space between the wagons, and then multiplied the sum by one hundred. Totalling up a further fifty yards or so for three or four diesel locomotives, the train was a mile and a half long.

With the setting sun behind me, I drifted along the edge of the ballast for half a mile, fetching up at the caboose. The guard leaned out and put me in the picture about how they would be here for another five minutes while a train further down the line cleared the tracks. Divided from the engineers up front by over 2,000 yards of ironmongery, he was on his lonely way towards Wyoming to load up from the open-cast coal mines that are ripping the face off swathes of that fair state. He had worked on the Union Pacific all his life, and his father before him. Now, his only daughter's husband had gone clean off the rails into the new world of information technology. The railroad man saw no dignity in the boy's calling.

'It's fine and dandy communicating quicker and better than ever, but in the end, you gotta have steel. No steel: no automobiles, no dishwashers, no street lighting, no ships, no buildings, no United States.'

'But surely, all this new technology has its place? Otherwise we'd be back with the Pony Express.'

'Sure it does, but this country was built on industry. Heavy industry. Making things that have a function, things that folks want to buy. You can't cook with a computer and you can't climb in it and ride it to California. This Internet craze will settle down in a few years and he'll be out of work. But the trains'll still be around.'

Something beeped inside his cab and he turned away from me to attend to the mysteries of his craft.

'Here we go, then. Be seein' you, Mister.'

A cloud of black exhaust appeared from the front of the train, followed five seconds later by the deep throb of a diesel beginning to pull. It took that long for the sound to reach us. From along the line of cars came the steady clanging of couplings taking up the slack and the squeak and rumble of truck wheels starting to turn. Twenty cars to the westwards, the train was in motion. In no time, the guard's van smoothly followed. I watched it shrink into the distance beyond town until it was lost in the dazzle of the setting sun.

Back in the Ol' Hickory, I slumped on the bed and stared at the ceiling. To a European used to ceilings plastered from wall to wall, the cladding that covers the joists in North America is startling. Often, ceilings are panelled with board or even polystyrene held up by narrow timber strips or a light metal framework. The sections can be anything from two feet square to half the ceiling, although the method of support remains the same. The smaller variety make working on the plumbing or wiring easier than levering up floorboards in the room overhead as most Brits are constrained to do when the central heating starts to drip black filth on to the best carpet. Yet even here, a downside lurks. Years before, I was hired to help renovate a Boston flop-house. I removed one of these panels, delighting in the ready accessibility, only to be showered with ex-mice and other dust-caked horrors that had opted not to die honestly out in the yard. Except at their best, which in roadside motels they often are not, these ceilings at first look home-made and untidy, yet after a few months they fade from the traveller's consciousness and become an unnoticed part of the indoor scenery.

As the coolness eased the aches of the day, I inspected the room in more detail and realised that it was a classic in quintessential American styling. To our eyes, the general effect is often dark, the walls lined with wood-effect composite material in preference to the stuff that comes from trees. As a lover of timber, I can never understand this preference for the laminates that proliferate even in smart homes. There is an intangible fifties and sixties feel to furnishings and light fittings, while the efficient, but aesthetically disastrous Venetian blind remains popular, often without a vestige of curtain to ease its starkness.

The Ol' Hickory was also typical in the bed-linen department, with tightly tucked blankets reminiscent of a post-war childhood instead of modern quilts. But the price was right, and in any case, the main decision to be made at bedtime in summer is whether to leave the air-conditioning on and suffer the stress-inducing racket, or turn it off and risk dissolving under a damp sheet somewhere in the mazy world before morning.

It seemed as though a train passed through Hoxie every half-hour between dusk and dawn, so that the long-standing importance of the railroad to American continental culture was rammed noisily home. Surrounded by the sound of heavy commerce, in the middle of the night, in a small town that only existed to be on the way to somewhere else, it was easy to empathise with the guard's frustration over his daughter's choice of husband.

In the first half of the nineteenth century, investment in the transport of goods and people by rail proved a winner for both fly-by-night gamblers and conservative shareholders. Funding could be raised for any viable enterprise and, as early as 1850, Washington was firmly connected to New York, Boston and even Maine by regular trains. In the antebellum South, branch lines forked away through the plantations, into the forests and across open grassland to join Charleston with

Atlanta, and Savannah with Chattanooga. Similar development was fanning out from Chicago, Detroit and the Great Lakes, but it was not until 1866, fifteen years after the California gold rush, that the momentous decision was taken to link the East and West Coasts.

From the East, gangs of Irishmen, black and white men from the defeated Southern states were hired by the Union Pacific. Construction teams graded the route ahead of the iron road, while in their wake came the unstoppable army of up to 10,000 track-layers and their pack animals. Behind these shuttled a back-up stream of trains, Typically, forty cars each carried ten tons of track, ties, spikes and timber sleepers, as well as domestic supplies for the navvies. Such a load would represent an advance of no more than a single mile of track.

As the thin, shining line crept west beyond the longitude of our present lodgings, the Central Pacific Railroad was pushing its own track eastwards from San Francisco, mostly with coolie labour from China. Their men are said to have refreshed themselves with tea, while the heavies of the Union Pacific were powered by whiskey. A subsidy of 16,000 dollars per mile promised by the government proved so inadequate when the Central Pacific hit the high Sierras that it had to be jacked up threefold.

Two years was all it took for these men of astonishing ingenuity and fortitude to fight their way across the Rockies. They had no technological support save dynamite and, with the exception of timber, all materials were delivered on their own trains, having arrived in California aboard square-rigged sailing ships obliged to beat around Cape Horn.

The straight roads across the plains of North America are still delineated by traditional telegraph wires on lofty wooden poles. These began with the first transcontinental railroad, carrying messages from station to station and bringing a huge improvement in efficiency and safety. As East Coast met West in the impossible remoteness of 1869 Utah, the telegraph was joined at the same time as the railroad track. Its commercial potential was obvious, but the first message sent from coast to coast is said to have been tapped out by a lineman leaning back against his leather strap high in the wind on his historic pole. 'Stand By! We have done praying.'

In the morning we sheered off from the railroad. Riding on rising ground towards Mountain Home, Arkansas, we soon found ourselves in idyllic countryside of the type we'd expected to see along the Tennessee-Kentucky border, but hadn't. Small fields interspersed with sweet-smelling copses of pine and neat, fresh-painted farmsteads. In one meadow by a stream three handsome horses were standing knee-deep in grass and wild flowers; one white, one caramel and one a yellow butterscotch colour. I swung Madonna into the roadside, dismounted and was leaning on the gate when Roz arrived. I'd stopped for her, really, because I knew it was a scene she would want to savour, but instead of exuding sweetness and peace, she was clearly uptight about something. I chose to ignore the signs, half-heartedly hoping the mood would lift. I should have known it wouldn't.

She joined me at the gate, but said nothing.

'Lovely riding,' I tried again. 'Nice and cool.' The temperature was easing as we climbed towards the hills, but I'd got something badly wrong.

'It probably is for you,' Roz responded, 'but until you stopped, I haven't been able to enjoy a thing about it. I have to concentrate so hard on these twisting roads that all I see is your back-end, the tarmac and the traffic coming towards me.'

'But there isn't a lot of that.'

'No,' she acknowledged, 'but every time one of those wagons goes past, I feel as if it's attracting me like a magnet. I daren't breathe until it's gone. It's terrifying, my back's giving me stick and there's something wrong with my wrist.'

I had known Roz for over a quarter of a century. We've seen tough times together, and I understood that she wouldn't complain until almost at the end of her resources, yet this all seemed over the top. I'd been riding as slowly as seemed reasonable, and apart from a truck or two every few minutes, the traffic had been almost non-existent. The road had been narrow and unusually twisting with an indifferent surface, but I had not seen any special challenge in the morning's ride. To her, it seemed to have become a nightmare of fear and danger.

'Try to be reasonable,' I began, falling headlong into another perfect masculine blunder from sheer frustration, 'this is like Utopia.'

I must have involuntarily raised my voice in frustration, because my wife came back at me with interest.

'Don't you shout at me!' she said with venom. 'You're big, you're strong and you've been riding since your voice broke. I still have to think about having the clutch on the handlebars, and every time I stop or start, I know that if I let the bike go down more than ten degrees I'm going to drop it. How can you be so bloody thoughtless!'

I shook my head in despair. It was no good arguing that I hadn't even thought about shouting at her, so there was nothing useful to add. Roz took this as dumb insolence.

'Have you any idea what it would be like to hold on to this bike if you only weighed 125 pounds?'

With a full tank and her travelling gear, Betty Boop topped the scales at over 500.

Without another word we carried on into the township of Hardy, parked up and went looking for some lunch. We had a serious problem, and we did not walk hand in hand.

Hardy is another small town, but unlike Hoxie, the main thrust of its effort is given over to entertaining visitors and relieving them of their money.

The clapboard Hardy Café on the narrow main street was packed full of families tucking into Sunday lunch, but we found a corner table underneath a plastic flowerpot with plastic ivy. On the wall beside us was a painting of a silver catfish dressed, like the diners, in blue dungarees and a cowboy hat. Between his whiskers, this fish was smoking a corncob pipe. I ignored his unwritten promise of fresh river-food and ordered the safe bet of 'Sirloin Tips', this time with ocra on the side. Then we addressed the main issue.

The bottom line was that quitting was no option. So long as the traffic was thin and the roads not too demanding, Roz was going to be content to come slowly to grips with the new discipline. If ever she was obliged to park the bike on an awkward slope, she would kick down the side prop to prevent Betty Boop falling all the way and when she was ready to start up once more, I would stand by to heave the heavy bike upright until Roz was letting in the clutch. I would also help out with the back-murdering manoeuvring that came our way every night as we wrestled the bikes into precarious shelter between the stanchions of motel half-roofs or the tree-roots around the tent. As she said, it wasn't that she hated the motorcycle. She'd always enjoyed fast cars.

'I'll just have to hang on through these hills,' she announced, pushing half a plate of tips to one side. 'It's got to be easier on the plains. The weather might be harsher, but looking at the map it's straight, straight roads for a thousand miles. By the time we reach the Rockies, riding Betty'll be a piece of cake.'

I kept on chewing my sirloin. If she'd made her mind up, life was going to be easier by far.

'I know you'll do what you can to help,' she added unexpectedly, 'it'll get better You'll see.'

And it did, for a while at least.

Out in the street, we walked straight into a yard sale. The proprietor, a huge man dressed exactly like the catfish, right down to the corncob pipe, was divesting himself of the family tools.

Among the usual selection of chipped chisels and beaten-up screwdrivers, was a complete set of caulker's equipment and a weird, three-pronged iron device on a stout broom handle. At a thousand miles from the sea, it was more than odd that a caulker had passed this way and left his tools behind. Caulking mallets could once be bought in any respectable chandlery, but the irons were, and still are, the sort of personal items a tradesman grows used to. They pass down through families and are rarely seen second-hand, even on the coast where this outfit must have originated. I asked the giant what boats he had caulked, and he did not know what I was talking about. I told him. He shoved his hat back on his head, rubbing his hand back and forth in the sweat standing on his broad brow.

'That so? Well, hot-dawg!' He perked up when I picked up the item on the stick.

'That's for diggin' out frogs,' he said broadly. 'Kinda useful for a frog dinner. But y'all know that. Bein' as you're from outta town, you can have her for twenty-five dollars.'

I backed off fast.

'Well, how 'bout ten bucks then. You won't find a better one,' he paused, realising he was missing the mark, 'but I guess you folks'll have one already back home?'

'That's right,' interjected Roz. 'Like you say, it's not as good as yours but it'll do us for a while. Besides,' she added archly, 'frogs aren't as big as they used to be.'

I knew she'd based this statement on the fact that up in Nova Scotia, where I had worked on an inshore long-liner, the fish were now far from what they had once been. A quarter of a century earlier, the boys and I had cruised into port in the evenings with a catch that started at eighteen inches and went up to three or even four feet in length. On a recent visit, our skipper, now long retired, told us there was a moratorium on line fishing because in the wake of the foreign 'vacuum' trawlers, people were taking cod hardly mature enough to breed. Mention the size of fish up there and you're one of the crew. Why not frogs too? Maybe the backwoods were frogged out.

Roz must have got it right, because the would-be salesman shook our hands like good buddies as we left, even though we hadn't bought a thing. It was good to see Roz back on top of the game.

Further down the road towards where we'd parked the bikes, we passed a used boot store of galactic scale with one-owner Texan high-heels lined up in pairs on the sidewalk like a Wild

West funeral parlour. All US bikers wear cowboy boots with their jeans over the top. A fashion so universal must have something going for it apart from looking cool. I had been thinking of changing my ancient World War II dispatch rider's boots (always worn outside the jeans, comfortable beyond price and tough as nails), which the locals called 'shit-kickers', for some *haute couture* and this had to be the place. Tragically, out of the hundreds on offer, one of the only two pairs that fitted turned out to be pigeon-toed. The boss suggested I bought them and wore them on the opposite feet for a month or two to straighten them out, but I could see me hitting the brake with the wrong boot, so I turned them down. The others were snakeskin, all style and no substance, but Roz treated herself to a pair of high, light brown 'ropers' with little Cuban heels and sexy lace up fronts. They were comfy from the start and looked great, but she wouldn't wear them riding, preferring the first-class protection of her full-on racing boots brought from a colder land. The ropers went home by mail.

The salesman took Roz's money, stepped easily through the usual opening gambits, then advised us that the main problem with the US nowadays was that the dollar had become more important than the people. A second man stepped out of a closet and agreed with him. He was someone you could not ignore.

The newcomer stood six and a half feet tall, with no fat on him. Good teeth, full lips and a broad smile, in a black shirt, black Stetson, dark blue Levis and boots with holes in the toes. In his huge hand he carried a cheap-looking, brand-new violin in a grip like a poacher holding a pheasant. I asked him about local country music as soon as I saw his instrument, but he did not play. Instead, he sold these fiddles for the incredible price of forty dollars apiece. He had just returned from Indianapolis where he had made a killing on a trunkful.

Unlike most Americans we met in the middle of the country, this man held opinions about foreign policy.

'You Brits did a great job down in the Falklands,' he said, and I sensed him sizing up whether he or I was the taller. 'People who walk into other folks' houses with guns and say "Git!" want putting away. We have enough of that stuff over here, but when whole governments climb in on the act, why, someone's gotta stop them. Your Mrs Thatcher, she sure knew how to call a halt. Best leader since FDR.' While pleased to hear this endorsement of my country, I wasn't sure how to respond.

'I don't know why we didn't do more to help,' said the store owner. 'That all wanted doing.'

'Jeez,' responded the big fellow. 'Them Brits didn't need no assistance, but we did tell some interfering busybodies to stay out of the ring.'

'Who was that, then?' I asked.

'I guess mebbe they didn't tell you guys,' he said, 'but some heavy hitter with a capital to the east of you was makin' all sorts of hints that they'd send their troops in to back up the bandits. The USA told 'em to stand aside from somebody else's quarrel, or they'd have serious trouble on their hands.'

The laughing eyes disappeared, replaced by Lee Van Cleef sighting down his Peacemaker in *The Good, the Bad and the Ugly*, and I believed every word he said. Behind that look was an iron will and total confidence in the power of his country to prevail in the cause of justice. I have met more sophisticated Americans who might call this fiddle salesman's attitude naïve, but I found it reassuring. There was not a hint of arrogance in him, and I knew who I'd rather have beside me in a bunker with red-hot shot flying overhead.

'You guys want music,' the salesman interjected, 'you'd best head for Branson, Missouri. That town's built on music. You go there.'

Back at the bikes, I noticed Roz touching her forearm carefully, and asked what was the matter.

'I've been bitten, I think,' she said, carefully unbuttoning her sleeve that was turned down against the sun. 'It's throbbing like mad.'

Her wrist had swollen to twice its normal size. Angry and puffy. It wasn't surprising she'd blown out that morning. She needed a doctor and she needed rest.

Hardy was a tourist town. Plenty of fancy 'Bed and Breakfast' homes charging more than we could afford. Camping was out of the question. The doctor was off-duty on Sunday, so we filled up the bikes and asked how far to Branson.

'Seventy miles, I guess,' said the elderly gas station attendant, leaning against the unleaded pump.

'More like fifty-five,' contradicted his sidekick, whittling a stick in the shade of a battered timber kiosk.

I glanced at my folded Rand McNally state map. It looked further than either of these estimates.

'I should say it's a full 150 miles,' put in the owner of a mud-caked truck from the other side of the pumps.

'Anyways, you keep right on goin' through the hills past Mountain Home, up 62 as far as Harrison. Then you hang a right in the centre of town and hit 65. You'll be four hours on them rigs if you don't hurry.'

'Yeah,' broke in the pump man laconically. 'Three hours, mebbe four . . .'

It was easy to forget that Americans on the road think distance in terms of hours, not miles. The heat was far less oppressive here in the hills, and the afternoon could only become cooler as the miles spun by. I looked a question mark at Roz.

'Let's go for it,' she said, zipping her leather and carefully fastening the studs over her bad arm. 'I'll take a break there. If it's no better, I'll find a hospital in the morning while you sort out some music.'

And so we wound our way through the Ozarks, disappointed at the lack of hillbillies and hoping for better from Branson; Roz nursing her throttle arm and me yearning for Oklahoma, Kansas and the wide open spaces.

chapter ten

the beginning of the big wide world

I don't know what I'd imagined for Branson, music centre of the Ozarks, but the reality was definitely not it. It had been a long day, with frequent stops to water up and for Roz to rest her arm, and the first we saw of the town was a long, deeply undulating strip that materialised around us out of the woods. Among the fast food and service stations were expensive hotels with smart new cars parked in the lots. Mini-theatres offered all manner of electrified country singers, retired pop stars, dance bands, everything except the clean, blue grass music we'd been hoping for. As we thrummed our way down the hill we realised that the place was a temple to tourism. We'd transgressed the travellers' line again, so with sinking hearts we retreated to the river where our luck turned. By the water's edge, we found a 'resort motel' that hadn't changed since the 1960s. The neat, individual lodges were arranged like a tiny village, with a loose square in the centre. The office was part of an older timber house. To complete the ambience, the place needed one or two '57 Chevrolets and a panhead Harley with a rider in a Marlon Brando cap. What it got was us. Nobody else. All the tourists were paying big bucks uptown.

I clattered up the steps to the check-in and banged the bell. A young woman of stunning beauty appeared, dressed like a football cheerleader in flouncy skirt, blouse and headband.

'Sure we have a cabin. It's thirty-five dollars, I'm afraid, but there's a fridge and cooker and a TV as well as the usual . . . '

good vibrations

Up the hill, the crowd were being charged eighty-five dollars plus for a bed and a bathroom. I took the room, sight unseen, and the girl thanked me. She had grace as well as looks.

We moved into the cabin, set to stay two or three days while Roz got well, then we chained up Betty and hopped aboard the Heritage to hunt for dinner. The Roundup had peanut shells all over the floor and an Appalachian harp on the wall. It hadn't been played in years. The steaks were large and tender but the booze was non-existent because it was Sunday. I needed a drink and Roz looked as though she'd kill for a whiskey. We threw a few peanuts around for the sake of good manners, then bopped home to the cabin where I had kept the last quarter-pint of Haggerd's moonshine for just such an emergency. We drank it between us and felt better, as he'd promised we would. It was full-strength lightning, not yet diluted for human consumption, so I took mine fifty-fifty and had sweet dreams behind the blinds. Roz went for the whole experience and didn't feel a thing till her arm woke her with a deep, dull ache at five. She gulped down a handful of pain killers and turned on the television.

I awoke two hours later to a time warp of a younger, simpler America that a casual visitor might imagine has been eclipsed by progress. Opening one eye carefully, I saw our room by daylight. A throwback to *I Love Lucy*. Chequered plastic cloth on an angular table with biblical tracts on the wall behind it, vinyl chairs, tartan sofa in orange and brown, the standard mock wooden walls and a screen door to an open veranda. Roz had the kettle on as she watched an ancient television set with round Bakelite knobs instead of digital tuning and a zapper. As if specially ordered to match the surroundings, a 1950s black-and-white comedy was showing. Andy Griffiths, strutting his stuff in surroundings that matched our own to perfection.

'How do you feel?' I grunted.

'Hung over, and no better.' She angled her head towards the screen. 'I keep expecting a pink caddy to stop outside full of young guys with army haircuts draped around girls with ponytails and sticky-out skirts.'

Then she showed me her arm.

We were in the hospital by 0800. At nine, we were out once more, surprisingly few dollars the poorer after the sort of service any Brit in a casualty queue with less than a broken neck would find hard to believe. We were loaded with antibiotics and reassured that Roz was only suffering from a buffalo fly bite.

'Lucky for you it wasn't a brown recluse spider,' the nurse had observed. 'They dig a great hole in your flesh. Sometimes, they're fatal. Take all the pills and have a couple of days' rest. You'll never know it happened.'

So we relaxed in our little home. I stocked up at the corner store and Roz started the pills. By midnight she was up alternately vomiting and prostrate with diarrhoea and I was awake with a badly burned leg that was my just reward for riding into town in shorts. A Harley exhaust burns just as badly as a Matchless or a Kawasaki. The difference is that while other bikes keep their pipes low down out of harm's way, Harley-Davidson site theirs where they will impress the bystanders and burn the skin off the legs of any clown who forgets.

At nine the following evening we were both feeling surprisingly improved. The swelling had almost disappeared from Roz's wrist and my burn had scabbed over, so we fired up Black Madonna and headed out towards a bar three miles away, where I'd eased my thirst on the foraging trip and met the bartender who had been out polishing his ancient Harley.

The parking lot in front of the bar was notable for black shadows and lack of neon lights, but the headlamp picked out a selection of wreck-status cars, an interesting white Italian Moto-Guzzi at least twenty years old with a leopard-skin seat, and one extremely smart Jeep land cruiser. Inside, it was almost as pitchy, but the air was alive with twanging guitars wailing somebody's grief on the hi-fi, cigarette smoke and the honest smell of booze. Jim the biker-barman kicked a deadbeat off a barstool to make room for Roz and pulled us each a glass of fizzy lager on the house.

It wasn't long before we were part of the general conversation at our end of the bar. Sitting next to us was a handsome man of around my own age with a leather vest, a long queue of grey hair and a major hair braid. Beside him was a girl in her thirties with hair redder than a traffic light, a major body and a 'go-get-'em' attitude.

'You guys headin' up for Sturgis?'

'No decision yet,' I replied dismally, avoiding Roz's eyes. 'I guess you're going?'

'We are,' said the grey-haired man. 'I've been a coupla times, but Red here goes most years.'

'Where are you from?' I got in first, for once.

'I'm from the East Coast,' said our man. 'Merchant seaman. I work three months, get three off. I love it up in Dakota. Cooler in summer, but don't mess with winter.'

Roz brightened at the prospect of sweat-free slumber.

'So you've ridden across this far, same as we have?'

'No way!' cut in Red, 'Rich has a camper van. We travel in that, sleep over in it nights. The Guzzi goes on a trailer. We take her down for a buzz round sometimes in the evening.'

'Don't you feel you should be riding all the way?' asked Roz, perhaps deliberating about a better way of doing this thing.

'Jesus no,' responded Red. 'Not on that ol' Guzzi. Have you seen the buddy seat? My ass would never stand it. Plus, it's cheaper this way. No room bills. Most people ship their bikes out to Sturgis one way or another. If you ain't riding there, where are you going?'

'San Francisco, then maybe back to Baltimore.'

'Sweet Jesus!' Red took another look at Roz. I had to say that if the two women had been assessed on image alone, it would have been Red cracking on across the prairie with her headband flowing in the endless wind, and Roz pruning lupins in her garden. But as Bernard Shaw's butler observed, 'You never can tell, Sir. You never can tell.'

Jim's girlfriend Kim now joined in the conversation. Red was dressed for the road, if provocatively, but Kim was in a cocktail dress and heels, long blonde hair and manicured hands. She was another reminder that things are often not what they seem. Her main interest in Red, Rich and the Brit contingent was the machinery. She turned out to be a motor mechanic, more interested in how a Harley can air-cool its back cylinder at desert temperatures than anything, except Jim himself, who cut a manly figure as he kept the punters' glasses topped up.

Nobody could say why it is that Harleys don't seize up in the heat, but Rich was soon extolling the virtues of the stylish Moto-Guzzi, whose own twin cylinders are arranged so as to poke out on either side into the airstream. Roz had lost interest before he started and soon Red had also heard enough.

'Jim!' She called along the bar, 'bring us all a rattlesnake!'

Jim upturned a variety of spirit bottles into a huge shaker, whirled it around a few times, then poured the contents into six large glasses.

'Better drink along with you guys, I guess,' he said. 'That way I know how bad things are getting.'

Roz had taken a cocktail of pills before leaving the cabin, and I glanced at her anxiously, but she was obviously firing on both cylinders, so I put the question of her sickness from my mind. The rattlesnake bit like its namesake and Red had ordered another round before the first had reached the bottom of our glasses.

'We'll all get together up in Sturgis,' she said, loosening up, but handling the booze like a professional. 'You'll change your mind, Roz. Bound to. Bear Bluff's the place to camp. I pitch my tent right under the cliff. There's plenty of action, but I never saw nobody get shot.'

'That all's at the Buffalo Chip campground,' put in Rich. 'You don't wanna go there. Not with a lady.'

'So how do we find Bear Bluff – if we ever make it?'

Before he could respond, a scuffle broke out at a table near the door. Four youths who, according to law must have been over twenty-one, began pushing and shoving. Standing by them was a girl perfectly turned out for stirring up the boys in shark-skin jeans with a chunky zip at the back and a black, lace-up bodice.

Jim watched them hard for ten seconds, then things simmered down again.

'Bear Bluff?' Red continued, 'Well, you go down towards . . . you take a right . . . Oh shit, I don't know. You can't miss it. Sturgis is a tiny town. Just ask anyone.'

After two more rattlesnakes I was facing up to the fact that I must either leave the bike where it was for the night or run the gauntlet of the cops. The looming buildings surrounding the bar were perfect for hiding bike bandits. All manner of people passed though Branson and I'd heard reports of organised gangs heaving half a dozen Harleys on to low loaders and driving them away. The drunken ride home was going to be the best of two bad options, so I decided that I might as well be shot for a bull as a calf, stood my corner and ordered more rattlesnakes.

'I'll do these.' A tall, elderly man with the regulation Stetson and perfect cowboy drawl joined our group. 'Tired of drinkin' alone!'

Cactus Jack stood six feet three, lean and hard with a bootlace tie and high-heeled boots under a pair of blue jeans finished off by a cow's-skull belt.

'Where you from?' Jim asked as we made space. I was struck by the relevance of this gambit between strangers who, on the face of things, have no more in common than having to choose between the same presidential non-entities. Never again would I open a conversation by mentioning the weather.

'Down in Texas,' Jack grabbed a stool, 'grew up over the border in New Mexico. Right now, I'm sellin' jerky. Used to be a cattle man, but my wife passed away three months gone. Home's kinda empty. I'll stay on the road for a year or so. Mebbe then I'll settle down again.'

We drank quietly for few minutes while Roz found out that 'jerky' is dried meat of the type that cowhands would victual on for the long trails before the days of refrigeration. Like the similarly redundant salt cod of the North Atlantic, its backers were guaranteed a market long after the product could have been consigned to history.

'That stuff jus' tastes so good.'

It was around midnight when the girl in the lace-up leather top over by the door started screaming at the guy next to her to take his hands away. In no time, the young men were laying into each other. One hit the deck and was taking a kicking, the others kept upright and were lashing out with their fists. No knives yet. Rich and I were full of drink and little use to anyone, but Jim came flying over the bar like a champion hurdler, powered up by a tankful of rattlesnakes. He waded into the war zone without hesitation while the rest of us were clambering to our feet to go and help him. All four fighters gave him their immediate attention, urged on by the girl who had caused all the trouble. Things turned difficult and one of the guys managed to pin Jim from behind. I lurched off my stool, but before I could take a step, Cactus Jack sprang into the action like an antelope. Ignoring his undoubted age and what must have been half a pint of whiskey, he grabbed two of the guys by the hair, literally cracked their skulls together and while they were still staggering, threw them out on to the street. The odds were now even and the other pair didn't wait to be asked to leave, but as they rushed for the door, Jim grabbed one by the collar.

'The check's forty-seven dollars, Mister,' he announced grimly, bleeding slightly from the corner of his mouth. 'I'll take fifty for cash.'

The man fished a bill out of his shirt pocket and scurried out, dragging the girl after him.

Jim straightened his collar, shook Jack solidly by the hand, mopped his face and served up a free round. Jack muttered something about the diversion having blown away a few cobwebs, and began to talk as only a man who spends too much time alone can.

Being raised on a New Mexico ranch back in the forties and fifties, he had been at once innocent and sophisticated.

'Didn't know white girls had fannies 'til I was eighteen,' he announced solemnly. 'Thought that was only for them Spanish women.'

I watched his eyes. He didn't seem like a racist, but then he winked at me. He'd done well for himself with the girls from the kitchen and had steered clear of the boss's daughter, that was all. Without a pause, he began describing the days when he and a partner ran cattle up to New York City on trucks. A thousand head at a time.

'We'd come blastin' up that ol' New Jersey Turnpike in a convoy like an army on the move. Cost a grand every time we gassed up. One station was just short of the George Washington Bridge. We was fillin' our tanks an' nobody came to clean my windscreen. I gave them a minute, then I told them to quit pumpin'. We was headin' back out on to the highway when the guy comes chasin' after me, cool as you like, an' offers me a discount.'

'You sure showed him,' said Kim.

'I sure did, and I told that mean-minded sonofabitch that there's more in life than a few bucks. Old-fashioned manners is what this country needs. Them guys making that fuss jus' now, they didn't have no manners. If they had, they'd have gone outside to settle up, not bothered folks enjoyin' a quiet drink. This guy sellin' gas, he had no manners either. So we hauled on out and the next station cleaned our screens, swept our floors an' checked our oil without bein' asked. That's what you want when you do business . . .'

Jack suddenly broke off. I hadn't noticed, but Roz had faded right out.

'Ma'am, you don't look so good,' he said gently. 'Why don't I drive you an' your man back home?'

'What about the bike?' I asked. My head felt like a pumpkin and Jack's offer sounded just the ticket, but I was determined not to leave our iron steed outside this bar all night, even locked to the stanchion.

'I'll open both doors,' said Jim decisively, 'crank her right on in here. The Guzzi can stop over too, Rich, if you want.'

And so Jim held open the batwing doors while I somehow wrestled Madonna up the steps and through the tables. Rich followed me in. He was in even worse shape and dropped the white bike on the porch. Willing arms dragged it up and soon the machines were on their props, gleaming in the low lights, smelling of hot oil and giving the bar-room a surreal air.

Jack led the four of us out to the Jeep, we piled in and whirled away down the night. As we fell out again in front of our cabin, Roz started throwing up. I put her to bed while the rest limped into the kitchen. We put our feet up and drank until the sun flickered over the window sill.

The following afternoon, I walked back to the bar to pick up Madonna. She was parked outside. No sign of Jim, no Guzzi, nobody there at all. Just a waiter I didn't recognise and a few drop-outs hanging over the bar.

An hour later I was cleaning the bikes outside the cabin while Roz pulled herself around. We had to leave this place sometime, and tomorrow was going to be the day. The partner of the manageress stopped by to admire the machinery.

'Saw y'all had a party last night,' he said with a twinkle.

'We got a bit bent down the road and some guys ran us back.'

'Everyone needs to cut loose now and then.'

He picked up a rag and started poking it between Betty's awkward cooling fins, squatting on his haunches. He was fit, clear-skinned and as true-bred Anglo-Saxon as his girl was Hispanic. As we worked together in the afternoon sunshine, we exchanged life stories. He had seen things I could only imagine.

He and his wife had married twelve years previously. They'd had a couple of children before drugs and hard liquor began to invade their idyll. Within a year, she was an addict and he a hopeless drunk. They'd fought, cheated and in the end divorced because, as he put it, their habits were incompatible and had become the pivot point of their existence. Still in love, they parted in despair and the children were taken into state care.

At his lowest ebb, he had somehow found himself in Branson and been given a job in, of all places, a rehabilitation centre. He was introduced to the church and began to take a grip of his life. Three years later he was sufficiently recovered to trace his ex-wife to a strip joint and persuade her to rejoin him. Under his guidance, she had straightened out and now the kids had been restored to them. They had, as my host said, given their lives to the Lord.

As I polished my crank case I thought what a success story this family was for old-time, Southern religion. The tracts in our room had seemed simple to the point of idiocy, yet here was the living proof. This man and his striking wife had been so deep in the gutter that all the experience of human behaviour would say there could be no scrabbling out. Now, in spite of everything, he was bringing up his kids in a clean little business someone had trusted him to look after. Neither he nor his wife had a hint of the 'holier than thou' anywhere in them, and in the morning I rode out reminding myself that it is unwise to laugh at a whole group on the evidence provided by an outspoken few. The 'Bible' Christians had done these people well.

chapter eleven

riding the plains

'Don't go to Kansas and Oklahoma,' had been the serious advice of many people as we proceeded west. 'They're so boring you'll fall asleep on the bike,' or, 'Once you've seen one cornfield, you've seen them all,' were typical reactions. After visiting Branson on the recommendation that it was a place not to be missed, we were starting to doubt advice of this type, though Branson had turned out to be a vital port in a storm despite itself.

Changes in American scenery come on a continental scale and tend to creep up on you. In a small island like Britain, they smack you in the eye. After fifty more miles weaving though the hills, we became aware that the land was slowly easing away into a gently undulating green infinity. We were dropping down on to the Great Plains at last. Ahead, dancing in the heat that was once more establishing a stranglehold, lay Oklahoma. To the north burned the vast expanse of Kansas, described by the historian Carl Becker as a 'state of mind, a religion, and a philosophy'.

This, at last, was prairie country, where once the grass stood shoulder-high, where the endless herds of buffalo roamed in symbiosis alongside Native Americans who both hunted and revered them. Hawks and buzzards sailed the skies while the winds blew hot in summer and bitter cold in winter. Groups of cottonwood lived out their 100,000 days, surviving only if they escaped the axe of summer lightning or the tearing death of the tornado, while the tall grass rippled and waved through the centuries like the sea.

One hundred and fifty years ago, an act of Congress declared the territory open to settlement. It would never be the same again.

The New World began here only six generations ago, but within two, most of the buffalo had been butchered as food for the new settlers and the army that protected their interests. The rest were slaughtered, an official policy designed to leave the Indians homeless, starving and bereft of the vital pillar of their culture. Much of the valuable carcass was trashed by the white man. The indigenous people had wasted nothing. Now they melted away like winter ice, retreating west and north. In the wake of this trauma a civilisation has grown up, and with it a radically altered landscape. *Ad astra per aspera*, is the state's motto, 'Through the wilderness to the stars.'

Today, trucks and combines bowl by where once the buffalo was king; small towns have replaced nomadic encampments, but the snows still come, and the floods after summer storms. Tornadoes rip up houses, greedy for more than the trees, and giant hailstones pound down on tin roofs, leaving their mark as a reminder that modern man is only passing on the prairie breeze. Beneath the corn crops, the towering silos and the occasional sprawling city, the grasslands lie sleeping.

We rode out on to this mysterious expanse in late afternoon. The worst of the heat was over, the roads ran straight at last and the bikes responded, seeming to change up a gear. Before we knew it, they had eaten up 100 miles of freshly harvested Oklahoma and had crossed the Kansas line.

As the Harleys forged ahead, the journey took on a bizarre attitude, as though time were in suspension. For hours we floated weightless across infinite sunlit fields, only to be routed later in the day by monstrous rain and hail. The sense of being witness to a history so fearful and so close never left my mind, while the easier riding soothed Roz's difficulties almost out of sight.

In Kansas we came across the two extremities of historical monument presentation in a country which specialises in excess. The first was at 0800 after an early start from Coffeyville in the south-east of the state. The second came a day later in, of all places, Dodge City.

Even since Kansas arrived on our itinerary, Roz had been anxious to visit 'The Little House on the Prairie'. For much of our daughter's early life, she was educated at sea by her mother aboard the traditional sailing boat that was our home. The exercise was successful, partly because Roz consistently presented the fact that life existed beyond the eccentricities of our immediate surroundings. Some of the vehicles for this leavening were the *Little House* books of Laura Ingalls Wilder, true stories of a pioneer family growing up in various frontier homesteads as the father tried to wrestle a living from virgin territory. Life in the Kansas cabin was precarious. Buffalo and Indians were still in residence and the wagon trains rumbled by, carrying those casting their lot even further from civilisation. A cottage has been reconstructed on the site where the family lived for one year.

We puttered down a lonely lane to the Ingalls' place across soft, undulating farmland. Not a cloud interfered with the sky and the dewy air was sweet with the scent of trees shading the cabin. It lay deserted in the morning sun, a statement of how to present heritage. Built of logs, caulked with mud and roofed with large shingles, it had a door at one end, a tiny window on each long wall and a stone chimney at the fourth side. It was secured with a simple padlock. A tasteful rustic sign gave a breakdown of the Ingalls' travels, while a small notice advised that the caretaker would arrive at nine. I was for taking a quick look around then pressing on, but Roz pointed out that we were in no hurry. So we eased our souls by lying in the still grass, gazing up into the endless blue. The bike engines cooled off, ticking and pinging, while an insect orchestra tuned up for a hard day's chirping as the players' juices warmed in the sun.

At ten minutes before nine, a pick-up stopped and a mature, weather-beaten man climbed down with a hint of arthritic stiffness. He walked with a stick, the complete plains farmer in blue denim dungarees and battered straw hat. His hands were broad, thick and work-hardened. Mr Hambling opened up for us and we brewed him tea on our bike stove which we all drank in the cool of the interior.

'Reminds me of 1944,' said the caretaker slowly, 'you Brits was always makin' tea as we battered our way into Germany.'

Mr Hambling fought with 101 Group Paragliders in Holland and onwards across the Rhine.

'Funny thing is, my descent is half-German, half-Irish. You might ask why I was fighting on the side I was.'

'And?'

'My country wanted me. That was enough.'

Happy to talk about his war, he went on to say that as he had fought and watched men of several nations die, only the Brits had impressed him.

'You guys are the only people we can rely on,' he said as we shook hands.

Heading towards Dodge City, Roz finally relaxed into riding at 70mph. By midday the temperature was up around 100 degrees and the road took on the quality of a hallucination. The illusion of water began only 200 yards ahead, becoming denser towards the horizon so that the ever-narrowing strip of tarmac and the immense fields on either side of it swam in the heat. The handlebars and the soft twist grip of the throttle provided a link with gravity, our bodies baking above the scorching engines mirrored the surrounding austerity; but at these speeds, the constant throbbing hammer of the V-twin engines smoothed out to a humming, high-speed resonance that released the brain from the general discomfort, creating a weird sensation.

Small farms flashed by, mostly in the distance up dirt tracks. More often, we passed abandoned wooden homesteads, all their paint long since burned off by the cruel sun, roofs falling in, with greenery searching every crack for a place to grow. Insects thudded into Roz's leathers and my open shirt, smacking into us like pebbles as they burst, and every approaching truck rammed home the message that if either of us made a mistake, our own vulnerable bodies would receive identical treatment.

The first sight a plains biker has of a converging eighteen-wheeler comes when the truck is at least three miles ahead. It appears as a smudge of colour several feet above the road, probably breasting a rise in the distance. Maybe it disappears for a while behind the next undulation, but converging speed is around 130mph, so it moves closer fast. After a minute, it has grown to a ridiculous height, its chrome reflecting the sun like flickering lasers, two stove-pipe exhausts belching heat and engine fumes at the angry sky. Soon, it stands 100 feet tall, teetering in the mirage and beginning to rock-'n'-roll. As for forward progress, none is apparent on account of the zero perspective of the head-on meeting until suddenly, when it is as close as the length of a football field, it becomes deadly.

Massive and roaring, it is on you in seconds, swaying on the uneven surface as it rushes by leaving glimpsed impressions of its world. The sun glinting off the windscreen and the driver's shades, his shirt sleeve flapping at the open window, perhaps a split-second sighting of the name of a far-off town painted on the door.

'Cheyenne.'

As it passes, it shoves a wall of hot air that picks up the motorbike and hurls all quarter-ton of it to one side like a broom sweeping a dead mouse off the back porch step. The blast is so thick you can feel it. Diesel exhaust, grit and gravel, with oblivion thrown in if you are napping on the job. Then it's gone, but every Freightliner carries a reminder of that slender thread by which we hang on in the land of the living.

Small communities clinging precariously to the road spun by as we ran due west immediately north of the state line. Straight, wide main streets, a few stores, a county police station with a 'full-size' patrol car outside, a doctor's surgery, a lawyer's office and a church. Side tracks were built up for 100 yards before giving way to the fields that have replaced the prairie, many with the solitary 'one-horse' oil wells which are to be seen everywhere in Kansas and Oklahoma. These bore-holes, anything from 100 to 1,000 feet deep, are milked by simple contraptions that look like small Victorian beam engines. On a quiet day, they can be heard alongside the birdsong, squeaking rhythmically as they slowly rock to and fro, generating wealth for the oil company and paying a percentage to the landowner.

For some, the fruits of the arrangement cover the grocery bill. In a few cases, several units supply a farmer's retirement income.

Every so often, an active well will stop to let the head build up once more, so the inactive pump far away on the grassland could merely be dormant, or it might be as dead as the windmill nodding like a sleeping sentry outside any of the derelict homes out on the prairie.

One afternoon after lunch in a prairie township, I decided to give my bike her head. There was no chance of taking a wrong turning, because there was no significant junction for twenty-five miles. Roz accelerated away with the sun high on her left while I waited in the shade of the bank for five minutes, checking my oil and tyre pressures. When she was six miles up the road I pulled out, noting that the cops were still at lunch, their heavy-duty Chevrolet cooking in the glare.

Out of town, the smooth road stretched away straight down the latitude with the telegraph wires drooping from their tall poles and disappearing into the distance like an art school perspective exercise. I accelerated up to eighty, listening to the staccato of the exhaust merge into a single drone, taking in the scene as Black Madonna got into her stride. All around, the baked fields reflected the burning sky like lakes. Parched trees floated on non-existent water, sunflowers flashed by in the ditches, and a group of bullocks stood in an ancient buffalo hollow, up to their flanks in what looked like a dewpond but was probably an illusion. Towering white clouds gathering for the afternoon storm painted their shadows over the land, while far away, tall grain silos glimmered like ghosts on the boundaries of perception. Lazy buzzards hovered, finger-feathers at their wings' ends eternally trimming their flight as they hung from the up-currents, seeking the casualties from the wild side that men do not notice.

At last the road was clear. Nothing in the mirrors but the shoulders of my faded cotton shirt. Time to open up. Without a hint of subtlety I wound my right wrist fully clockwise until the throttle hit the stop. Unlike a modern sports bike, the Harley didn't leap forward in a crazy adrenaline rush, she just sat down on her fat back wheel and steadily surged ahead; 85, 90, 100, 105, chasing Roz into the mirage of the highway. The bike was flat out now, nudging 110, all trace of the classic Harley-Davidson 'chumpa-chumpa' sound lost in the wind noise and the deep roar of a big engine running as fast as it is meant to, freed for once of the fetters of speed limits. The wind was ripping me away from the handlebars but I held tight and let her go, high as an eagle. The familiar vibration of the bike rammed itself straight up my spine until she was part of me and I of her. No bends, no traffic, no cops, just the champagne of life on the edge, ten miles north of the Oklahoma line.

It seemed no time before Betty Boop appeared ahead, a splash of yellow beneath Roz's black leather jacket, trundling along at seventy. They were riding the heat haze fully three feet above the tarmac and I ran up behind them as though they were standing still.

Late that afternoon we rolled into Medicine Lodge. Directly westwards from here, the land falls away a little so that the town seems elevated. We were tired from the heat, but a mock stockade on the outskirts of town beckoned with the promise of a museum, so we stopped to find out what they had to show us. Like the glorious road that led to it, the museum was deserted except for the lady curator who asked us for six dollars apiece. Twelve bucks would buy us a good dinner in these parts, so I expressed reluctance to part with the cash. The curator understood. Her own life was in limbo until she could save enough to get back to Alaska. Money was hard to come by and you had to keep hold of it, but it was still going to be twelve dollars.

'Tell you what, mister, you take a look round and if you think it's worth it, pay me when you come out. If it ain't, just leave quietly.'

This sporting offer made me feel as mean as I was. I handed her the money straight away and did not regret it. Out attention was called to all manner of odd artefacts, but the item that was worth every cent and a good deal more just to look at was a peace treaty. This document hung in a glass case. It was signed by a representative of the 'Great White Father in Washington' and a number of Indian chiefs on behalf of their people gathered around this stockade. The names of the dispossessed rang like the thunder that was beginning to rumble overhead. Black Kettle, Standing Bear, and Woman's Heart. The paper with all their marks on it in lieu of white man's writing looked almost fresh, hardly mature enough to be a museum exhibit. Dispassionate fate had been drawing its cruel curtain across this part of the prairies around about the time my grandfather was weaned in a Victorian manse in the security of central England. Not long after signing up to what Black Kettle hoped might be a lasting compromise with the white man, he was ridden down by Custer's soldiers and shot dead on his pony with his wife behind him.

As we were leaving, the museum was closing. The cleaner turned up early for her shift and told me her grandparents had homesteaded here in Kansas after arriving by wagon train.

She'd read her grandfather's diary, she said, and he had believed it would take a thousand years to pioneer and populate the West. In fact, the usable land was subdued in less than a century.

Just around the corner we dragged the bikes under a motel porch. Inside, surrounded by such recent violent events and the descendants of those taking part, we shared the sort of dinner the cleaner's grandfather would have been grateful for. Another companionable plate of canned beans.

After we had 'done the dishes', we stepped outside to eye the weather. One glance at the afterglow of the sunset removed any desire to venture afield. The sky was in torment. It was clear at the land's rim, but above us and towards the dying light the clouds were writhing. Lightning flickered, and far off we could see distinct cones of whirling greyness groping downwards as nascent tornadoes tried for full-blown status. The cloud base bulged and seethed as would-be twisters probed earthwards before retreating back into the mother cloud, not having quite managed to form. Against the lurid sky in the extreme distance, two columns looked as if they might make it, but after a few more minutes the night shut down the show. We went inside, double-locked our door and turned on the 'Weather Channel'.

Throughout our travels, the television Weather Channel was our constant companion and valued assistant. There is no foreign equivalent to this remarkable service, which exclusively churns out meteorological information, national and local, twenty-four hours a day. With storms always around the corner, it was both entertaining and important to keep in touch with the announcers, some of whom already seemed like old chums. These celebrities did their best to keep us dry while glorying in the outrageous nature of the weather pudding served up to much of the American population. That night, a jolly chap in a pale grey suit joyfully advised the nation of 'humongous storms' in southern Kansas. Ten minutes later, after a break to check up on the astoundingly low prices offered on furniture at our local superstore, his state equivalent came on the air. This proved to be a charming girl with a worried expression who gave it to us straight:

'Storm Warning tonight. Extremely heavy rain expected west from Wichita into eastern Colorado. Tornado warnings for Comanche and Kiowa counties.'

Roz checked the map. These extensive tracts of land lay immediately west of Medicine Lodge, so we hadn't been seeing fairies out there on the porch.

Thirty minutes later the heavens opened, with unimaginable rain and almost continuous lightning. The gushing roar of the water pounding on to our roof made watching television impossible, so we reluctantly switched off. Thanking our stars we had not tried camping, I got up, padded over to my pack and poured us a shot of Wild Turkey.

'What on Earth can life have been like in a teepee with no other option?' said Roz. I myself had been considering what it must have felt like to face such conditions from a covered wagon, but before I could reply, the unmistakable chatter of a full-sized Harley sounded immediately outside our door. There was no problem about hearing that through the downpour. Since absolutely nobody could be riding voluntarily though the wall of water tumbling from the matt black sky, the noise could only be some opportunist stealing Madonna. I hurried into my jeans and leather jacket, slipped my feet into deck shoes and stepped out looking for trouble. The Heritage hadn't been touched, but out of the madness of the night a man wearing only leathers and a headscarf for protection was wrestling an ancient 'panhead' Hog under the portico. Behind him, still out in the rain, was a long, yellow Honda tourer, a proper motorbike. Astride it was a black figure looking slightly unsteady.

Relieved that the situation demanded assistance rather than a confrontation and ashamed of my paranoia, I dived out into the deluge. With the thunderclaps and the rain there was really too much racket to talk, but words were unnecessary to see what was required. Together, the man and I grunted and heaved the two heavy motorcycles into the comparative shelter in front of the next room. Once inside, he gave me the upturned biker's handshake. Roz appeared at the door with the whiskey and we all necked a slug.

Steve was around my age. With only his riding jacket and chaps for defence, he was so wet he looked as though his skin had been leaking. As the puddle around him grew, however, his main concern was for his companion. Nell already had her helmet off, and as she kicked out of her boots and began to peel off the layers of her highly professional wet-weather gear, her eyes were fixed on Steve with a mixture of gratitude and adoration. First came a crash-resistant waterproof; next, a Balaclava headpiece that ran down over the shoulders. Beneath the outer layer she wore black leather chaps that fitted loosely over extremely tight jeans. When she turned around to take them off, I realised for the first time that American riding chaps do not encase the buttocks like full riding leathers, but somehow lace across them. You don't see these in Europe, probably because they are banned for being worse than provocative. As she wriggled out of them and the jeans to reveal tight-fitting full-length underclothes, I realised with astonishment that this girl was dry. Steve made for the shower. Nell reached for the whiskey again.

'That is one hell of a man!' she announced as the rain continued to cascade down the roof, drowning the sound of Steve's life-saving ablutions. I couldn't argue with her judgement. He'd held on to his figure well although his black beard was streaked with grey. His hands had been oily from some mishap with one of the bikes, and his eyes were the darkest brown, looking out through the grey curls plastered to his face. He had stared into extreme distances for a long time. As for Nell, she was young, blonde, and slender, with film star teeth, blue eyes and high cheekbones. Like a Swedish immigrant from 1880s Minnesota.

'How did you two get together?' asked Roz. Even their bikes looked incompatible. His was black and battered from thousands of miles and forgotten adventures, almost a museum piece from the 1970s; hers, the latest model and, apart from today's fresh mud, clearly squeaky-clean. The Honda was as yellow as Betty Boop, but bigger and meaner.

Nell sat down on one of the two beds. She looked deeply knackered.

'He picked me up on the roadside back in California. I have to get back to Missouri by tomorrow night. I'd over-reached myself and I was washed out. Steve rode along with me all day. In the evening, he said he'd see me home.'

'But that's thousands of miles there and back. Was he going that way?'

'I don't think so. But it's all the same to him. He's an ex-'Nam US Marine. He just lives on two wheels.'

At last, a full-on biker. This guy was no dude on holiday.

'I have to be back at work in thirty-six hours,' Nell continued, 'I'm a school teacher . . . '

'Godalmighty!'

' . . . and my headmaster said if I was late one more time I'd be looking for a job. I love my class, so it's Missouri or bust. But I'd never manage without Steve to keep the pace going. It seems easy with him up front.'

'How far do you make in a day?' queried Roz, seriously interested now.

'We've run 500 miles since breakfast this morning,' Nell replied casually. 'It was OK, but we've seen some stuff. He brought us over the highest pass in North America.'

'Where's that?'

'I don't know. Somewhere in Colorado.'

Roz was turning this over in her mind when Steve stepped out of the shower room. He looked meadow-fresh, but his clean vest was saturated from a day in his battered saddlebag.

'Rain's slowed us badly,' he said, hanging his kit over the door. 'Reckon we carried this storm all the way from the Rockies. It's taken the legs right off us. If it doesn't move on, we'll have to live with it all the way to Missouri.'

An alarming squall shook the building and rattled the door.

'You did OK today, Nell,' he continued. 'I thought that wind would blow you clean off coming down the mountain.'

We left them to their intimacy and tried to get some sleep, but it wouldn't come. For a short while the lightning eased, but soon it returned. The storm took on a near-human malevolence in the small hours as I dozed in a world where Steve was leading a wagon train, trying to live peaceably alongside the Indians while greedy whites undercut him at every turn. Nell had turned into a pioneer woman, fresh from the East Coast, recently widowed and in dire need of protection.

A further lightning attack woke me and suddenly I knew who Steve had been reminding me of. It was another ex-Marine, as light-complexioned as Steve was dark, but both carried the same powerful aura of competence. Clint was his name. A blacksmith by trade, we met him working in a shipyard in Connecticut shortly before Roz and I fell foul of a New York tycoon during a piece of dirty dealing that seemed set to rob us of our boat. Back in the mid-eighties the vessel in question, seriously damaged in a collision for which we were subsequently found blameless, was all we had in the world. She was also home to us and our young daughter, so we were not about to give up without a struggle. Matters rapidly deteriorated into a lawsuit. One bitterly cold day, an ugly-looking customer turned up on the catwalk and, in the course of what might have been casual conversation, pointed out that it didn't cost much money down in the Bronx to have a nuisance rubbed out. I didn't take this too seriously until my car was torched. It was then that I called Clint. He arrived before dawn, kitted up for trouble.

For a number of nights he and I huddled at the aft hatchway to the boat while my family stayed locked below decks further forward, waiting for the knocking at the entry that might presage serious violence. It never came. Perhaps someone had decided that destroying my car was enough, but when Clint drove his truck into the downtown New York City boatyard on that bleak winter's night he had been ready to risk his life to do what he believed was right. There is more of this spirit alive in America than is generally broadcast to the outside world. We hear about massive drug problems, organised crime, psychotic serial murders and the greed of multinational business – and all of it is authentic – but are told little of the silent majority. Lying in the storm at Medicine Lodge, I remembered them, and was glad.

It was still raining at first light, but I thought I detected movement outside. Roz heard it too. She clambered from her bed to boil the tiny kettle which she always carted in off the bike because motels rarely feature in-room tea-making facilities.

'If they're really leaving in this rain, the least we can do is offer them a cuppa,' she yawned. 'Why don't you give them a hand with their bikes?'

I opened the door. Down the slope, the highway was running like a river. Steve was manhandling his Harley out on to the parking lot, his sodden cowboy boots squelching with each struggling step. I helped him, then together we turned to the yellow Honda, which daylight revealed to be a really lovely bike. By the time we had them both facing the right way we were soaked through. Roz nipped between the rooms with four teas in a drawer she'd pulled from the dressing table.

'I suppose you'll be going to Sturgis?' she asked as we sipped.

'I'll mosey on up after I get Nell home,' replied Steve. 'See you there?'

I shuffled my feet and Roz looked at Nell.

Nell stared out at the dirty dawn and was more reticent.

'I promised to get together with some guys I met in a gas station in Reno,' she said as calmly as though she'd come across them at her local package store. 'So maybe I'll make it. Don't know what I'll tell the head this time, though. It gets harder and harder. Guess he thinks I'm some sort of moll.'

She pulled her helmet over the balaclava and started the Honda.

'Let him think what in hell he likes,' she said. 'Maybe see you there.'

Revving positively, the school-ma'am exited neatly from the forecourt into the gushing stream that had been a road less than twelve hours ago. Steve kick-started the panhead, nodded to us and followed her towards the wide Missouri. It was 6:30 a.m., so Roz and I went back to bed.

When we awoke, the rain had stopped and the whole world was steaming. According to the Weather Channel, there had been almost six inches of rain since the previous evening. Roz turned to me.

'That Steve,' she said, 'he's a hero.'

I glanced at her sideways. Perhaps he was, but Nell was a very attractive woman.

'When I took in the tea, both beds had been slept in!'

Down the hill by the river bridge, we found a householder leaning on his garden gate. Both he and his house were under water to thigh level. The plastic deer he had selected as his yard ornament was self-consciously standing up to its neck in the red, flowing tide. We stopped to sympathise, dry-shod on the levee that must have been thrown up for occasions such as this, and noting that he looked far less miserable than his situation permitted.

'Aw, shit,' he said, gazing ruefully at his antelope, 'things are going to be a mess when this goes down, but at least we didn't get no twisters. Them poor guys over in Comanche County had their homes blown clean off the ground.'

We commiserated; then, like tens of thousands before us, set our eyes west down the undulating highway towards Dodge City. Gas stations were far apart now, and running out of fuel became a serious possibility, especially for the Sportster, but we made it across the uncultivated range lands on Betty Boop's last gasp.

We hit Dodge City mid-afternoon. The town is well-known for its historic position at the head of the Chisholm cattle trail to Texas, for saloons, gambling and gunfighters, and for Boot Hill Cemetery where the townsfolk buried the remains of those who died with their footwear on. Railroad yards and cattle fattening stations were the first impressions of this sprawling, low-rise town on the prairie. Roz had no special interest in the place, but I was drawn in by the name alone.

I was sorely disappointed. Boot Hill was consigned to the ranks of mediocrity, and the famous streets had been reduced to theme-park status within a compound that tourists were paying good money to enter. I stood on a handy crate and peered over the wall anyway, hoping to catch a glimpse of what was going on. Wild West buildings strung out 100 yards or so along a street, with tourists meandering aimlessly around the bogus frontage. A bored-looking girl sauntered out of a saloon togged up like a film extra, and the sound effects of a phoney altercation filtered around a corner.

As I stepped in despair from my orange-box, I found a passer-by inspecting the red ensign of the British merchant navy strapped across the pack on my bike. Surprisingly few people had commented on this unusual item of window-dressing, and even though he ignored the far more unusual UK licence plate, he still deserved my attention. After the standard preliminaries, he told me that he was from Kansas City. He was on vacation in his RV and he knew what he liked.

'If you're heading west, don't miss Colorado. Most beautiful state on the planet.'

Quite how he could be so sure of this was unclear, since he also told me that he had never been east of the Appalachians or west of the Rockies. Taking the easy line out of the conversation, I thanked him for the advice and rejoined Roz who was taking life easy in a bar full of railroad men and cowhands in the authentic Dodge City. She was not surprised at my desolation over Boot Hill, but came on strong when I mentioned Colorado.

'Places we're advised to visit are turning out to be bad news,' she stated. 'We almost never like them. Nobody said, "Don't miss Medicine Lodge," but it was a winner. So many people have told us to go to Colorado that the whole state must be log-jammed with tourists.'

'You can't tell me every historic site is a fallacy. What about Mystic Seaport?' I reminded her about the reconstructed ship-building village in far-off Connecticut that is an example to the world on how to handle heritage.

'I think we need to learn from all this,' she said firmly. 'Mystic's great; so is Jamestown and there are plenty of others, but every time we go looking for organised history you get hacked off and say we're sinking into tourism. And it's true. We are. You'll love the mountains, but you'll hate Colorado. I've been looking at the map.'

I took a long draught of my fizzy beer and said nothing. Incongruously, my mind was diverted by a wobbly ceiling fan that looked as if it would crash down on the drinkers at any moment.

'The direct route to Dakota from here passes though Nebraska.'

I missed the hint about Dakota, and fell on the route instead.

'But absolutely nobody goes to Nebraska!'

'Don't you think that might mean it comes with a zero nonsense factor?'

I couldn't argue.

'How about this? You want to go to Sturgis and I'm not interested in hairpin passes in Colorado. Why don't we head up to Dakota through Nebraska, see the bikes, check out the Indians and give the snow peaks a miss?'

'Let's do it.'

chapter twelve

pounding the prairies

When the 1854 Kansas and Nebraska Act opened up the central plains, 50 million acres of virgin grassland became available in Kansas alone to the first-comers to stake their claims. Many settlers made a success of their farms, but an equal number returned to the East, or even to Europe. In the early years of the twentieth century, another boom time for immigration, fifty out of every hundred immigrants to the US from Italy, Russia and the Balkans went back home again. Out on the plains, some homesteaders were defeated by their own indolence, others became sick and a few fell foul of dispossessed natives or whites working to a different agenda. Many collapsed under the pile-driver of the climate.

Tribulations crowded in from all sides. Prairie fires destroyed crops and left famine in their wake. Blizzards scourged the plains in winter, and rainstorms washed away whole homesteads. If the deluge missed you, the drought would not. Sometimes lasting from one winter to the next, these parched the harvests and their desperate cultivators. The drought of 1860 saw a fall in state population of almost thirty per cent.

Alongside these apocalyptic forces strode destitution at the hands of Man. In the very early days, border raiders encroached on the young settlements. Next, Kansas found itself in an equivocal position during the Civil War, suffering ugly guerrilla action from both sides. Outlaws, rustlers and the foreclosing banker followed with such ruinous effect that one retreating pioneer is said to have announced wryly, 'In God we trusted.

In Kansas we busted'. But for total destruction, no adversaries, either human or natural, could compete with the humble grasshopper.

As Roz and I approached Nebraska, these hefty insects became a serious menace. They bounced off our leathers and wrecked the paint jobs on the leading edges of the bikes. If they caught us in the face we bruised, and the 'crack' as a heavy one hit the helmet at 60mph woke the dozing rider with a start. It occurred to me that it wouldn't take much for this substantial population to swell out of control, so we investigated a roadside library and dug up facts that made the plagues of Pharaoh's Egypt pale in comparison.

In 1874, the previously moderate grasshopper nation found conditions particularly to its liking. In response, its numbers exploded to cosmic proportions which ate their way clear across the state.

According to Mary Lyon, ' . . . this day there was a haze in the air and the sun was veiled almost like an Indian summer. They began toward night, dropping to earth and it seemed as if we were in a snowstorm where the air was filled with enormous flakes.'[6] The green army landed to a depth of four inches or more and blanketed every speck of ground and foliage. Tree branches collapsed under their weight and even when the frantic plainsmen covered their vegetable plots with tarpaulins, the insects munched straight through the oiled cloth. They attacked anything made of wood, even kitchen utensils and furniture. Curtains were left in shreds and any clothing out in the open was eaten. Adelheit Viets had her dress eaten clean off her back. The material had a green motif. 'The grasshoppers settled on me and ate up every bit of green stripe in that dress.'[7]

So thickly did the pestilence fall from the skies that the numbers extinguished a burning field lit to ward them off. They even stopped a train.

When they had gone, the water tasted of grasshoppers.

Our first fifty miles out of Dodge City led down a white, shining road across deeply undulating, untamed grassland, then onwards through a waving prairie of high sunflowers the colour of Betty Boop. We passed fields watered from the subterranean aquifer by giant irrigation machines that would dwarf a football field. Late in the afternoon we stopped to watch a team of harvesters and their enormous combines converting the client farmer's labour into saleable wheat. This crew were among the many who move north with the sun, following the seasons, harvesting America for the world. Right of the sunset and coming ever closer lay Nebraska. A tourist-free zone.

As we crossed the Nebraska line, the change in road surface and hence in the impression of less spare money was dramatic. The surface switched from motorcycle heaven to rough concrete, occasional stretches of tarmac and intermittent gravel. The eastern half of Nebraska is comparatively populous, although the towns are still spread out. The west, particularly the north-west, is sparse in the extreme, with roads spanning fifty miles and more between unmarked junctions.

Crossing the state from east to west around seventy miles north of the Kansas line flows the Platte River, a main tributary of the Missouri. South of its fertile, tree-lined valley, the plain becomes 'dissected', which is to say, hilly land with moderate undulations and salient ridges. These survive from a higher, more ancient plain now eroded by wind and water. The impression is of poorer soil than Kansas, and of remoter country.

The town of North Platte lay across our path to Dakota. It was an obvious stopping place, but McCook came up first. This community of some 8,000 inhabitants is one of western Nebraska's larger settlements outside the river valley. We cruised around hunting a bed and rejecting several for being too soft or too dirty, before signing the guest card at the small, privately run Sage Motel. Sonia, the lady who welcomed us was an extraordinarily positive individual, glowing with conviction and mental health. Above the bed was a tract we hadn't yet encountered. Rather than offering the usual 'store-bought' wisdom, this one was written personally. I read it out to Roz as she brushed her hair.

"'Because this motel is a human institution to serve people and not merely a money-making organization, we hope God will grant you peace and rest while you are under our roof. May this motel be your second home. May those you love be near you in thoughts and dreams. Even though we may not get to know you, we hope you will be as comfortable and happy as if you were in your own home.

"May the business that brought you our way prosper. May every call you make and every message you receive add to your joy. When you leave, may your journey be safe.

"We are all travellers from birth till death. We travel between eternities. May these days be pleasant for you, profitable for society, helpful for those you meet and a joy to those who know and love you best.'"

It was signed, 'The staff and management.'

That Saturday night, for the first time, we didn't lock the bikes. We slept deeply and awoke refreshed to find a ten-year-old girl playing with a skipping rope in the yard outside. She was wearing her Sunday best, a patriotic knee-length stars-and-stripes frock, with white socks, button-down shoes and a pink hair ribbon. Sonia came out of the office, also dressed for church. 'Breakfast, Sweetheart!' she called to her child, then she saw me. 'Good morning, Thomas,' she greeted me. 'Did you sleep good?'

She must have read my name off the registration form, because my full handle is used only when I'm in trouble. Coming from her, it had a satisfying, biblical ring. Thomas, the doubter. Suddenly I was seized with a nostalgia for the Sundays of morning church that had been the time signals of my childhood and adolescence. The open face of the little girl, the honest message on our bedroom wall and the mother going about her Lord's Day routine touched a nerve somewhere in my agnosticism.

'Would it be possible for us to follow you up to church?'

'You can come in the car if you like.'

We dug out clean shirts and climbed into the Dodge.

The Church of God was all I expected. Although less militant in its exterior manifestations than back in Tennessee, prosperous-looking places of worship in all the plains towns had augmented the 'God-spot' radio programmes, implying that Christianity, rather than the bars, was still the core of social living. Smartly clad folks met us, pumped our hands and scurried away to advise the preacher. He obliged by greeting 'Friends from Overseas' after the first hymn, rather as our own minister used to welcome visiting African church dignitaries back in 1960s Manchester. In some ways, Roz and I were as far removed from his flock as the self-conscious Nigerians had been from Lancashire, yet the clearly drawn values of the community reminded me irresistibly of my upbringing. Not for them a slide from the post-war climate of moral certainties into the present-day ethical maze. In south-west Nebraska, still heavily influenced by religion, the American idea of 'what's right' is understood, even if human frailty means it is not always followed to the letter. Here in the bright, packed Church of God, we were aeons from the insecurities of more fluid societies.

Further hymns were now sung lustily, then our preacher, youthful in his middle forties and an auctioneer on his 'day job', socked it to the congregation in a voice like Moses booming down from Heaven's gate. A powerful country message with the tang of the open range on its breath. 'Blessed is he that cometh in the name of the Lord,' rang the text.

The exposition started off with solid biblical theory, but lest any might accuse the congregation of being 'Sunday Christians', the preacher was soon calling for testimonies from members of a team who had spent their vacations working in downtown Chicago with disadvantaged black teenagers. 'Let the Lord get to them before the drug gangs do!' was the message.

I could only marvel at these people, sufficient amongst themselves in their close-knit community and knowing almost nothing of what went on outside the US, giving their time at some personal risk to offer a starting chance to hard-bitten youngsters from another universe. Next, we heard from Sonia's sister who was teaching English in Romania ('Now where in heaven is that?') and spreading the Word of the Lord as part of the deal. It is a mistake to draw conclusions about America as a whole without recognising the effect on the national character brought about by the tens of millions of regular, enthusiastic church-goers.

Meanwhile, five miles out of McCook on the dusty roadside, a very different sort of plainsman had been trying to flag a lift since breakfast time. Riding north after church, I recognised him as the man who had stayed in the next room the previous night. We'd said 'Good evening,' but that was all. Now he was wearing a Jesus T-shirt, jeans and a felt cowboy hat. Flowing yellow hair curled out from under it and his narrow face drew personality from a huge moustache and a miniature beard developed from the central section of his lower lip in Buffalo Bill Cody style. He was carrying a small, ex-Army satchel and what looked like a metal detector. My pack left me strapped for space on my buddy seat, but I was too intrigued to ignore him, so I swung around and stopped alongside. As soon as I killed the engine I realised that, for once, the prairie wind had dropped and the heat was becoming oppressively damp, despite the cruel sun.

'Where you bound?' I asked.

'You guys took your time starting,' he observed laconically as he mopped his sweating forehead. 'But you're the best of transport. This humidity's killin' me. I'm headin' up for the old Jones place. Track must be around thirty miles north.'

'You familiar with the turn-off?'

Every few miles, dirt lanes wandered away into the hills. Some were marked by a lone mailbox. The rest could have led to the rainbow's end.

'Nope. But I reckon I'll spot it. You runnin' about sixty?'

I nodded.

'I'll time us. I'll know the place.'

We gave him a drink of water, then reorganised the luggage to make room on Black Madonna. He hopped aboard, jammed down his hat and away we went across the fractured plain, the bike note deepening as we powered up hills, and settling back to a sweet purr dropping down into the valleys. My washed-out green cotton shirt flapped in the heat and my forearms burned an even deeper brown above my hands, wet with sweat inside skin-tight black leather riding gloves. The road was so empty that Roz came up alongside, using the whole highway to maintain a safe distance in case either of us weaved. Betty was a grand sight, pounding the prairie as she was borne to do, her buckskin tassels flying in the slipstream. I thought about the die-hards back East who'd said the bike didn't have the guts for the long haul. From the general bike scene around the larger towns, I now understood why they thought so. Most 883s are used only for short-range pottering, but then, so are a lot of full-sized Hogs. It was all a question of perceived image and nothing to do with the facts. The sunshine Harley was performing far better than any traditional bike I'd ever owned. There was no question of Madonna leaving her behind. There was still a long way to go, but so far Betty Boop was gobbling the job.

Exactly half an hour after we'd picked him up, the hitch-hiker dug me in the ribs. I leaned the bike into a run-down track to the left and we climbed off as Roz propped Betty on a carefully selected piece of ground that was hard enough to hold the stand. The silence after the engines would have been oppressive but for the chirping of the grasshoppers.

'You got relatives up there?' I asked. The lane was grown over and could not have taken a vehicle for months.

'Nope. Never knew the people. Reckon they've been gone twenty years or so.'

I looked across the prairie. We were on a high section. If there were any valleys in the vicinity, they were well-hidden by the tall grass. There was no indication that anything had changed since the Indians and the buffalo left, save for the roughly metalled road and the telegraph lines withering out into the distant haze. It was none of my business, but curiosity bettered social caution and I asked him point-blank what he was up to.

Robert was a treasure hunter, a modern-day prospector. He was broke, unemployed and homeless, but he had hit a winning streak on the Keno lottery. He had also met a woman up in North Dakota who drank his whiskey then told him about a stash of buried silver coins on the abandoned Jones farm.

'People there died,' he said. 'He had a cancer. His wife hung on five years on her own. The woman I met was with a group of hippies – come up here years ago lookin' for the simple life. They didn't find it, but they discovered the old lady and they didn't like that at all. She'd been dead three weeks, the sheriff said. Coyotes had been in. Seems they didn't have no children. Preacher came up next with some folks from the town. They took away what was left an' they buried her.'

'So how do you know about the coins?'

'There was a letter the old girl had been writing. It wasn't finished. "Dear Eliza," it said, but there wasn't no address, so the woman kept it. She showed it to me.'

As the story grew ever more improbable, it transpired that the unsent note had mentioned the silver and that it was buried 'good and safe', but that there was no indication of its whereabouts. The hippies hadn't even looked, but on the strength of the tale Robert had spent his winnings on a metal detector, bought a week's rations and headed for the booty. He didn't mind telling us, he said, because our bikes indicated that we were well enough heeled not to consider shooting him for his metal detector.

'Besides,' he added, patting his satchel meaningfully, 'I'm ready for trouble.'

Fascinated, we walked with Robert up the track to the clump of cottonwoods a mile from the road which hid the remains of the Jones place. The inevitable windmill still hung on to two of its original twenty blades by the side of the weather-board house. A porch wider than the living room of our English cottage must once have been a source of pride to Mr Jones, but now the screens had blown away on the endless winds while the wooden steps had rotted and broken under the weight of winter snow. Somebody, perhaps the burial party, had cleared the homestead out comprehensively. Maybe the job was completed by other fortune-hunters who dropped by some time over the last quarter-century, but not a stick of furniture remained in the parlour; even the beds had been taken. Weeds were growing up through the floorboards and the roof had fallen in at the rear, showing an impassive sky with the first clouds of the day beginning to boil up.

I stood in the back kitchen and thought about Mrs Jones. No farmer's wife in her day made a positive decision to remain childless, so one way or another she and her husband had carried the burden of barrenness through their life together in this remote homestead. The rose wallpaper was peeling away under the onslaught of the weather but the cooking range where a lifetime of meals for two had taken shape was still defying nature. Above it was the sole surviving sign of warm human life. A calendar given out by a North Platte agricultural supplier. No monthly picture, just a tear-off four-week planner. March 1968. She'd clung to life through one last winter, but had finally given up the ghost, perhaps in the last blizzard of that year. Nothing was written on the day squares. It was her time to go.

Out in the yard, the mood was less gloomy. We ate oranges from our saddlebags while Robert told us his plans. The money he was about to dig up was already earmarked to finance his next venture which, he hoped, would take care of his needs forever.

'What happened is no secret,' he said, 'but I've worked out where the gold will be.'

'What gold?'

'The gold that was sittin' in a Pony Express depot out in Wyoming. It was on the way through when the place was attacked by Indians. The office was hooked by wire to the transcontinental railroad track. The telegraphist was the last man alive. He banged out a message that he'd buried the gold in a Dutch oven. Then they scalped him. The cavalry found the bodies, but they never found no gold.'

Robert had discovered a plan of the station and decided that anyone in his right mind would have buried the gold across a shallow river whose waters ran just below the buildings. He was also confident that nobody had yet searched the area with a metal detector. The problem was, he had to have a fourtrack to reach the remote site. It was hard to imagine Mr and Mrs Jones' life savings amounting to even a clapped-out Chevrolet pick-up thirty years on. I suggested a trail bike, then we left him alone with his schemes. We also left him our water, because he had none, and without it he looked set to join Mrs Jones in the local cemetery before he made good. An hour later we were drinking our fill in North Platte.

We quit town at breakfast time after meeting up with three middle-aged adventurers on the spree from their suburban wives. Like every other motorcyclist for a thousand miles, they were bound for Sturgis, but their message was in total contrast to the last intelligence we'd received. When they heard Roz was bound for this centre of biker violence, our backstreet heroes warned us to watch out for gangs, not to venture anywhere near Buffalo Chip Campground and not to ride out after three in the afternoon, because of the militant high-velocity drunks. They asked what type of firearm I carried, sucked their teeth at my unarmed irresponsibility, then blasted off up the valley in a cloud of blue smoke and insecurity.

I glanced towards Roz.

'Don't worry about me,' she said. 'They're probably just another bunch of guys who've been watching too many videos, but if things really do get rough up there I'll move in with Steve. You can look to yourself and Nell will have to lump it. Nobody will bother you, though, as long as you don't smile. You look so macho you'll be inconspicuous.'

Thirty miles up the potholed road we ran into solid evidence that the theory of travel and tourism Roz expounded in Dodge City was bang on the money. The same holds good at sea. If you are the first foreign yacht ever to visit some far-off outpost, be it in Norway, Russia or the South Sea Islands, the locals will come looking for you full of curiosity. It only remains for you to be pleasant and they will open up. Arrive after the same place has been overrun with visitors for a decade or two and, with a few notable exceptions such as the Azores, the main interest the natives have is how many bucks they can screw from your pocket before you give up and leave. The central United States has seen little in the way of casual callers off the beaten track, and less of motorcycle travellers. The great plains are of almost oceanic proportions. A couple biking in from a different world on the other side take on the status of deep-sea wanderers and are greeted with generosity.

The country people of Nebraska love to put one over on the city dweller. When he learned that we knew New York, the proprietor of the solitary service station in the tiny settlement of Tryon, just had to tell us about how he had faced down a hard-nosed New Jerseyman. An ex-trucker, he'd once carried a load scheduled for delivery before the next evening just west of the George Washington Bridge. Even using the interstate system, the timing had proved too tall an order, and after driving non-stop for thirty-six hours, our man found himself approaching the bridge at the close of the working day. Perhaps understandably, he missed his exit in the fourteen lanes of the New Jersey Turnpike, was unable to turn around and ended up having to pay twelve dollars to cross the Hudson River into Manhattan. The toll really got to him, but he worked through the streets, recrossed the bridge and arrived at the drop just as the storemen were leaving. The slick manager told the Nebraskan that he'd have to come back in the morning as they didn't work out of hours for a delivery driver who hadn't called in that he would be late. Disgusted, the driver grabbed his repeating rifle from the back of his cab and secured their attention by loosing off three rounds into the door of the showroom. When they returned from their hiding places, he announced that he would rather tip the load into the Hudson than wait until morning for their convenience. Seeing that he meant it, they opened up, took in the cargo and bought him a beer. The following month, they sent in a far larger order which, he said, went to show that New Yorkers weren't as bad as people said, so long as you gave good return for their rudeness.

'Love the bikes,' admired a young rancher filling up from the other side of the pump.

'Do you ride?' I asked.

'Only an off-roader for cow work,' he responded unexpectedly, 'but I'd sure like a road machine one of these days.'

'You mean you round up cattle on a motorbike?' asked Roz.

'Sure thing,' he replied. 'We still keep a horse. Use both together sometimes, but the bike's cheaper. More fun too,' he added with a self-conscious grin.

He joined our conversation with the garage man and Roz expressed her concerns about the Sturgis event. Neither man even knew where Sturgis was, or had any interest in its dubious claim to fame.

'You guys in a hurry?' the farmer suddenly asked. 'Come on down to the ranch in the morning. Me and my pa have a load of heifers to get to market. You might enjoy the action.'

Prices in town were now almost embarrassingly low and we were charged just twenty dollars for a homely room. Leila, the owner, gave us coffee and lemon cake. She wouldn't take a cent for her hospitality. Instead, she sent me to Sowders' Store ('Western Art, Rocky Mountain Jeans, Hats, Short Orders, Sandwiches to Go') across the street to have my boots re-soled, then told us that the rancher must have been Kirk Neal, who runs six sections with his father fifteen miles north of town.

A 'section' of land is equivalent to a square mile, a system of measurement adopted for the original survey of the West begun by Thomas Jefferson and completed in the late nineteenth century. At that time, plains townships of thirty-six sections were designated on a geometrical pattern before they were settled or, in some cases, even thought of. The arrangement, together with a number of early military highways of Roman straightness, goes some way to explain the grid-iron framework of the prairies.

After supper we ambled down a side street, past the three or four homes that bordered it and out into the wild land beyond. The smell of the earth was strong in the moonless darkness, and the stars burned sharply. Half a mile from the buildings the faint sounds of the settlement faded out. There was no traffic noise and zero light pollution. The whisper of a breeze had sprung up with sunset, the grass rustled quietly and somewhere far to windward a cow lowed. Gigantic nature seemed to be pressing in on the 100-year-old township, calling in ghosts from the former cattle trails. According to our map, the population of the 800 square miles of McPherson County was 534 souls. Maybe 100 of them lived around Tryon. The rest were spread very thinly indeed. Cherry County to the north of McPherson, named after Lieutenant Samuel A. Cherry, murdered in 1881 by one of his own men, is two-thirds the size of Wales. Its only town of more than 200 inhabitants is Valentine at 2,826. Western Nebraska is not troubled by overpopulation.

chapter thirteen

ranchers and farmers

The fifteen miles north to the Neal ranch after breakfast the following morning gave scant time for reflection on the change of country from the fractured plain and open prairie we had been crossing for two weeks. Twenty thousand square miles of western Nebraska is made up of arid sandhills more or less held together by sparse clumps of coarse grass. Before the white man began to settle the area it was the home of the Pawnees, until an epidemic of imported European smallpox in 1831 wiped out over half their population with more deadly efficiency than the carbine ever did. The powerful Sioux moved into the vacuum, and it was them that the first settlers and cowmen had to contend with. The area was known to exist because it bordered the well-beaten Oregon Trail in the Platte Valley, but it was not until the late 1870s that reports from wandering cowboys of lush valleys among the sand led to the arrival of the cattle barons. By the mid-1880s, herds of up to 50,000 head roamed the sandhills, but the land failed to regenerate from this range-plundering. Having denuded much of the grazing, the legendary barons moved on, leaving the sandhills to less ambitious ranchers who began nurturing the difficult land.

We swung off the pitted surface of Highway 97 at the Neal mailbox and my morale sagged as I saw the track winding into the hills ahead. I knew what Roz would be thinking.

'Oh, hell! Another dirt road and I can't dodge this one.'

Up until now, Roz had managed to avoid following me far on to an unmetalled road, but this time there was no choice. Having to hold the Harley on its feet along the western highways was bad enough, but the rutted, semi-graded surface of dirt paths half-destroyed by winter weather was off limits. I felt some frustration as a result, but hung in without too much complaint, grateful that my partner had the guts to come this far and hoping that her resolve would not crack. If she came off, even unhurt, it would set her back a month. It might also bend the bike.

But she didn't tumble, and soon the ranch house appeared about a half-mile from the road, nestling deep into a small valley. The modern-style bungalow was surrounded by outhouses, screened by a group of densely foliated cottonwoods and sided by a large corral full of bellowing beasts. As we came into view, we saw Kirk talking with a slim, broad-shouldered man on a trail bike. He waved us over and introduced Laverne, his 'old man', who had inherited this ranch from his own father and grandfather.

As he clambered off the Yamaha, Laverne moved with surprising fluidity in his high-heeled boots and blue jeans, his legs slightly bowed from long years in the saddle. A few years earlier, he had left the ranch free for his son and moved into a 'buy-it-from-our-showroom-and-take-it-away' house a mile or two down the track. At around sixty-five, he could have been the perfect client for an off-the-peg retirement home. Instead, he worked the cattle as number two. This morning, he was here to help load the heifers on to the truck, when it arrived. The breeze plucked at his green check shirt, but didn't trouble the tall hat clamped above his weather-burned face as if it had grown there.

Laverne was straight from a John Wayne movie, except for the motorbike where once a horse would have stood. Kirk represented the new fashion in cowboy gear, herding in a sweatshirt, comfortable pants and baseball hat.

Kirk packed Roz and me into a museum piece Chevrolet pick-up for a tour of the spread. We lurched away slowly across the uneven grass of the sandhills, climbing unsteadily to the top of a high mound from where Kirk assured us we could see thirty-five miles.

'We can fatten six to eight cows per 100 acres here,' he announced to our astonishment. We knew of dairy farmers in England who made a living 180 acres 'all up'. The widely spread cows were a gauge of the poverty of the land.

'Those heifers down in the corral,' he continued, 'they're crossed Hereford and Angus with a few Charolais. There's sixty-five of them and they're around a third of our gross annual output.'

'What'll happen to them?'

'Truck'll come around lunchtime. They go to auction in North Platte and on to a fattening yard, then it's the dinner table.'

It was an unsettled day. Squall clouds loomed, missing us but casting their moving shadows so that the hills seemed to sway like waves on a green and yellow ocean. Not three miles off, a black curtain of heavy rain blotted out the small building Kirk was indicating.

'That was the only schoolhouse in the neighbourhood until they opened the new one in Tryon a year or two back,' he said. 'I was educated there. All grades in one class, from eight to sixteen. Now kids have to travel further. The schooling's better but there's no bus like there is most places.'

The Appalachian foothills. Heading into moonshine country.

Roz and Betty Boop in north-west Kansas.

Nebraska. A barn behind the deserted Jones farm. But was there any hidden silver?

South Dakota. The Korn harvesting operation 'standing down' for a break.

Kirk, the Nebraska rancher, herds his cattle 1990s style.

Glacier National Park. Occasionally, motorcycle mirrors reflect
something more inspiring than a flashing blue light.

For all my long-faced British common sense, the boys and girls
rolling into Sturgis were as great a sight as their machinery.

The Little Big Horn memorial with the graves of
unknown US Soldiers who perished with Custer.

The greatest wonder of the world's in Uncle Sam's fair land,
It's the big Columbia River and the big Grand Coulee Dam.

Death Valley. Black Madonna stands by for a one-way ride into hell.

Bryce Canyon at dawn. 'A uniquely feminine experience.'

'Santa Fe'. Every schoolboy's vision of the American railroad locomotive.

Arizona. Navajo country viewed from high on a Hopi mesa.

Entering Logansport, Louisiana. A world away from smart, neighbouring Texas.

Shrimp boats in North Carolina. Shades of the 'Hungry Neck Yacht Club'.

Hurricane damage in North Carolina. 'No gas today, Madam.'

'That must place a huge burden on the mothers,' observed Roz. 'The distances seem enormous.'

'To some extent,' Kirk agreed. 'The state government understands the problem though. Kids are allowed to drive themselves to school from their fourteenth birthday, and there's no shortage of land to learn to drive on beforehand. It's just to school and back though. No joyrides until you're sixteen. One kid drives thirty-five miles each way every day. Mind you, they have it easy now. Some of my pa's generation had to make it to school on a clapped-out horse, two or three brothers and sisters all on the same animal, through snow and all.'

For a moment, we gazed at the huge expanse of this young man's property. It was not wealthy in money terms, but it conferred a powerful sense of identity and a healthy life for his family.

'Kids are pretty safe on the highways,' he said. 'McPherson's a dry county – no booze that is. Most folks are proud of it.'

He threw the pick-up into gear.

'You like machinery? Come and visit my spares department.'

After a few more hills, we arrived in a large field where half a dozen vintage tractors stood open to the weather, all the same antique make and model, all facing downhill. Stretched hoods covered their two-cylinder John Deere power plants; steering wheels stood high above everything with connecting rods to the front end that extended through clear air above the engine casing.

'Laverne and me have been collecting these for years,' Kirk said, jumping from the beat-up truck and scrambling on to the nearest tractor. 'This here's the working one right now. When anything fails, we just tear one of the others down and use the best bits. Haven't bought a tractor part in years.' The saddle was all metal, brutal cold on a winter's morning, hot enough to burn your backside in high summer. The front wheels were set centrally, almost touching one another and effectively making the machine into a massive tricycle. All in all, a most unusual vehicle.

This was practical conservation, I thought. Never mind if the things are pollution monsters. Far more greenhouse gases would be generated in building and delivering one new tractor to replace this line-up than the whole bunch would produce in their long life yet to come. I suggested this idea to Kirk, who agreed, pointing out that it is far greener to keep a good thing going than to scrap it when a store-bought replacement would only do the same job a wee bit better.

'So why are they all facing downhill?'

'Haven't got a decent battery between them,' he chuckled, 'but there's usually one with enough "go" to lick up the spark if you bump start it down the slope. If it doesn't fire up before the bottom, your problem ain't the battery.'

I looked down. The old girls must have suffered from permanent vertigo.

'Do you breed your own cattle?' I asked as we drove back for lunch.

'We use four bulls,' Kirk replied, 'the heifers going out today are last spring's calves. If you don't get greedy and overstock the land, they fatten up good. We grow some alfalfa here, you see,' he said, 'it's restorative for the land. Kinda holds the sand together and fertilises it. Makes great cattle feed in winter.'

'What about water?'

'With all these storms around you'd think we'd have it to spare, but we don't. The ground's dry, but there's plenty of water 200 feet down. We pump it up with windmills.'

He gestured towards a large galvanised vat fifteen feet across, standing by a windmill in a hollow. Cows were drinking from it.

'Once a young bull gets to the right age,' Kirk returned to the favourite subject of procreation and winked at me, 'they get tested – know what I mean? The best, a very few, get the plum job with a lifetime of willing virgins, the rest go visit McDonald's.'

'Some choice.'

Back at the house, there was still no sign of the cattle truck, so Barb, Kirk's wife, served up lunch for us with her two young kids, and the new baby. We bowed our heads as grace was said, then we ate home-reared beefsteak, fried then braised, with mashed potato, sweetcorn and gravy. Food for a hungry man. As Barb and her children were clearing away, the world's longest articulated Freightliner truck (a 'semi') arrived with a belch of exhaust and a whining of gears. It manoeuvred somehow so that its trailer was hard by the corral. The tractor end was immaculate in blue paint, complete with coach stripes. Gene, the driver, seemed like a long-term family friend. He probably was.

Kirk and Laverne set up a fence to guide the cows into the truck, then performed unusual feats of gymnastics armed with electric prods to chivvy them aboard. There was no question of 'age before beauty', here. Both men walked across the backs of the packed cattle to move the herd in the direction they wanted. There was little resistance. The cows stamped and banged their way up the ramp into their two-tier accommodation, accepting their fate without fuss. The warm, animal smell of the cattle reminded me of childhood visits to the zoo, the one element Western movies always miss out.

The truck tailgate slammed shut and Gene pulled out up the track. The rest of us, kids and all, piled into the family station wagon to follow him to the North Platte auction sales. I couldn't help noting the roof of the wagon, which looked as if it had been beaten out like a sheet of copper except that the indentations were around three inches across.

'What happened to the car?' I asked.

'Hailstorm this spring,' replied Barb. 'Hang on. I'll show you the stones.'

She ran back into the house and returned holding lumps of ice fully the size of tennis balls.

'I shoved a few in the freezer. These were bigger when they landed, but of course they melted a bit as I carried them through to the kitchen. They can injure you if you get caught out. If they come in summer, they can wreck a crop completely.' She inspected the hailstones closely for a second or two. 'Sometimes it's like war out here.'

The auction was in full swing when we arrived. Squeezing out of the car beside the barn where the business was done, the first thing to hit was the almost overpowering reek of cattle. Barb left the kids to play outside the building, and nobody worried about them because there was nothing to fear. The rest of us entered through a sort of lobby and worked our way up to the back of the arena where we found space on the plank seating. The baby perched on Barb's lap and behaved like a proper trooper. The reek of cows was even stronger inside than out, as a pair of cowboys under the lights beneath us chased in a small herd. The calves galloped clumsily around the fifty-foot ring for the appraisal of cynical buyers seated beside nervous sellers in rows like a small circus, six or seven deep. To a man, they wore cowboy uniform, their high-heeled boots up on the seats in front, some with spurs. All had the tall, white hats except for a few of the younger sellers. They smoked cheroots and perused their song sheets as the auctioneer announced the next lot.

'Fine bunch of steers. Haven't drunk water in two days. All grass fed. Local reared. What'll yer gimme?'

At this, which was a request for a starting price per pound of cow ('pure meat – no pumping them up with water'), his preamble faded out into the classic auctioneer's song.

'Fifty cents, fifty cents, an' a five? Gimme five? Gimme five?' and so on. After a minute, the rhythm had become mesmeric, the pace had quickened and we could not understand a single intoned word. I nudged Kirk.

'What's the price now?'

'I dunno,' he shrugged. 'Can't hear anything the guy's saying. It's like this every time.'

'Who's bidding? I can't see anyone raising an eyebrow, let alone a finger.'

'Can't tell you that either. These buyers are all pros. They ain't farmers. They come from the conglomerates. The auctioneer knows every one. But don't ask me how the deal is done. I just supply the beef!'

On the day, Kirk and Laverne secured 60.5 cents per pound for their beasts, which worked out at around 540 dollars for a typical cow. Business was lean, but it was about what they'd expected. Kirk was philosophical, Barb said they'd get by. She was relieved. They had feared worse, but it was still hard times on the range. Two years previously the same cattle would have been fetching ninety cents per pound, and her household bills never went down.

After the sale, we cruised across the gigantic, roughshod parking lot and elbowed our way into a restaurant heaving with cowmen and their families. Beef was top of the bill and everyone was choosing it. The meal was a sort of private Harvest Festival for everyone there, and when ours pitched up, Kirk invited us to join hands with them to give thanks for the safe arrival of the herd at market and the sale of the cattle. Laverne poured himself a tumbler of water, cut up his steak ready for the fork, and told us a tale.

'Prices might be low,' he started out, 'but so long as you're fit and well and you think straight, there's always some poor guy worse off. Take High Plains Sam; used to hunt out our way in my Grandpa's day. He didn't think right. He suffered from optimism, and he ended up dead.'

'What happened to him, Grandpa?' asked Kirk's son, tucking in to a 'kid's portion' that would have shamed many a London restaurant.

'Well . . . Sam wasn't a young feller and he was deathly feared of tornadoes. He was all alone up there, and he was scared one would blow him clean away an' nobody would ever know. Sam had this theory that buffalo had a sixth sense about tornadoes and never got hit. He wasn't the only one, either. Plenty of the early settlers built their cabins right by a buffalo wallow, because that was where the beasts went when there was tornadoes around.

'One day, Sam knew there was going to be big twisters. He could see it in the sky and feel it in the air, so when evening came around, he made straight for a buffalo wallow he knew. There was still buffalo up on the hills then, but when he arrived, they was nowhere in sight, so he spread out his bedding and hunkered down for the night, feeling pretty pleased with himself.'

'How'd he make out?' asked Kirk who, incredibly, seemed not to have heard this story before.

'Everything went fine until around midnight,' continued Laverne. 'The storm's rumblin' all round him, but High Plains Sam could sleep though worse than that. Trouble was, the buffalo out on the range suddenly decided that it was tornado time and took up the same idea Sam had. So here comes the whole herd, galloping into their wallow right on top of him. Folks who found him said Sam was flatter 'n a frying pan.'

'Laverne! That is one awful story,' burst out Barb.

'Depends on how you look at it,' he replied. 'Sam might have been trampled to death, but he got one thing right. He never did get blown away by no tornado!'

The day after we left the Neal family should have been an easy one. We had 100 miles of sandhills to cover before we reached the Nebraska border settlement of Merriman, then possibly a further thirty or so to Martin in South Dakota before we saw any gasoline, so we rode into Tryon to top up. Anywhere in the United States, achieving a brimful motorcycle tank involves a contest of will and ingenuity against devilishly clever nozzle 'safety' cut-offs. The regulations owe more to the need for gas vendors to be protected against litigation on the remotest of contingencies than they do to common sense, but I suppose they do stop suicides from hosing red-hot engines down with gasoline. These 'safe' nozzles aren't a serious issue for car drivers with twenty-gallon tanks, but for the biker of sound mind, they are a dangerous menace. At the generally slow American speeds, the range of the Heritage was a mere 160 miles, while the Sportster, even with the special 'highway tank', switched over to 'reserve' at around 120. After that, how much it held was a lottery. The manufacturers certainly weren't letting on. This would be of no concern to most of their customers as they cruise the palmy boulevards of California and Florida, but out here the last teaspoonful could save a long, hot walk, so we kept cheating the system until the fuel was up to the rim.

The pump attendant shook our hands as though we'd been acquainted all our lives and we realised that by now the whole community would know about us. Someone had given us a good school report.

The road to the north across the hilly, deserted cattle country ran alongside a railroad line and soon deteriorated almost to dirt track status. Theoretically metalled, it was in such poor shape that we slowed to 20mph to lessen the crunch if either of us came off on the longitudinal ruts that were picking up our tyres and throwing the bikes from side to side. After ten miles of this grim riding a train horn sounded almost on top of us. Glancing over my shoulder, I saw a Union Pacific freight train rumbling past, heading up towards Canada, overtaking at a combined speed of around 10mph. The engineer gave us another two blasts. 'Whooooo! Whooooo!' The haunting sound went through me like a shot of moonshine and it took the train over five minutes to clear us.

Twenty miles down the road the bikes were back up to speed so that we found ourselves overtaking the same locomotive. This time the guys gave us four deafening notes. They were leaning out of their cab, lapping up the macho Harleys. Just us, them and the American highway.

Half an hour later, I wasn't feeling so elated. I stopped to take a photograph and Roz pressed on ahead. When I remounted I reckoned she was five miles away, so I hurried on as hard as I could on a surface which was again deteriorating. I didn't see Betty Boop until I almost ran over her. She was on her side by the ditch, engine stopped, and no sign of Roz. The road was bending slightly to cross a bridge over a rare streambed with water in it.

I hung on the brakes with my heartbeat in limbo, realising in an instant this was what I had been dreading all the way from the coast. Running back to the yellow bike, I was struck by how small and vulnerable she looked lying in the dust, but what I desperately needed to know was what had happened to my wife. Was she in the ditch with a broken neck? Had she wandered off somewhere with a snapped wrist, or crawled into cover with a fractured leg? The selfish thought formed for a second that the trip was going to end here in the pounding heat just south of Sioux country, but in truth I couldn't have cared less.

Weighed down with remorse for dragging Roz along all the way from the New Forest to dump her bike here on the lonesome prairie, and beside myself with anxiety, I called out, dreading silence most.

'Down here!'

I scrambled towards her voice and, to my inexpressible relief, saw her sitting happily by the water, boots and socks off, dangling her feet in its bubbling flow.

'What the hell?'

'Come on down. It's lovely and refreshing.'

'Are you all right?'

'I'm fine. It was so damned hot I just stopped to bathe my feet. Betty fell over when her stand sank in the sand. I felt stupid just waiting for you and I certainly can't lift her up, so I left her. I hit the 'kill switch' for the engine and turned off the fuel. I think she's OK.'

'Thank Christ for that,' I mumbled, and I meant it. Specifically.

An hour later we were in South Dakota. As if cut off by some great planner's knife, the sandhills gave way to fields with crops ready for the combines and we floated down a road like a silken carpet. The change was startling, but so was the price demanded by the glitzy motel on the busy Route 18 that runs west out of Iowa, through Pine Ridge Sioux reservation and on to the wilds of Wyoming and Laramie. After the past week, we felt so out of place on the wall-to-wall carpet of the lobby that we walked right into the oven again. Thirty miles along the highway we hung a left to retreat into Nebraska. The road here was in better shape than the one we'd used to make our northing, but it still wasn't much. Half an hour down its length with the sky looking like something High Plains Sam would have appreciated, we finally arrived in the frontier town of Gordon. We signed for the last available booking at the realistically priced Colonial Motel, grateful by now to find any lodging at all. The fancy place up in Dakota had also been busy, in total contrast to our experience out West so far, where nobody ever said, 'No room.'

'Why is everywhere full?' I asked the manageress.

'Crops are coming in,' she explained. 'We got the usual truckers, plus a commercial traveller or two, but that outfit next to you are harvesters from Missouri. And there are others.

They'll be around for a couple of weeks. They come every year. I'm expecting a new crowd in around midnight.'

We walked across to our room and shoved the bikes under the veranda. As we unlocked the door, the rain crashed down and we drew lots for the first session in the shower.

By the time I was cleaned up, the deluge was over. Fresh out of booze, I ventured down the street to the liquor store where I was sold a 'quart' of Teacher's Highland Cream, forty-three per cent export strength. The whisky was a long way from home and, glancing up the scrappy thoroughfare sided with shoe-box buildings of indeterminate age, some wooden, most of composite brick and concrete, I reflected that I was too. An assortment of light industries lined the road, while grain silos and other small towers of less obvious function made up a distinctive skyline. As always, heavy electricity wires criss-crossed at random from rough pine poles. Apart from me, the sidewalks were empty, and no traffic disturbed the evening's powerful scent of rain, so I walked back to where the Colonial Motel stood at the intersection of 'Main' and the road north to Dakota. The motel's substantially constructed rooms were arranged around an 'L' shaped forecourt to one side of a sprawling parking lot half filled with trucks and mobile farm machinery.

The neon lights were just coming on as I stepped up to our door. Outside the next cabin four men and a boy were sitting on the step sipping cold drinks. Just as the bikes leaning on their stands were our own badges of identity, these guys were distinguished by a huge, jacked-up pick-up that was somebody's pride and joy. Maroon coach-painted and immaculately clean, its running boards stood three feet above the ground. On the door in distinctive script was the legend, 'Korn Harvesting Services'.

'Fine motorcycles, Mister,' offered a handsome man in a blue sweatshirt. Square-rigged with curly, sandy hair, even features, a moustache like mine and a seemingly permanent grin. This was Wayne Korn, prime mover of the family firm. The other men were Pokey the truck driver, short on teeth but long on heart, and Cody, a broad-handed farmer from the same neighbourhood. The lad was Travis Korn, aged twelve. Travis drove one of the three combines along with Cody and Wayne. According to Pokey, he was the best operator of the three: 'Works his line as straight as a bullet.'

The team was completed by Wayne's father who ran the grain collector, the vital link between the combines and the trucks. 'Grandpa' was a Korean War veteran who provided a sort of moral overview to the team.

That night we drained the Teacher's in the cool darkness that followed the rain. The boys were staying at Gordon for the same reasons as us, and it was decided that we would hold on to our room for a while and travel to work with them across the Dakota line in the morning.

The time spent with the men from Missouri passed in a whirlwind of impressions. Roz sat in with Cody, and I with Wayne, perched high above a wheat-field the size of an English town in air-conditioned detachment. The juggernaut combines mowed, threshed, and every so often offloaded into Grandpa's collecting skip trailing behind a tractor. The patriarch rushed the shipment across the stubble to where Pokey waited in the chilled cab of his Freightliner to swing on down to the elevators in Gordon.

Agricultural versions of the heavily metalled fire engines of Middlesboro, the combines seemed never to halt. Like Martian combat tanks from the *War of the Worlds*, the three alien monsters marched, distorted by the hot air, as they steadily harvested the land. Chaff and dry dirt blew off behind them like smoke. Ahead stood the golden wheat waving in the prairie wind; astern, stubble that would soon be ploughed under, leaving no trace of the flowing bounty they had swept up into their safe, mechanical arms.

'Hey! Check out my coyote!' Travis' piping voice squawked out over the inter-connecting VHF radio. Wayne and I craned our necks to the youngster's combine and saw the yellow creature, half-dog, half-wolf, loping down-sun, flushed from cover by the whirling blades and joining the jack-rabbits bounding away across the newly shorn land.

'Guess having the boy along keeps the rest of us young,' Wayne said in a rare show of paternal affection.

'You do the job year after year and you forget the wonder that's in it. Takes a kid to remind you. There's more grain here and up in Canada than our own people can ever use. Sometimes, I forget that me and the boys and these farmers are feeding the world.'

The combines strode on across the plain, the trucks shuttled the grain to the silos and two days passed like the haze welling out behind the vehicles. In the evenings, we hung out with the farmer and his family, whose faith in the arid soil and their own luck make all this happen, through years of plenty and years when a one-hour hailstorm just before harvest wipes out a whole crop. The single-storey farmhouse stood inside a tiny garden beside the barn where Gary still kept horses. Ten yards from the parlour window, beyond the wire garden fence, the fields began, completing the permanent intimacy with the ever-cycling crop and raw Nature, always lying in wait to punish weakness, indolence or misfortune.

Seated at the long table in the clean, modern kitchen we talked of the Native Americans that I was passionate to visit and whose lands border these farms. Nobody had much time for the indigenous inhabitants of Dakota, especially Gary's father who had lived alongside the Sioux all his life. He had a distinct manner of speech that might have been a throwback to the days before the combine and the tractor revolutionised life on the prairie.

'The Federal Government pays them Indians . . . 1,200 dollars a month,' he said without bitterness, pausing before mentioning the sum of money, then picking it out as though it were spoken in italics. 'They're given houses, food and free education, and what do they do? They . . . spend . . . half the money on beer. And the rest? Why . . . they blow it to the wind . . . that's what they do.'

I almost began to ask a stupid question stemming from theories of equality I had heard back East, then had the sense to cut off a piece of my steak and shove that in my mouth instead. None of these intelligent, responsible people argued with what was clearly considered self-evident. Offering a different point of view would have been irrelevant, pointless and damaging. I'd learned years before that for a short-term guest to criticise a host's strongly held opinions is not only rude, it can cut off further communication as surely as drawing a blind. Besides, a stranger's remarks are generally seen by the man in the front line as ill-informed, and are discounted.

'You wait and you'll see,' continued the farmer, his face lined to the bone by seventy sub-zero winters and the desiccating winds of as many blazing summers. 'Go to Pine Ridge and see how they live. It's a shame how they . . . waste . . . their land.'

The Weather Channel promised storms by the evening of the third day, with fifty per cent chance of hail. The combines pressed on with renewed effort as the clouds gathered. This was the fourth day the Korn boys had worked this farm. They had known the family for years and were apprehensive for them, but you can no more rush a combine than you can a sailing ship. Wayne and Travis kept to their cabs and I accompanied Pokey to the elevators where the atmosphere was so dust-filled that no man could work there and hope to survive for long. Masks were required, of course, but masks are rather like crash helmets to a Western American motorcyclist; to be worn when absolutely unavoidable, but otherwise shunned as a restraint on freedom. The inside of the hoist was like a cathedral, dark and echoing. Above us, the silo soared skywards like a round-topped spire.

Roz had been fascinated by the sight of the wheat being churned around and whirled into the maw of Cody's combine, so she stayed in the cool cab, contemplating the catharsis of the year as the storm clouds gathered, chatting of family and the practicalities of living life in Missouri. Cody's even temperament had survived the tragedy of two lost chidren. He kept himself busy, he said, which helped balance his mind. As Roz talked the day away with the quiet man of the outfit, he told her Wayne and he were considering making an offer on Betty Boop if ever she became redundant. They'd both sampled her around Gordon and, like the rest of the world, seemed to have fallen in love with her. Roz suspected that this idea was equivalent to the acquisitive infatuation sailors feel for all manner of unlikely items thay see in far lands. 'These guys remind me of seamen,' she said to me late one night. 'They're staring at the horizon, but really, they're thinking of home.'

The last of Gary's grain came in half an hour before the storm broke. Watching the precipitation sweep towards us like a scythe riding on gale force winds, we rushed the bikes and Wayne's truck into the barn to keep them from the otherwise inevitable damage. We beat the weather by seconds. The stones were not the tennis ball-sized grapeshot we'd been shown down in the sandhills, but they would have done well as musket balls and would surely have destroyed all our paintwork. The hailstorm blew off to leeward after fifteen minutes, leaving us all hanging about shell-shocked. Gary looked as though he could hardly believe how closely he had been let off the hook for another season. The rest of us were glad for him, but fearful for his neighbour. The hail had mostly scattered off the road and piled into the sides, where it was melting as fast as ice in a cooking pot. The gleaming truck was stuck behind the bikes and Gary's car, so Wayne borrowed Betty Boop and chugged away up the road while the rest of us drank coffee with the farmer's wife. He was back in a half-hour.

'Sure enjoyed the ride, Ma'am,' he said to Roz, polite as always, but for once not smiling. Then he turned to the company. 'But the next job's a mess.'

The boys agreed that the best they could do was rally round, help the poor guy salvage what he could and hope his insurance didn't renege. What remained of the job wouldn't take up all the time allotted for it and so far they had had good fortune from the weather, leaving them a week or more ahead of schedule. It was even possible that they would win enough days to go back to see their families while they were waiting for their next crop to ripen up on the Canadian border.

'Can't I stay on here, Dad?' demanded Travis immediately. 'You know Ma'll grab me for the start of school if we go home, and you need me to drive.'

The parallel with my own daughter's upbringing was obvious. Year after year, she had been a week or three late for the autumn term so that she could complete some voyage or other in the family boat. She had taken no harm. Even if his wife disagreed, Wayne clearly thought as we did. Travis could well miss a fortnight's schooling, his father said to me later.

'I was just testing to see how he really felt. We'll hide him away clear of the schoolroom until the job's over. The plains will take up the slack.'

Roz and I returned to Gordon for the last time after sharing an impromptu harvest supper with the whole team. As my headlamp blazed ahead into the starry night, I realised that watching the Nebraska cattle families and the plains farmers living their compromise with the ancient prairies was giving me the beginnings of an understanding of the underlying strength of the United States. Roz had remarked in Baltimore that America is too close to its past to recognise itself. In these parts, it seemed almost as if the past had never finished at all, and that the life the settlers risked everything for had been found and kept. My overall impressions had been very different in the multi-cultured cities of the East, and I concluded that the ordinary people of the plains were somehow cleansed by the unavoidable certainties of Nature which confront them every minute. Theirs is the life of freedom, secured by service to the family, the nation and their god, that the Constitution of the United States foresaw.

chapter fourteen

a close call on the reservation

I settled into my personal, vibrating semi-consciousness, reflecting as I rode that even the Colonial Motel had turned out to have its dark side. I was suffering from back pain that morning as a result of several bad nights in a bed that for the money should have been a lot more comfortable.

'Lumpy,' was the verdict.

Apropos of nothing in particular, Pokey had told us that the manageress had used our room while her apartment was being renovated. The day before we left, she was not in her office when I went to settle in advance for our final night. Various people were hanging around the check-in, and finally the owner of the place showed up to find the manager's apartment stripped and the cash-box empty. The good woman had 'done a runner' with the proceeds.

'She always treated us right,' Wayne said as he started up his sparkling truck. 'Nice lady.'

That last evening, Roz and I had given up trying to convince ourselves the bed was tolerable, so we chucked the mattress on to the floor, always the last-ditch answer. As it had come away from the base, the mattress revealed a stash of a dozen or more empty bottles of gin and vodka tossed at random between it and its supporting springs.

I was still chuckling about the excesses of our unusual hostess when we came up with a throng on horseback following the high roads towards Pine Ridge. The altitude had been imperceptibly rising for hundreds of miles as the plains rolled towards the Rockies so that we now enjoyed blissful relief from the noonday heat, with cool mornings and evenings. For some reason I could not identify, once inside Indian country, the land actually felt higher and, as the outsiders had promised, the organised wheat-fields were replaced by unkempt, yellow-brown prairie. The first indication of the travellers was a tailback of traffic along the two-lane highway. Next, a dust cloud could be seen rising ahead. Finally, we trundled past a hundred or more full-blooded Native Americans, men, women and children, meandering towards the town. Perhaps a third straddled ponies, the rest were on foot. The ponies were athletic-looking creatures, light-coloured with bold brown or black markings. The horsemen went bareback. Many had long hair with coloured headbands like the Apache warriors of my schoolboy comic books; one or two wore feathers slung point-up. Beads and brightly patterned cloth swung in the sunshine, and there was a joyous lack of formality in the way the group moved amongst themselves. A mounted man trotted by, half-turning on his pony's back to joke with a bunch behind him, youngsters scampered here and there, almost between the horses' feet, women swayed along chatting amongst themselves, and the whole crowd ebbed and flowed out on to the blacktop, seemingly unaware of the traffic jam. Like just about everyone else in North America, however, they registered the bikes, waving and calling as we trickled slowly ahead.

The Indians could have been heading up to Medicine Lodge 120 years ago to meet Black Kettle and Standing Bear, such was the effect of their costume and the totally non-Caucasian dynamics of their interplay. They reflected the high sun softly from their buckskin and wampum, we shot it back off our chrome and steel like helio mirrors, yet with the styling of our leather saddlebags, our scarves drifting in the wind and the essentially 'Western equestrian' seating position of the Harley-Davidson, we were far more in harmony with the scene than any of the air-conditioned cars and their white inhabitants.

Why this tribe were on the road remained unclear for only a short while. We were low on fuel when we arrived at the settlement of Pine Ridge, so our first stop in the main town of a reservation the size of Yorkshire, was the local filling station which was also the most significant building around, part store, part restaurant and automotive centre. Before we had even opened our tank caps, a heavily built young Indian descended on us aboard a 1971 Harley held together with wire and string. Sid Half-Head wore no helmet, his long braided hair flowed over his leather shirt and his breath suggested he'd enjoyed a liquid lunch. We had met one or two Indians back at Gordon, handsome men with high cheekbones, cowboy kit, dark ponytails and perhaps a thin necklace of wampum beneath the open necks of cotton shirts. Sid didn't have their figure, but he had the broadest face I'd ever seen off an Inuit. There was no doubting his ancestry. He admired our top-of-the-line modern machines, which were clearly beyond his wildest financial aspirations, without even a tinge of envy.

'Evolution engines,' he nodded, referring to our motor units, a marque introduced comparatively recently. 'They as reliable as folks say?'

'We've come all the way from the East Coast and they haven't missed a beat.'

Sid shook his head and I inquired about the travelling tribe now weaving its way into town.

'Sioux nation pow-wow,' he announced with pride. 'Starts tomorrow. Folks'll be gatherin' from all over. North Dakota, Montana; Iowa even. Plenty here already.'

We parked the bikes and ambled across the street with him to the yard of a wooden building where four young girls in full tribal regalia were being quizzed by a group of female elders. Neither Roz nor I could make head or tail of the proceedings. I turned to ask Sid, but he had bored quickly and split, leaving us on our own in a small crowd of local onlookers. The girls seemed to be giving résumés, after which they were cross-examined on what appeared to my mind the most banal issues.

'They're being assessed for the Queen of the pow-wow,' a mid-range voice spoke up from my elbow. Looking down, I found myself pressed against a well-endowed Indian woman of around thirty. She looked me in the eye, paused, then continued, 'To be selected is an honour.'

This fine-looking lady promptly introduced herself and started to fill me in on her experiences on the back of various motorcycles, complete with intimate details. When she picked up the fact that Roz was there too, she turned from me and started work cutting her down to size. Roz's Spitfire-pilot father, her childhood in the caravan at the end of the runway, the 'Clergy Daughters' public school and the heavy-duty motorcycling suddenly sounded excruciatingly middle class when our friend announced that although she had rarely left Pine Ridge, she had taken full advantage of the educational opportunities offered to Native Americans and had a degree and was daughter to one of the tribal elders. What clinched her superiority was being the great- granddaughter of one of the young chiefs who forsook the white man's imposed reservation. They had chosen instead to live free with Crazy Horse in those dangerous years leading up to the annihilation of General Custer in the summer of 1876. Together with Rain in the Face, Black Foot and a number of other sub-chiefs under Sitting Bull, these warriors are among the most charismatic men in American history, but their triumph was so inevitably brief that few of them survived to see their ancestral hunting grounds turned into wheat-fields. The Oglala Teton Sioux chief, Red Cloud, managed an uneasy compromise, persuading his people to subsist on the Pine Ridge Reservation, but Sitting Bull was ultimately assassinated and Crazy Horse lost his life in suspicious circumstances. In 1890, Black Foot was cut down with hundreds of his unarmed kinsfolk, many of them old men, women and children, in the determining massacre by the US Army at Wounded Knee.

All this remained in the back of my mind as the young lady worked out that ours were the two bikes parked over the road. Turning her back on the beauty queen competition, she took my arm and asked in a matey sort of way for a lift to the field on the edge of town where the pow-wow was apparently gaining momentum.

'You have to be there,' she was saying. 'Big party, music, dancing, and great conversation. You can pitch your tent by the teepees.'

Roz expressed an understandable ambivalence at this offer. 'Isn't it just for Sioux?'

'The pow-wow is for anyone feeling the spirit move them,' responded our self-appointed tour guide serenely, leading the way across the stream of traffic to the bikes. From the safety of air-conditioned cars, RVs and virgin four-tracks, passing tourists stared at the Indians, but few made the move to come out into the open. It crossed my mind that perhaps they all knew something I didn't, but it seemed churlish to refuse this enthusiast a lift.

'You two go ahead,' Roz said, unconcerned, 'I'll follow on behind.'

I reorganised my kit somehow and the girl, no mean weight, hopped up on to Madonna's buddy seat. She hugged me around the waist as I kicked the bike into gear and opened up for the West End of town. I could see Roz in my mirrors, a light and a yellow flash. She was a long way astern.

By the time we reached our turn-off, the way my passenger was pressing into my leather-clad back was hinting that perhaps a pow-wow was one of those affairs where 'anything goes'. There's no doubt that bikes do things to some women and unfortunately a Harley engine, even a smoothed-out Evolution version, can act like an overpriced vibrator to anyone straddling the buddy seat. Fearing the worst, I held back, willing Roz to give it some throttle, but she had disappeared temporarily from my field of vision and the girl behind me was raring for action.

'Come on!' she urged, breathing in my ear, leaning forward and nudging my right elbow with a helping of unmistakably female chest, 'it's just at the bottom of this hill and across the field.'

Filtering in from the side, an endless convoy of ponies, trucks and ancient cars, mainly American, was lurching down a long, steep slope, rutted and deeply muddy, towards a water-meadow studded with trailers, tents and a handful of tall teepees. Slipping the clutch and riding the back brake judiciously to stop the heavy bike sliding from under us, I hung on as we jolted down the slope. The V-twin growled sexily as I blipped the throttle to avoid a series of potential collisions. The frame responded with its wicked high-resonance shudder. I dreaded to imagine what the monster was doing to the ancestral hormones.

At the bottom of the incline, we set course for a group of teepees on the far side of the wide pasture. By the time we got there, any semblance of tread in my road tyres was crammed with mud and the traction was reduced to zero, but the chief's great-granddaughter was getting a bang out of hollering to her chums. If we'd collapsed in a greasy puddle I don't think she'd have minded one bit.

As the pair of us dismounted, I peered anxiously astern for Betty Boop, feeling like a wagon train survivor praying for the cavalry. To my exquisite relief I saw Roz riding precariously through a crowd of appreciative but well-oiled young braves. Not only was the Sportster still on her feet, despite the abysmal going but Roz's arrival lifted me from what had all the makings of a diplomatic disaster.

There was no sign of the elders keeping a lid on the action. The teepees were empty, the trailer crowd was ripping into the firewater and heavy metal music was reverberating around the valley from hidden speakers of major proportions. Despite the carnal attractions of my passenger, I had been hoping for some serious discussion about the life of an Indian in today's United States, but fate and the bottle seemed to be conspiring against such enlightenment. Roz searched for a patch of ground hard enough to support Betty's side stand as I tried to engage my passenger in meaningful exchange, but she had lost interest and was proposing a lift back to town. Perhaps this was because of Roz's persistence; more likely, I thought, my presence was no longer required now that she had made her triumphal arrival on site. Whatever the reason, I was persuaded to mount up, pop her on the back once more, and drop her where I had picked her up. Roz muttered something about seeing me there. As I hacked away across the boggy field with the Indian girl's powerful thighs once more clamped around my hips, I reflected that I'd have been much better off with Laverne's trail bike than the heavy, skidding Heritage. Despite the non-event now subsiding to its anticlimax, I couldn't help speculating disgracefully on the potential outcome had I been a lone rider. But that was one thing I'd never know. The dark-haired beauty hopped off at the gas station, awarded me a warm, wet kiss and was last seen deep in conversation with Sid Half-Head over a can of Coke.

I waited five minutes for Roz. After ten, I was seriously worried and had just started the bike to go look for her when she arrived from around the corner covered in mud. Seeing her reappear from those direst of straits made me realise how much I loved her, but she was not in a mood to be told. Instead, she indicated for me to follow, opened her throttle and blasted away eastwards across the plain at an unprecedented speed, ground-up dirt spitting from her tyres. She didn't falter until we were twenty minutes outside the reservation. Only then did she stop on a swell of the sunset prairie, miles from anywhere.

'Sometimes I really wonder about you,' she said, her eyes steely. 'The first sniff of a girl and you gallivant off into some God-forsaken jamboree with me tagging on like a spare part.'

Still filled with admiration for her nerve, I tried to remonstrate that to refuse would have been rude, but this was no acceptable excuse.

'And then you leave me in what looked like a World War I no-man's-land surrounded by drunkards. The bike was totally bogged down. If she'd gone over, God only knows what would have happened. I've strained my back holding on to Betty, so I'd appreciate the fanciest berth in Dakota for tonight. I need a hot bath and a comfortable bed.'

Ten miles on we pulled in at the tourist joint we had turned our backs on a week before. Travel had been a tough option that day and, as a mollified Roz pointed out, tourism has its place in a secret corner of every journey. We parked our filthy Harleys among the polished motorcars and tucked into a proper dinner surrounded by vacationers from everyday jobs. These were the people whose faces we'd seen peering through vehicle windows that afternoon. The following morning, I chatted with some of them in the lobby and was not really surprised to discover that they were ordinary folks from Middle America out to see their country. Their Pine Ridge experience had been dramatically different from ours. Many of them were now pressing on to the Little Big Horn battleground, or into the Black Hills to visit giant statues of the heads of Washington, Lincoln and other presidents at the Mount Rushmore monument. Sturgis was being avoided like a plague city. Since no one seemed interested in Wounded Knee, we decided to go there.

As soon as we re-entered the reservation on the secondary route leading to Wounded Knee, the pot-holes became so deep and erratic that some stretches of road represented a major undertaking. Set back from the track, shabby trailers and basic houses were surrounded by wrecked automobiles, rusty cookers and other debris, an untidy contrast to the neat homes of white farmers a mere thirty miles away. 'Low morale', would be a simplistic deduction, yet when we stopped by the roadside to take in the scene of poor soil, buttes and shallow canyons, two beaten-up local cars had swung by within five minutes to check brightly whether we needed help. Both drivers were Sioux, the second a woman.

'We're fine, thank you,' Roz reassured her. 'We just stopped to admire your beautiful country.'

And it was true. The deeply scoured valleys and gulches might have been unproductive, but they were lovely in the cool morning.

'Beautiful country, yes,' responded the woman, arms wide, 'this is sacred ground. The Black Hills and all this land are the burial place of our ancestors. It was given to us and will always be holy.'

'What I don't understand,' Roz remarked after she had driven away, 'is that if the place is so sacred, why dump rubbish everywhere like modern-day gypsies? Why is there no respect for the environment?'

I could only suggest that perhaps nomadic Indians, and gypsies too, had always left their refuse behind, but that in pre-industrial times, everything must perforce have been biodegradable. Perhaps when they came back to a summer camp after a six-month absence, their leavings had more or less returned to the earth. Living free with the land and its creatures as a part of the whole order, rather than being forced to subsist on its surface as consumers, must have cast a very different perspective on such questions. A hundred years is a short time to change a path of thinking that was part of this nation's genetic framework long before the Army ground it into irrelevance at gunpoint with government approval.

Perhaps the last word on the Indian philosophy of land ownership should go to Crazy Horse. 'One does not sell the earth on which the people walk.'[8]

At Wounded Knee, we stood alone at what must be one of the most dignified monuments in the United States, a Stone Age people's equivalent of the wall memorial in Washington to the dead of Vietnam. A small enclosure has been cordoned-off above the shallow valley where, a day or two before Christmas 1890, the Army opened fire with field guns on a final group of free Indians under Black Foot, who were actually in the process of handing in their arms and coming on to the Pine Ridge reservation. One of the few survivors was Black Elk.

'I did not know then how much was ended. When I look back now from this high hill of my old age, I can see the butchered women and children lying heaped and scattered all along the crooked gulch as plain as when I saw them with my eyes still young. And I can see that something else died there in the bloody mud, and was buried in the blizzard. A people's dream died there. It was a beautiful dream . . . the nation's hoop is broken and scattered. There is no centre any longer, and the sacred tree is dead.'[9]

From four-foot withies driven into the hard earth, a few scraps of coloured cloth floated on the summer breeze. One or two simple statements were carved on low stone tablets and a plain stone monolith marked the centre, but the essential message is in the fragments of material caught in the endless wind. What the fluttering fronds mean to the people who maintain them I do not know, but for me, they mark a position fixed in time; the watershed between a philosophy that accepted the land as it was and the new one of recasting it to accommodate man's special needs.

a close call on the reservation

Our next stop was to be Whiteclay to replenish our booze. Alcohol sales are forbidden on the reservation and this settlement immediately off Indian Territory was said to fill the gap in the market. Riding the bumpy road to the drink store, I deliberated the impressions of the Sioux. My thoughts centred on the confusion of identity that seemed to beset the most famous Indian nation of them all. The stark perfection of the Wounded Knee memorial failed utterly to gel with the drunks at the pow-wow, and it was clearly true that for many Native Americans, in this area at least, liquor provided an important life support system. In the absence of sales points on the reservation, the hamlet of Whiteclay has given itself over to servicing this requirement. It consists of little more than a sun-beaten open space with the right stuff on sale. As we trundled to a halt, the place smelt as though something had died around the corner and been left there for vultures who had not fancied it. No habitation, no church, no doctor's surgery and no school disturbed the seedy dispensing of booze.

When we shut off our engines, a small gathering of sullen men rose to their feet from benches outside the stores and came lurching over towards us, weaving from drink but distinctly menacing. Roz glanced at me for confirmation, then she thumbed her starter button and we turned tail. Facing up to strangers in circumstances that imply a potential threat always takes moral fibre, and I for one had run out of the commodity for the time being. It was a sad end to a remarkable two days, but rather than face a meaningless conversation or something worse with these ruined men, we sped towards the wilderness of the Badlands into which Crazy Horse's parents had carried their son's body. His grave was never revealed.

chapter fifteen

style or substance?

We chose the least-used route through the thousand-odd square miles of the Dakota Badlands. In the hot afternoon, it took no imagination to work out that before the trail was driven through and the odd motor vehicle passed by, dying of thirst or exposure in the wildly decayed wilderness of cream-coloured clay would have been simple. The division between the marginally cultivable Indian reservation and the totally unworkable Badlands was dramatic. The grass petered out while the terrain took on fantastic shapes as though painted by Salvador Dali. Wide, flat-floored valleys and narrower canyons carved out by the weather spanned the miles between almost vertical, stratified cliffs rising to the surface of the plain above. The low-lying areas were littered with crazy towers of clay and flat-topped 'mini-mesas' a hundred or more feet high that cried out to be explored.

Immediately inside the southern boundary, a dust track wandered off across an area of sparse, coarse vegetation to a tiny wooden church. Roz rode on along the partially metalled road as I, always a push-over for a chapel or a bar, pulled over to investigate. Seemingly irrelevantly placed miles from any habitation, I doubted whether even the coyotes came to church here. As I parked Black Madonna, I took off my shades to get the full effect of the still-high sun, but the light shining back from the pale-coloured cliffs and the peeling white clapboard of the walls was so strong it hurt my eyes. I slammed them back on again and forswore reality.

The chapel bore the same signs of semi-regular use one notes on the churches of country parishes in England, where ecclesiastical cut-backs require vicars to service three or four congregations. Notices announcing 'Holy Communion, third Sunday in the month,' and 'Flowers next week, Mrs Tidy,' were absent, but the timber steps were in good repair. The heavy door was unfortunately locked, but the board announced to any who should pass by that this was the church of 'Our Lady of the Sioux'. It was my last fleeting connection with the modern-day survivors of the tribes of the northern plains, but no priest appeared to explain why the building existed in so obscure a location, or who were the worshippers who made the stupefying journey to mass.

Back on the road, the tarmac was shimmering in the midday heat. I strapped my leathers across the back of a bike and gave Madonna the gun to catch up with Roz, only to succumb to another dirt track ten miles later weaving away into a narrow canyon. The dust had been pounded hard and flat by storms, so riding wasn't too difficult, although over-confidence would soon have had me off because the stark light was not picking up any holes and corrugations clearly enough for me to anticipate at over 15mph. I stopped my engine in a side gulch, and stood for a few minutes experiencing the totally lifeless nature of the place. Nothing whatever moved and the only sound was the bike cooling off a fraction from running temperature to the blood-boiling ambient heat of the surrounding air. My black, studded machine was in perfect harmony with this outrageously American scene, and I reflected that if you threw in a friendly rattlesnake the picture would make the cover of a Harley-Davidson brochure.

I could have sat on my haunches all afternoon watching the shadows grow, but Roz was running further away each minute and as usual, we'd no contingency meeting plan other than that we'd be in Sturgis that night. This typically loose arrangement, however, was going to be even less use than usual. We hadn't seen a bike apart from Sid Half-Head's since we'd entered the reservation, but there had to be thousands of them fifty miles north of us. Unless Roz stopped to wait for me, which there was no guarantee of her doing, finding her in town was going to be like looking for a small bolt in a well-stocked workshop 'bits box'. Reluctantly, I fired up and gave the engine all the gas it could guzzle.

I was soon seeing double from the high-speed throbbing of the engine, but even so there was no glimpse of the black and yellow flash far ahead until our obscure track ran into the main drag at the imaginatively named junction of 'Scenic'. As we merged with the highway that led through Rapid City to bikers' Mecca, we at last filtered into a river of spotless motorcycles which grew ever denser as it flowed westwards.

For any lover of traditional American engineering, the sheer mass of steel, chrome and tooled leather pouring westwards was worth a long, hard road to be a part of. Founded in 1903, Harley-Davidson's history is older than many parts of the modern country, and even the spread-eagle logo could serve as a national call to arms. Harleys prevailed here by an overwhelming percentage, with cool dudes lounging back on customised 'choppers' riding as easy as Captain America himself; grizzled veterans in ancient leathers barrelling along with grey beards flying in the wind; smart city types cruising on 'store-bought' one-offs, while an occasional 'rat-bike' wreck surged along in defiance of the laws of mechanical ageing.

'Highway pegs' in lieu of conventional footrests were standard equipment, allowing the feet to ease out almost to the front wheel. The resulting laid-back mode makes for comfort in a straight line, but can be so unsuited to ambitious bend-swinging that the attitude has given Harley riders in Britain the reputation for posing. Removed from nationalism and prejudice, the unadorned fact is that so long as it isn't taken to the sort of extremes that are normal in Sturgis, the position is safer than it looks assuming you aren't in a hurry. Out West where the roads run straight all day and half the next as well, the tables are squarely turned on the sport-biker. In 'Marlboro Country', it is the man crouched over a high-speed 'crotch rocket' that seems vaguely ridiculous, on a mission to prove something.

The one thing that struck us immediately we joined the stream was how slowly everyone was riding; 50mph, maybe 60 for a treat, was maximum. To me and to Roz too, now that she was starting to relax, travelling on a powerful motorbike so slowly seemed somehow rude to the machinery, and so we blatted merrily on, overtaking almost everyone in a non-aggressive sort of way.

As we passed each bike, hearing its booming thunder as the sun sparkled on chrome-work and coloured the flying leather tassels, I couldn't help but check out what our brothers and sisters were wearing. In sartorial terms, I felt like a farm boy at a society wedding. Most of that remarkable procession was togged up in fashion gear, and I had to admit it caught the eye of the beholder a whole lot more effectively than our fundamentalist leathers. It also assisted the air-cooling of the suffering body, but the protection factor of a thin sleeveless jerkin, a headscarf and a pair of jeans with rips across the knees approaches absolute zero, even against grasshopper attack. The truth was probably that nobody rode at a sensible speed simply because it hurt too much, even if you stayed on your wheels. Actually sliding in the gravel in such kit would be too damaging to contemplate. Yet for all my long-faced British common sense, the boys and girls rolling down that road were as great a sight as their machinery. The disdain for crash helmets was universal, but stylish hats or caps, flying ponytails, brawny arms showing off acres of tattoo, neck chains and cowboy boots with huge ring buckles were uniform for the younger men. The old-timers were better covered and looked as if they had ridden farther, but it was the women who really seemed to have a death-wish.

Every so often we overtook a lady on her own bike. Some were riding 'safe', others making a statement for freedom by wearing next to nothing in the golden sunshine. Comparatively secure in her full-face helmet and leathers, I could see Roz peeking in disbelief at the black leather bikinis, minimalist buckskin jackets revealing cleavages with all-over tans and at least one set of the sexy, black, North American chaps with the open behind worn over nothing more than a G-string. One false move among the tight group she was riding with and the lady's manicured bum would look like a field of burnt shell-holes. I could almost feel Roz shuddering. Such valkyries in control of their own destiny were, however, in the minority. Most of the fair sex trundling west were perched uncomfortably high up behind their men, the young ones with their feet so close under their behinds that they hung on only by splaying their bare legs in a manner only the simplest could misconstrue.

Beyond the classic 'strip' of Rapid City, the smooth surface of Interstate 90 rose steadily for thirty miles to the Sturgis turn-off under a shoulder of the 7,000-foot Black Hills. It had been a long day from the luxury of our overnight refuge, but the last thing we wanted at the 'Greatest Motorbike Show on Earth' was a wholesome, family camping place. Zealously searching for action despite our fatigue, we scoured the outskirts of town for the forbidden venue.

'Buffalo Chip?' I asked the leader of a group of half-shaven road-burners drinking beer under a threadbare tree. He looked hard at me for a few seconds, dragged at his roll-up, then spat in the dust.

'If you gotta ask, Mister, you shouldn't be goin' there.'

His cronies made 'Mr Cool' expressions and flexed their tattoos. I met their stare with a nonchalance I did not feel, nodded and opened my throttle.

'Give it one more go,' suggested Roz.

Our next human road-sign was leaning on a smart new custom model filling his trendy peanut tank with 'Premium Unleaded' and taking the sort of care with the hose that would normally be reserved for a nitric acid dispenser. With such a pitiful fuel capacity he'd never have made it across the Badlands, and he had no more clue about the forbidden campground than we did. He even fished a plan out of his pocket that indicated where a homeless biker could unroll his bedding. Still he shook his head.

'Ain't no Buffalo Chip on this map,' he said, 'but there's a good place right here behind the pumps. They got showers, dancing, the lot.'

And so, by chance, we pitched our tent beside a Dutch couple on a similar expedition to our own. Marek looked at home on his 'Springer-nosed' Harley with Death's Head handlebar ornaments, leather vest and riding cap. Marlika rode pillion, but had reached a similar conclusion to Roz about motorcycling long distances in her underwear.

'I think we should form a chapter of uncool bikers,' she proposed in almost-unaccented English as we glugged a quick bottle of Wild Turkey to get in the mood. At 9:30 we marched across to the dance.

The barn was full of atmosphere and the music vibrant, but nobody stood up from the trestle tables to bop around, no voice was raised either in wrath or delight and the booze was going warm on the shelves. We necked a few beers to be polite, then the band hit us with 'Mony, Mony' and Roz couldn't take any more idleness. We hopped out on to the floor followed by the Dutch contingent, danced the number through and sat down again. People looked at us as though we hailed from Mars, so we gave that up and struggled to join in the table conversation over the sound of the redundant band. Perhaps not surprisingly, this proved to be 100 per cent Harley-Davidson. Nobody talked about threading the high passes out of Colorado in soft snow as Nell had, and no-one was gossiping about sex, drugs and demolition derbies. There were no 'Nam vets stretching out their pensions on the highway, just part-time bikers discussing 'Screamin' Eagle' carburettor parts and chrome custom fittings. You expect people to voice their enthusiasms at such gatherings, and Marek and I had some interest in the subject, so we stuck with it for a quarter-hour. Then Marlika leaned across. A lovely girl even though she was covered up.

'Roz and I are going back to the tents to drink the other bottle of whiskey,' she announced to the assembled teetotallers.

'I spent all day on the back of the bike and I don't want to pass the night talking about the thing.'

Marek glanced at me.

'We'll come along too,' I responded quickly, relieved to be out of the tedium.

Back at the Khyber Pass, Marek splashed scotch into his plastic Coke cup. As a transport driver who had fired himself to make the trip to America, he was an expert.

'They have trains full of motorbikes coming from all over America to nearby towns,' he announced solemnly. 'And there's trucks galore. There's still a few who really ride out here. You've met some, so have we, but folks like us are a minority. These are mainly middle class people. Most of them don't have the time to do it right. They have to get back to their jobs. There are a few reformed ravers, but even those guys are middle-aged with kids now. The wild times are done.'

As he spoke, a gust of cold air swept through the tents from the lowering bulk of the Black Hills. Within a minute, a katabatic wind off the mountains had risen to near gale force and tents were blowing away. I ripped open my saddlebag and fished out my sailor's coil of line to fashion a storm guy. Marek was contriving a similar lash-up for his own outfit as a flock of 'superlite' igloo motorbike tents somersaulted like tumbleweed in the moonlight. Bikers in various stages of undress scattered in disarray across the dusty campground like infantry in rout before an avenging Chief Touch the Clouds. The flimsy shelters wrapped themselves around trees, pick-ups and motorcycles. One shot clear away past the well-lit toilet block and out the gate, pursued by a hobbling shadow in a forage cap, pulling up its pants with one hand. For an hour or more, chaos was king until the storm died as suddenly as it had risen, tattered tents were re-established, and all was peace except for the constant drone of unsilenced V-twins that continued day and night.

'I think that's the most action we're going to see here,' predicted Marlika, and she was right.

The morning after the tent-storm, we mounted up to hunt for some of the people we'd met along the road. Having failed miserably to locate Buffalo Chip, we fared no better searching for Bear Bluff with Red's campsite under the cliff. Hoping for better luck with Nell, Steve and the rest we filtered into the mob of rumbling, roaring bikes cruising into town.

Here, the crush was drastic. The broad, Wild West main street of Sturgis is designed for a winter population of around 5,000. Now it was home to what was effectively a nation of bikers.

'There's something like 200,000 machines here,' I overheard one long-haired knight of the road tell his companion.

'Someone else just said that,' observed Roz, *sotto voce*, 'but it must mean the number of extra people here, including all the hangers-on. If it was bikes, that would mean half a million humans, and there certainly aren't that many. There's an awful lot, though . . . ' she tailed off as an even denser mass of approaching metal deafened us. The street was virtually impassable as we struggled to wrestle Madonna into a parking space. Two hundred thousand or not, the effect was monstrous as bikes and owners strutted their stuff in the blazing sunshine.

Phenomenally executed tank art abounded. Paintings of Indian chiefs heroically greeting the sunrise shouldered up to neighbouring bikes where half-naked babes reclined in the inviting poses normally reserved for the noses of World War II American bombers. Bikes with buffalo horns instead of handlebars crushed against sidecar outfits that seemed to contain all the owner's worldly goods, right down to the dog, all kitted out in scarf and goggles. Side panels painted with liquid fire competed for attention with tanks bearing the US flag with a dagger or machine gun and motifs such as, 'Free Spirit', or, 'Live whole and die free'. Vast trucks with their diesels idling to keep a cool cab were parked immediately off Main. Superheated gases from gleaming exhausts distorted billboard sides decorated with ghost horsemen, buffalo herds and biker cowboys that would have outfaced the most cynical of art critics.

Towards lunchtime, the strip became so crowded that it was virtually impossible to ride down it, let alone make a pass at its length in a motor car. The only tourist we saw trying was lost without trace. We refreshed ourselves in every bar, elbowing alongside the posers, the enthusiasts and the occasional genuine hooligan, but we never found our friends.

'I'll bet you they've all vanished into the same legend as the gang warfare and the mob sex,' I said to Marek, who had also failed to find a Canadian he was hoping to run into. In a final effort to dig out some deep-down human colour, the four of us jostled into town on our last night to try our luck in the once-infamous 'Broken Spoke Saloon'.

We jammed the bikes into the side parking lot soon after midnight and shouldered our way to the bar through massed, uniformed motorcyclists sipping small beers. Another great band was blasting away for all it was worth along the only solid wall. The other three sides of the huge room were open to above head height, allowing drinkers to wander in and out more or less at will, while affording those inside an uninterrupted view of the world's most spectacular motorcycle parking lot. Interesting bikes were suspended from the upper walls, mostly Harley-Davidsons, but one 'Indian' graced the scene with its 1930s styling. I was pleased to note a British Norton and, of all things, a Matchless, a lifetime away from the Mersey Tunnel. Amongst the metal were charts of North America covered in markers indicating sites on prairie, mountain, desert or in towns where 'fallen brothers' had met their violent ends.

Marek stumped up almost as much for a round of drinks as Roz and I had recently paid for a full night's lodgings, and we squashed into a square yard of floor space. The bodies were so densely packed that taking in an overall impression was impossible, but it was safe to say that although fashions in here were even more racy than on the road, the action was slower than the last bike at an Angel's funeral. Shapely women accompanied some of the boys, as usual wearing imaginatively revealing variations on the traditional biker gear. Two close by had opened their jerkins to reveal breasts straight from a tabloid newspaper, but despite the provocation, none of the brave lads were fondling them.

'Keep your eyes down, boys,' Marlika had spotted Marek and I shaping up. 'If you so much as tweak a nipple, you'll be sued for sexual harassment. You're not in Amsterdam now!'

At the bar, a couple of aggressively unattached girls were either searching for love or touting for custom. One, a tall woman whose face revealed her to be around forty, still had a figure like Miss America. Clothed modestly in a halter top and tight jeans, her roving eye brimmed with promise. Her blonde chum was shorter but more than made up for her lack of stature in all other departments. Her cowboy hat set off a 'come-on-boys' grin and her faded jeans were so tattered they were literally falling off her tanned bum. As we drank our cloudy beers, we watched several guys plucking up courage to tackle this pair, but after an hour there was no sign of close contact. Nobody danced, although the drummer of the band had clearly been sent by God; nobody was shot, although it seemed more than likely that a number of those present would be armed, and if there was any casual sex going on, it was in the cosy privacy of some RV.

'I don't know why Americans can't let themselves go properly,' said Marlika suddenly. 'It's bloody frustrating. Look at this scene. It's the best in the world. But where's the action?'

'I've known plenty from this side of the ocean who could walk on the ceiling after a few pints,' I argued, although really I was right behind her.

'They're all in your memory,' Roz put in. 'We knew some lunatics in the old days, but the puritans seem to be winning now.'

'They certainly know how to set a scene though,' Marek growled, 'and look at this waste of talent.'

He had hit the spot with his last remark. All the rest was idle talk. Like him, I'd been trying not to think about the possibilities of this bar for a single man who knew what he wanted. In the end, our wives took pity on us and we were led away, seething with frustration. Muscling back to the bikes, we dragged them out of the tangle of ironmongery and the four of us roared off into the night.

On a whim, without even discussing a plan, we steered into the Black Hills, gaining altitude all the way. We clattered through the gold-rush town of Deadwood, where Wild Bill Hickok was gunned down from behind as he played poker in Saloon Number Ten, on through the active mining community of Lead, tucked deep into its system of conjoining valleys, and made a further ten miles towards the Wyoming Line, then stopped in total darkness.

For the first time in four days, the only motorcycle noise was that of our own machines cooling off as we split a full hip flask of Bourbon. It was cold in the still night, and fresh with the scent of the pine trees. We shrugged down inside our gear, huddling together for warmth. Suddenly, the eerie howl of a timber wolf rang out around the mountainside above us. A second took up the refrain, with more joining in until the hills were echoing with the ancient cadences. My spine shivered as the supernatural sound rose and fell under the circling stars. For a while, I tried to gauge whether the pack was heading our way, but soon I realised that these secret inhabitants of the sacred mountains were going about their prehistoric business with less interest in me than I had in a rabbit back in the Badlands. Left undisturbed, their descendants would be wailing their melancholy song long after both me and all the motorbikes in the world were dead and rotten.

chapter sixteen

the great divide and the deep green redwoods

A moment arrives about half-way through a month-long ocean sailing passage when the mariner stops looking back to the previous existence before departure, and starts considering the possibilities of the destination. This is an emotional effect over which a sailor has no control. Coming on watch, he settles to the helm and chooses his steering star, only to find himself thinking about what he will order when he hits the first restaurant on the new continent, or what mountain he will climb. At the same time, the troubles and joys of his past life begin to fade into history. Then he knows the procession of days is working on his soul. Traversing Wyoming and on up through Montana, Roz and I experienced the same phenomenon. We recognised the signs, asking each other whether pioneers and settlers lurching down the Oregon Trail had had a similar impression.

Mountains almost the whole length of both Americas lay across our path and the country was opening up into views that seemed to encompass half the planet. California and the West Coast were still a thousand miles away, yet we had come so far that, quite unexpectedly, our initial destination felt within reach. For me at least, the succeeding days continued to deliver meaning enough by virtue of the road flashing below my boots, but the journey had adjusted my mindset and I realised that, like the stormy sea passages that had preceded it, it would leave its marks on me.

Perhaps it was significant that this powerful response coincided with our arrival at the Little Big Horn, the site of the confrontation between Custer and the Sioux. That crucial encounter was the inevitable conclusion of the increasing scale of mining activities in the Black Hills, which the US government had guaranteed would remain undisturbed forever. Repeated betrayals, broken promises and the sickeningly predictable shooting down of women and children finally left those Indians who had rejected the reservations with no effective choice. In large numbers they came upon Custer's troops. Under the wide skies of Montana, inflamed with impotent injustice, they showed the man who had opened up the 'Thieves' Road' into the Black Hills what they were capable of. The aftermath of this humiliating annihilation of the white man was one of systematic revenge upon the Indians, culminating in the Wounded Knee massacre.

Despite their effective combat credentials, the Sioux and their allies the Cheyenne proved as powerless to stop the European expansion into even a small part of the West as had any other Native American. One of history's great expansions was in full marching order, backed by a well-organised political and military system. The Indians never stood a chance.

As we breasted the rising prairie, Big Horn County was as impressive as its name, with huge panoramas of undulating hills covered with waving grass and dotted with bushes of darker green. The sun shone from a cloudless sky and tourists flocked to a visitor centre occupying a stretch of ground that would have brought delight to a buffalo in search of a fruitful afternoon. Under a large sun awning on the putative site of the general's last stand, a bus-load of these good folk were receiving the word about Custer over the Tannoy. Signs pressed us to go the same way, but we ignored them and strolled across to where rows of immaculate headstones marked the graves of the fallen. These appeared to be white men only but, in fairness, it may be that the Indians disposed of the bodies of their own dead elsewhere.

Walking the battlefield was forbidden, but a minibus offered tours. Cutting our losses, we returned to the bikes instead, thinking how much better the Sioux had managed their memorial at Wounded Knee. Next, we side-stepped the gift shop and made five miles across the otherwise deserted prairie. The only sounds to break into the rushing whisper of the breeze were occasional shouts from a distant cowboy working a small herd of cattle. Only the ever-circling birds were as they must always have been.

After the Little Big Horn, the 'California-bound' feeling firmed up. I felt I could almost smell the sea. We expanded our daily runs, and without any prompting I found myself humming an obscure folk song I once heard sung by two middle-aged sisters. It is the story of a woman dreaming of leaving New York State – her 'home away from home' – pleading to go with her man to the paradise of the northern California coast. The heart of the message is the desire to travel alongside him to Mendocino. Closing her eyes she hears the sound of the sea, and nothing else matters any more.

The roads we chose were poor in surface, but as the foothills of the mountains approached, the vistas grew and grew until it seemed we were seeing the world through a fish-eye lens. I swear the plain tilted up at each edge, so vast was the area we were trying to take in with our small-scale English eyes. Despite the pitted roads, we were both running at 70mph or more now, Roz watching for every bump and niche, me keeping an eye open for the now common deer or antelope which can snuff a rider as efficiently as a rifle bullet just by leaping out of a ditch under his front wheel. Every bartender had a tale of some poor brother who ended up in deadly embrace with a buck that fate sent his way at the wrong moment. A 'fashion biker' crawl made some sense in this respect, but the high plains of Montana blew such considerations to the winds. The craving for freedom that is an integral part of the speed illusion drove us on with open throttles. After a while, I became almost drunk with the unfolding scenery which must surely be among the world's finest, retreating to my California fancy with the McGarrigle Sisters, their journey seemed to parallel our own as they passed South Bend Indiana to career across the Western Plains, ultimately tackling the distant barrier of the high Rockies.

One more sagebrush-scented day gave way to the mountains rising in majesty across the skyline. Climbing steadily, we negotiated 'Suicide Pass' and rode over the Great Continental Divide less than twenty-four hours after traversing the incredibly wandering Missouri for the last time. From now on, the rivers would be trending westward. More fuel to the California fire.

Still coming to terms with the downhill feeling, we stopped at a railroad barrier shortly beyond the Divide where a locomotive had come to a temporary halt. When it had pulled its unusually short train away with the standard roar of exhaust, rippling clank of couplings and whistle of turbos, we were confronted by the 'Last Chance Saloon' across the tracks. I wheeled into the forecourt of this low-slung, tarred shanty at the foot of a steep, wooded incline to stretch my legs and was shortly being interviewed by a large man who had burst out of the batwing doors into the sunshine.

He ignored me for a moment as he perused Black Madonna, then he spoke.

'Where you from with them plates on your bike?' His breath was pure Budweiser.

'England.'

'Thought so.' He deliberated this improbable information with agonising slowness, then concluded, 'holy shit,' so deliberately that each syllable took a full second to fall from his lips. He clamped his 'Mom's Donuts' hat hard over his eyes and drove away on a red tractor. Although not talkative, he seemed a nice man, so I concluded the bar couldn't be as bad as it looked and persuaded Roz to break her 'no beer' principle while riding. Although the days had cooled off with the rising altitude, even at 6,000 feet it was still ninety degrees in the midday sun, so selling the idea wasn't hard.

'Just the one . . . '

Inside, the place seemed as dark as night, probably because there were no windows. Accustoming my eyes to the gloom, I made out two spare stools at the bar. The bartender scored high marks for not opening with, 'We have . . . ' and listing a dozen types of bottled beer, none of which I had ever heard of. This conventional politeness pervades American eating and drinking establishments and after the novelty has worn off it can drive a traveller to booze. Such courtesies were not on the agenda at the Last Chance, so I tried my cool US Biker act.

'Gimme two Coors.' It sounded extraordinarily rude to me, but our man clearly expected nothing else. He served them up without comment.

'You guys from England, did I hear?' The man beside Roz was leaning across her. His mate on his far side was also taking an interest. I had seen them walk by during the crux of our conversation with the Mom's Donut man outside.

We confirmed that we were.

'You ridden all the way on them fancy rigs?'

Roz's glance flickered my way.

'Depends what you mean by all the way?' I responded carefully, suspecting this to be a wind-up that might need slick handling.

'Like, from your door to Montana.'

I looked hard at Roz and let her reply.

'We had to fly the first bit, you know,' she said, 'and the bikes came over on a boat, but we've ridden from Baltimore.'

The hillman nodded, reassured to have us placed.

'Figured you'd never have biked it from England. How it is here, you see, we're suffering sore from them states back East.' He was sure now of the nature of his audience and was readily backed up by grunts from his sidekick.

'Suffering?'

'Sure. Suffering. First, we got them comin' out here an' buyin' up all the best properties. Montana's our state, but they're tryin' to turn it into some goddamn National Park.'

I had no problem sympathising with this, but the man looked at me suspiciously, convinced already that I was some sort of subversive from Massachusetts, or Rhode Island, or England.

'This Clinton's the worst of them,' he continued. 'Taxes are crap. Gas is huge money . . .'

'It's five dollars a gallon where we come from,' I said, getting fed up with this. I'd just filled up at a dollar thirty-five. Petrol hadn't cost as little back home since the 1970s. 'Besides, you have no sales tax. You must be one of the few states that can say that.'

'That's all shit,' he rambled on. Five dollars for gas was the tallest tale he'd ever heard, his expression said. 'The worst of it is, Clinton wants to take our guns. That's fine for him livin' safe in a city back East, but he don't have to face no grizzlies or cats in the backwoods. How we supposed to defend ourselves if we ain't got no guns?'

The barman brought more beer for our advisors, though I saw no order pass between them, nor money on the table. I thought about the firearms and the nights waiting for the hitman back in New York City. I almost laughed, but the drunk was still talking.

'Them grizzlies'll eat you for pleasure,' he went on, warming up as soon as he saw Roz flinch, a classic bully, feeding on the signs of vulnerability. If only he knew, I thought. 'And the cats . . .'

'Cats?'

'Yeah. Cats. You know – mountain lions. They take twenty, thirty kids a year.'

'Two or three, I heard,' I interjected, having read the handout offered free at the state line.

'You'd 'spect politicians to say that,' put in the second redneck with a sneer. 'They don't want to put off no tourists, see?'

'Anyways,' continued his mate, 'you folks wanna watch out for bears in these mountains, 'specially with a woman. They love the smell of women. Particularly at what you might call "that time of the month".'

'An' they love the stink of sex,' Roz had clearly had enough as 'number two' made his play for ruining her trip, ''course, if you're properly armed, bears ain't no worry . . .'

Roz finished her beer, setting the bottle down with eloquent dignity.

'I'll speak to the Governor,' she said evenly, watching their eyes drop from hers, 'because after what you've told us, I can't believe all state parks don't already have large 'No Sex' signs at the entrances.'

We left in tight order and camped that night by a rushing river in the impossibly named 'Deadman's Gulch'. No grizzly, puma, or any other wild thing disturbed our uneasy slumber, but as usual we hung our victuals in a tree rather than bring them in the tent with us and encourage unwanted animal visitors.

Despite recognising the rantings of the Last Chance drinkers for the rubbish it was, even Roz was shaken by our encounter with redneck Montana. I lay beside her on my crippling air-bed, listening as ever for the dreaded rustlings in the trees, casting my mind back to a graphic statement by another American upset by President Clinton's attack on the gun culture.

Back in Kansas, not far from Dodge City, we had discovered a strange crop on a dead-flat field. Instead of corn, squash or alfalfa, the land was sown with closely packed plywood statues representing leaders of the nation. These brightly painted cartoon sculptures were, according to the accompanying sign, the work of one M. T. Liggett, an artist so confident of receiving no hate messages from the passers-by that he even left his phone number. President Reagan was let off lightly. His caricature was unflattering, but the legend was simple. 'Best,' was all it said. President Clinton did not receive such generous treatment from this pithy social commentator. The most powerful man in the world was depicted as 'Bubba Bill', all pink bare flesh, pot belly and striped red boxer shorts. A pennant with the word, 'Hero', dangled from exposed, diminutive 'privates' and he wore a yellow hat. The attached sign read, 'Commander-in-Chief – Yellow Beret Draft Ducker.'

Further down the long line of images, beside a cryptic representation of the popular maverick candidate Ross Perot, was another burlesque of Mr Clinton, this time with a full written indictment:

'The right to own a gun is being lost to a yellow-livered cowardly jackal that was too damned gutless to carry one during the Vietnam War. More than 58,000 men died with guns in their hands while the lousy bastard dodged the draft at Oxford. Character doesn't matter???'

We hoped that Mr Liggett loved his neighbours and that they put up with him, because this extraordinary assertion of the right to say what one thinks had left us gasping. Free speech is one thing, but it was hard for us to believe that this sort of massive licence wasn't somehow illegal. But if it was, the sheriff obviously agreed with its content and looked firmly the other way.

I was glad on the whole that we'd met the two human mistakes in the Last Chance Saloon. Things had been going almost too smoothly on the social front since my encounter with the small-time drug pushers in Tennessee, and it shook me from a silly complaisance that everyone in America must be the sort of person you'd like to know. There were plenty more ghouls under the same dirty stone.

Two hundred rugged miles later, we camped by the town of Hungry Horse below the mountains around Glacier National Park. Hard by the Canadian border, the neighbours proved more amenable than the boys from over the hills. Through the woods from our tent was a trailer in which a girl called Renee lived alone with her large timber-wolf/husky cross. One snarl from Greta would have deterred any interloper, unless armed with a machine gun, but when you got to know the beast, she wasn't so bad. Perhaps it was the ancient domestication in her sledding half that made her desperate for a rub on the stomach.

The best part of the day in Glacier proved to be its beginning. In order to make the distance and be back to our tent before nightfall, we hit Going-to-the-Sun road in the crisp air of first light wearing full leathers over fleeces. Ten miles on, the sky flushed pale pink as we crackled to a halt at the park barrier, but the pole was up and the ticket desk unmanned. I nurse a deep-rooted objection to paying for experiencing the undisturbed works of the Lord, and was delighted to read a sign that announced that the staff would not be turning up before 0800. There was nothing that said, 'No admittance before breakfast', and no honesty box gaped hopefully at me, so we breezed full ahead through the gates and wished the guardians of the mountains a comfortable lie-in. Not a vehicle disturbed the peace as we stopped by a lake for a sandwich. The road stayed quiet until later in the morning, giving us a ride to cherish for a lifetime, despite a nasty brush with the seamy side of tourism towards lunch. Rounding a sharp bend, we simultaneously spotted what had to be 'The Greatest Mountain Valley View in the West' and crunched to an unscheduled standstill in a gravelly pull-off. We propped the bikes by a number of other vehicles and I shed a layer or two of clothing while Roz fished out her camera.

'Why don't we pop down there a little way,' Roz nodded towards a steep trail disappearing through a copse of twisted pines, 'the angle will improve . . . Shame about that disgusting motor launch,' she added. My own eye had also been upset by a square, unlovely vessel plodding across a stretch of otherwise unsullied water far beneath us.

Fifty feet or so below, we arrived at the exact spot to capture an image, only to discover four other photographers setting up their gear. Unlike Roz with her travel-worn SLR, these guys had spent serious money and were out for value. Tripods proliferated, with exposure meters and hardware I didn't even recognise. We bade the chaps good day and nipped further down the slope in front of them for a picture which, while not losing the offending craft's unruly wake, would at least mask the unspeakable boat from the lens.

'Would you get the hell outta my frame!' a corpulent individual shouted from up at the viewpoint. 'I've been waiting twenty minutes to get that cruiser dead centre.'

Roz smiled thinly at him and clicked her shutter before we headed off into the bushes to take care of a more pressing requirement. One problem with motorcycling in chilly conditions is that however conscientiously you have abstained from drink, each approaching rest-stop takes on such an urgent importance that you hardly have time to cross the legs after dismounting.

Having dealt with the necessities of nature, we toddled back up to the bikes and scooted off, leaving the quality photographers still pondering over their meters. In due course, Roz's snap-shot produced a picture she could have sold to any discerning manufacturer of boxed chocolates.

As the day progressed, the snow peaks, deep valleys and blue lakes grew increasingly spectacular, while bend-swinging the tough gradients fed us exhilarating helpings of that dynamic oneness with gravity that the folks looking out from cars could never know. Pressing onwards and upwards, the narrow roads became gritty and challenging, but the rear tyres dug in well under the chain of command leading via drive belt, gearbox, crankshaft and con-rod to our throttle hands. Wheel-spinning a powerful machine under these conditions is all too easy; it is also emphatically not what you want, so it's 'gently on the throttle' as the bike winds her way up the hairpins. An aware rider can feel the rubber biting, and a really good one will sense that critical millisecond before it lets go under hard acceleration, backing off the power just in time. Controlling a Harley-Davidson on a rough road is less demanding than a hard-revving sports bike, but it still requires concentration and nerve. The nicest aspect of the business is the massive torque of the V-twin engine. Travelling uphill at well under 30mph, I could trickle the gas into Black Madonna in fourth gear and, instead of sulking, she pulled smoothly from impossibly low revolutions. Each individual power stroke made its own thumping statement, while her exhausts delivered the classic 'one-bang-every-lamp-post' rhythm that only the mechanically heartless could fail to appreciate.

We returned, exhausted but well-satisfied, to our camp after sunset, passing through packages of freezing air sliding down the slopes straight off the snow. The bears, cats and infinitely more dangerous rednecks did not put in an appearance that night, perhaps because we were in Greta's territory, but we lit a fire and built it up again after supper to be on the safe side. Some sort of weather front ran through after dinner, shaking the tent as we tried to sleep, but we must have nodded off in spite of it. I awoke at two in the morning with the wind blown out and the moon picking up the distant glaciers on the peaks. The bikes cast monstrous moon-shadows in the clearing and our fire had subsided to a smoulder. I left it to die completely. The small beasts of the undergrowth were still under the huge sky. The night was too beautiful to disturb.

Two days later after breaking camp at Hungry Horse, we were crossing the high plateau of Washington State with the sprawling town of Spokane and its Harley-Davidson dealership well behind us. One of the many hidden expenses of a big motorcycle is that the painfully pricey rear tyre will typically run bald every 3,000 miles. Betty Boop proved an exception to this rule, but Madonna made up for her. Equivalent power to a medium-sized car ripping up the road through a few square inches of soft-compound rubber is not a formula for high mileage, especially with a 240-pound Brit plus full kit adding to the load.

The Spokane dealer had his spread on the main drag into town, a never-ending, stop-go road with traffic lights, inadequate signposting and multiple lanes of heavy traffic ganging up for a bike-swatting mission. The stress volume was further turned up by a busy railroad with freight trains rumbling and clashing by only yards from us. We missed the 'H-D' sign the first time and were saddled with two U-turns to set matters straight. By the time we swung in outside the air-conditioned showroom, Roz had already blown much of the confidence she had worked up hacking over the mountains, so I treated Betty to a full fluid change and general check-over while we read the papers and Madonna received her new tyre. Betty came out with flying colours but I knew I was going to have to give further cities a resounding 'miss' and pray for an easy passage down the California freeways into San Francisco. I was nursing a real concern by now that the switchback of Roz's spirits would go into terminal decline there, causing her to bail out of the trip at the Golden Gate.

Out on the far-stretching fields of eastern Washington, such fears were banished to the back burner. Mile followed mile in a steady, easy flow across soil little better than powder baking under the pounding sun. Surface water was non-existent and dust was everywhere. Dust in your boots, dust in your eyes, dust in your morning coffee. Dust storms roamed the low hills climbing out of the high plain while whirling dust devils noiselessly stalked the fields, the lonely burial grounds and the roadsides. When we stopped the bikes every hour to drink the warm water from our packs, the wheat ran clear up to the unfringed tarmac at our feet. In contrast to English cereal crops where little or no earth can be seen between the tight-packed stems, half a foot or more of arid soil separated each stalk from its brothers. Just as huge tracts of Nebraska struggled to support herds that a couple of hundred acres would handle in a more comfortable climate, farm buildings in this harsh country stood vast distances apart for the same reason. As the land flickered by in 100-mile stretches, small, weathered farmsteads, blurred by the heat, would appear amidst trackless sections of thin wheat.

One of our rest stops came at the high junction of two perfectly straight roads. A hundred feet below us and more than a mile away was one of these groups of simple buildings. It was so remote that I could see no trail leading up to it and for a moment I took it for another derelict witness to enterprise defeated by the ever-changing climate of economics; yet this one bore the distant signs of working. Its wind pump spun away the years to the relentless drive of the bone-dry breeze, while a tractor, smaller than a child's toy in the distance, moved out of the deep shadow of a low barn, catching a second's light in a glint of metal or glass. Immense irrigation machines crept imperceptibly across a field beyond the house and I realised that they must be the secret of economic survival, but as to where the water originated I had no notion. I glanced across at Roz who was inspecting the map, propped my bike and peered over her shoulder. We were discussing which road to take south-westward into Oregon when out of the corner of my eye I saw the words, 'Columbia River' and 'Grand Coulee'. They tugged at some ancient memory under the litter of my mind, but for a few seconds they meant nothing. Then I realised they were an echo from childhood back in the 1950s, when the self-proclaimed 'King of Skiffle', Lonnie Donegan, had recorded a hit single called the 'Grand Coulee Dam'.

I relaxed on my saddle, giving the near-forgotten phrases a chance to stitch themselves together. Suddenly, like a zoom lens pulling into focus, the refrain thudded back to me, powered by the insistent beat of common time set by a long-gone washboard.

In the misty crystal glitter of the wild and windward spray,
I fought the pounding waters, and met a watery grave.

When she tore their boats to splinters and she gave men dreams to dream,

On the day the Coulee Dam was crossed by the wild and wasted stream.[10]

That a British rocker should choose such a subject is less improbable than one might imagine. The number arrived only ten years or so after World War II, a period when the developing rock-'n'-roll movement was heavily influenced by American themes, including 'The Battle of New Orleans' and 'The Rock Island Line'. I never heard the song from anybody else, even in America, but it goes on to glorify the damming of the great river and spell out the benefits to the populace. The delivery was one of the triumphs of an era when 'pop' music was branded as subversive by a parental generation, yet often consisted of nothing more sinful than three or four teenage musicians shuffling on stage with an acoustic guitar, a washboard and a tea-chest base.

Forty years later, in Washington State, Roz and I had already missed the main turn-off for the dam, thinking in strategic terms of Oregon and California. But the 'Grand Coulee', which was surely supplying the irrigation hereabouts as well as power for much of the North-West, was a mere forty miles away via a thin blue line on our map. Lonnie Donegan was shortly to receive a belated OBE and for the sake of the pleasure he had given my generation, I couldn't miss it. Sweeping aside any considerations of additional distance, I swung Black Madonna on to the side road, told Roz I'd see her at the dam, and opened the throttle. We had only just fuelled and at 90mph I'd be there in less than half an hour, so I let the bike rip, ever higher across the wide wheat-fields and away into the semi-desert above. As we pounded off the miles, more of the music came beating back,

Now the world holds seven wonders that the travellers always tell,
Some gardens and some towers, I guess you know them well,
But now the greatest wonder is in Uncle Sam's fair land,
It's the big Columbia River and the big Grand Coulee Dam.[11]

The dam came into view on a down-grade from the plain, the man-made blue of the vast lake stretching away eastwards. So enormous was its grey, curving bastion that, like the prairies of Montana, its true magnitude was masked from the eyes of someone from a smaller, tighter country. When it was completed in 1942, the Grand Coulee Dam was the largest concrete structure in the world. Apparently it still is, and its width is such that four ships the size of the Queen Mary could lie in line astern along the top. Power lines criss-crossed the cobalt sky, sagging from immense pylons as they fanned out across the plain. So far below that even thinking about it made me dizzy, the barely tamed Columbia River plunged off down its gorge towards the Pacific, churning in rage at the bold interruption of its journey.

Few tourists passed this way, so I stood alone, gazing, until Betty Boop sizzled up alongside, ten minutes behind me. By the time she showed up I was sunk deep into the surreal aspect of this massive feat of engineering. From somewhere in the depths came the deep, understated whine of a gigantic generator delivering its life-force of volts to the cities in the north-west.

Washington and Oregon, you can hear the fact'ries hum,
Making chrome and making manganese, and white aluminum . . .[12]

All powered by the same Columbia River that was watering otherwise unusable fields. Although the place seemed deserted, it was the beating heart of this end of modern America. A catharsis of natural force harnessed by superhuman endeavour. Add a pinch of artist's licence and many whose lands were not drowned in the new lakes would agree with Lonnie Donegan, hymning the dam as 'the greatest wonder in the world'. By rights, his song should have swept America and he ought to have retired rich on the back of that number alone. But those were the days when football players earned little more than coal miners, and a hit single was not yet an automatic passport to unimaginable wealth.

Cranking up and heading back southwards, we sweated through another seventy miles across the plain before dropping a thrilling 2,500 feet down a deep, rock-strewn gully into the Columbia River Valley. Here, incongruously after the all-American farmers grittily growing cereals in the baked fields above us, a grinning Mexican boy handed us peaches from his roadside stall. He was selling them by the piled-up crateful.

'How much for just a couple?'

'*Qué?*'

'We just want to buy one peach each.'

'Why you want only one peach? A box is cheap. Try them.' I gestured to the bikes.

'We just want one to eat now. It's hot.'

The Mexican saw our transport problem. He ruffled his black hair.

'Not so hot as yesterday. Take two each. No charge.'

The peaches were full of juice and no fruit ever tasted better.

This little scene seemed the first breath of the West Coast, but before the cool Pacific breezes and the projected idyll of Mendocino, we still had to cross the desert of northern Oregon and the coastal ranges of the Rockies.

We started out at 0530 in a pleasant fifty-one degrees as the first crack of pink was flushing the eastern sky. In the penetrating beams of our quartz-halogen headlamps, the unashamed near-desert featured the ubiquitous dust of America, dressed up with sagebrush clumps and spiced by the occasional pair of reflecting red eyes as some unidentified creature sloped off home before sunrise. As the sun came nearer to breaking the horizon, we began to make out escarpments and distant hills. Soon we were riding down a dead-straight road that must have run for ten miles on a flat plain between the Squaw Butte Mountains. Exact mirror-image crags stood ahead on either side. We passed between them as the sun appeared, casting impossibly long motorbike shadows alongside us, and climbed off at an isolated fuel stop that announced its incorporation as 'Wagontire, Population 2'.

The altitude of this remote settlement is around 4,500 feet and in the crystal morning air the whole operation would have served well in a television advert for aftershave. The next gas promised to be at least 100 miles away, so we filled up and clumped into the diner-kiosk to pay. We still hadn't seen a vehicle on the road since rising, but a useful Honda cruising bike was parked by the door.

Inside, a handsome, middle-aged man in biker uniform with headband but no tattoos was wolfing hash browns, bacon and eggs. The food smelt great, but we were saving money and clung to our resolve to picnic later by the roadside. I did buy a coffee, however, and Roz sat down to a glass of canned juice served up by one of the town's two inhabitants.

'Didn't I see you guys at Sturgis?' opened the lone rider.

'I can't believe you can recognise us, but we were certainly there,' I responded. 'Are you heading back to California?'

'Nope. I been down there already. I'm heading back up towards Seattle.'

'Lot of miles. Aren't you off-course so far inland?'

He chuckled. 'I go where the Lord sends me,' he said. 'Got the call to come this way. Guess I'm on course to meet someone, but I sure don't know who. Perhaps it's you?'

'What do you mean?'

'I got a small disability pension,' he waggled a hand that was short of a few fingers, 'so I don't have to work all year. I cruise the highways and help out where I can. Spread the Lord's word too, among the brothers.'

'Wouldn't you get more ready acceptance from the doomed if you rode a Harley-Davidson?' I asked sincerely, then kicked myself because the 'witty' remark sounded like a modern-day Pharisee mocking Christ. The man's response would surely have pleased his leader.

'I used to ride a Harley,' he said, 'had a nice shovel-head, but I've found that pitching up on a Honda creates just that touch of controversy. It got you spiked up didn't it?'

I had to admit that I'd been ready for a touch of word-fencing.

'Sometimes, it works out good,' he continued, mopping up the last of his eggs with a forkful of potatoes. 'One time last year I ripped open my rear tyre. It was a write-off. The only bike dealer within range was H-D, and the gentle soul who ran the joint refused to let my rice-burner in through the door. He'd take my money for a new tyre all right, but he wouldn't touch the job. Not even on his forecourt. His guys thought it was all very funny, but they were OK and in the end they persuaded him to let me do it myself out back, using the shop's tools.

'But that wasn't the end of it. Being a Harley man, he had no metric wrenches. Wouldn't let them under his all-American roof. Said once you invited those things in you might as well burn the flag. I said nothing, because "half-inch" ain't so far from "thirteen millimetre". You can always make 'em fit.'

'I suppose he had the neck to charge you for the use of his tools?'

'He wanted to, but his fellas wouldn't let him. So just before I left, I tipped him twenty bucks. Nearly drove him crazy, he was so mad.'

'You didn't convert him then?' asked Roz.

'You get to know the right time for preaching, and that wasn't it. Expounding the Word to folks you just ripped one out of don't usually work out. I saved him for later. Actually, he ain't so far from here. Maybe you guys were sent to remind me about him . . . ' He scratched his head.

As we left, our friend gave us his benediction.

'Ride with God, and watch out for rednecks.'

'Best of luck with that sinner!' called Roz over her shoulder as we opened the creaking door and walked on to the forecourt.

Back out in the desert, the heat was building fast as we cruised south through the 10,000 square mile arid emptiness of Lake County. Occasionally, a track would wander into the wilderness, marked by a mailbox on the corner. All these had been the subject of successful target practice by passing motorists and were full of holes, as were the occasional road signs and warnings. We pulled off for breakfast at a box that had been blown clean off its post by something with the punch of a howitzer. It had not been replaced and from the way it lay half-covered with whitish dirt in the shallow ditch, its owner had long since lost interest in the morning papers. As we trundled up the lane into the sagebrush, dust clouds streaming off our tyres, the macabre thought struck me that perhaps he had received the same treatment as his name board from some ill-wisher. Nobody would have heard the shots, and it would be many hours before help could arrive, even if summoned by telephone.

After a mile, the ungraded surface became impassable to road bikes, so we dismounted at a pile of consumer rubbish which included a cooker and a large refrigerator on its side. We used this as a table to lay out our crackers, 'squeezy cheeze' and fruit, setting up our stove on the ground. The selected item of kitchen furniture was of the heaviest grade, looking as if it had been built with resistance to machine-gunfire in mind, but even this monumental chunk of industrial architecture had received the attention of the local marksmen. With grim fascination, I inspected how the heavy-calibre slugs had punched through both sides, cleanly on the entry face but jagging open the steel where they had exited. There was something graphic about this manifestation of firepower that strengthened my resolve to do almost anything a man with a gun asked me to, should the situation ever arise.

Just in case I forgot, I took a photograph of our table, using my expensive 24/80 zoom lens. I packed away the camera body, placing the lens neatly on the fridge in its fine leather box. I only realised I'd left it there when I wanted it for a panoramic view two days later. By then, retrieval would have involved a round trip of 800 miles and we decided to let it go. It looked as though it never rained on that refrigerator and I doubt that it is visited from one year's end to the next now that it has been shot to bits, so anyone else who breaks his fast on its pocked work-top will be one lens the richer, particularly if his camera has a Nikon bayonet fitting.

By the time the lens fiasco was discovered, I felt we were on the last lap, with only hundreds of miles left to the coast and Mendocino. The route we had chosen for the final leg twisted through the smoke of summer forest fires, ever upwards through steep-sided woodland. The smoke went on for two days, yet we never saw the flames. Winds were light at this time, so rather than billowing in clouds, it took the form of a thin brown mist smelling of camp fires that pulled visibility in to three miles or less. Somewhere, devastation was in progress, but not where we were. The road, meanwhile, was giving away nothing by way of peace of mind. Precipices plunged first on one side, then the other, regular earthquakes left serious damage not dealt with promptly enough by Uncle Sam's road gangs, and gravel stretches abounded. Gas stations were anything up to 150 miles apart and human activity was almost non-existent, although signs here and there warned of bears. To add to her troubles, Roz reminded me that she was now at the lowest ebb of her monthly cycle. I tried to be sympathetic, pointing out that at least the smoke had at last cleared but, like most men at such times, I failed to get it right.

She was near despair after dropping Betty Boop, mercifully without significant damage, on a hideous stony bend in front of a view of Mount Shasta she should have been soaking up. 'I never get to enjoy the scenery. Always it's the damned road surface. Look at this place. I swing around the bend and half the tarmac has been ripped away by a 'quake. In case you can't see it from behind your shades, there's a 200-foot drop right here where I'm lying. They probably had railings before the road fell off the cliff.

'And the nights are worse. Trailing around looking for some crummy motel full of fleas, or praying a bear won't snap me up when we sleep in the open.'

I tried to cheer her up, reminding her we were well into California with the coast so close we were feeling the cool air from the sea.

She ignored me.

'The whole thing has degenerated into an endurance test,' she groaned. 'I get up in the morning, I'm still aching from yesterday, we load up the bikes for the hundredth time and then I grit it out all day. And it goes on and on. We're six weeks out from Annapolis and we haven't really stopped. I don't want to play this game any more!'

'Well, we're going to rest soon,' I responded, making an instant decision based on fantasy. 'We'll find a quiet place north of San Francisco, up by Mendocino on a beach. We'll move in there and just unwind until you're ready to go on. It'll be half-way. You'll be so glad you've achieved the crossing you'll forget all this stuff.'

I don't know if I believed it. From her expression, Roz certainly didn't, but there was no option for her. I too was aching badly across my shoulders, but according to the map we must soon see the Pacific. Like Xenophon 3,000 years before us, watching his Greek infantry craving a view of the Aegean after their long wanderings in Asia Minor, I hoped to God that it would change the mood.

Wearily, we crested ridge after wooded ridge, each time expecting the ocean, and always seeing more mountains until even I was mesmerised by the insistent throbbing of my bike.

Down a slope, engine comparatively quiet, brakes squealing occasionally from dust in the pads, popping sounds of backfire set up in the exhaust by the altitude. Up the next grade, throttle open, pistons working, blatter of exhaust echoing back from the forest or the rock walls. Another summit. Still no sea. Shut the gas down, ease on to the big footbrake pedal, forget the front brake. It doesn't do much on a Harley, and if you lock up the wheel on the gravel you'll be sliding in the stuff. Body weight thrown forward by the braking and the downgrade, handlebars bucking through the potholes, wrists screaming. I felt for Roz, but left her to her pain. The only way to keep my own mind from slipping down my neck was to shut off my head, watch out for the long drops and the busted lengths of highway and wander into the dreamland of northern California painted journey's end for the McGarrigle sisters. Here, their character lived out the remainder of her life, still looking westwards as the evening light died away across the ocean. Her satisfaction was perfected by each subsequent dawn over the redwood groves behind her, the woman rising with the sun until one morning her song was stilled and she rose no more.

Where, oh where were these immense, legendary trees, harbingers of the Pacific, the greatest and almost the oldest organisms on Earth? Surely we must be into them soon. Desperate for Roz's sake to be finished with the escarpments and hairpins so as to cruise in among these marvels, I kidded myself that each of the progressively tall pines we passed must be one of them. It was true that the conifers grew loftier with every fifty miles, and as we lost altitude for what must surely be the last time, we were passing trees taller than any I had seen anywhere. These must be them, I convinced myself, marvelling at their girth. But they were not. They were merely hefty Douglas Firs of the type that had once made the West Coast famous for its mast-making timber. The experience of riding into our first redwood grove was different altogether.

Towards evening, we were spinning through varied woodland along the foot of a valley. Suddenly I had the eerie sensation that I was cruising into a fish tank charged with air instead of water. The sound of the bike seemed muted and the light was plunged into a restful green. Motorcycling into this unmistakable aura, I looked around for its source, and slowly became aware that I was moving through trees as tall as modest New York skyscrapers. I think I had not recognised them because the girth of the redwood trunks was not comparable with any tree in my experience, including the ancient oaks of the New Forest. The height beneath the canopy dwarfed the neighbouring primary growth firs. I shut down the bike, listened to the stillness and gazed aloft for several minutes to readjust the meaning of 'tree' in my mind.

Like most of the redwood groves, which have survived the frantic onslaught of nineteenth and early twentieth century lumbering, this one had a small visitor centre and a tiny campground. Two families were pitching their tents almost shyly. The small timber buildings were tasteful, unobtrusive and in keeping. I hardly noticed the people. In the context of trees 350 feet high, they practically disappeared.

Walking among these colossal plants, a sense of deep peace descended on us. Roz's angst was soothed and my own anxieties about the rest of the journey seemed to fall away. The very ground in this dim, green place was soft to our tread, with clean bracken and the gently decayed needles of centuries of autumns. The trees grew sometimes singly, more often companionably in close groups of two or three, their shafts soaring straight through a verdant vault higher than the greatest cathedral nave, to where the coniferous branches spread out far above, cutting out direct sunlight and completing the impression of protection. We walked on tiptoe and spoke in whispers, leaned on the trunks and touched their foot-thick bark. The youngest of the fully grown trees might well be 500 years old. The gnarled elder statesmen, their top hamper riven by countless lightning strikes, could have been standing tall when the Romans still ruled Britain. The century and a half since the California Gold Rush has flowed by them almost unnoticed. Our own waxing and waning could never be more than a rustle in their eternal branches.

As I sat on the dry, sweet-smelling mould, breathing in this enhanced perspective on my own length of days, I recalled the sense of a lesson learned at my father's knee. I had not been picked for the first team football at my junior school. Sport was everything to me then, and to be confronted with my own mediocrity was almost more than a child could bear. As I wept out my disillusion, he sat me down and said simply,

'I know it's hard to understand, but remember that however bad things seem, nothing that happens to you will change the way the world will be 100 years from now.'

Surprisingly, it helped. Even at the age of ten.

Dad had died two years before Roz and I set out across the States. He had striven for a fairer society all his days, and I had suffered worse failures than my first ever selection board, but the giant, slow-breathing redwoods hadn't even noticed. Secure, until recently, beyond the mountain ranges and the windward passage around Cape Horn, the fleeting years steal by them in decades and centuries as they grow from cone, to sapling, to adult majesty. Even their dying takes hundreds of years, sinking finally to the ground without sadness, complete only in their return to the soil.

We lay down amongst the trees that night and awoke in the shining, verdant dawn, readier for the road and the last day to the Pacific.

chapter seventeen

changing times on the west coast

The morning was clear as we packed up our sleeping bags under the floating roof of the trees, and the early rising sun never managed to superheat the day as it had been doing across the continent thus far. We motored out into the open at low revs in our leather jackets, revelling in the champagne quality of the air. We were still wearing them when we entered a contrasting redwood grove many miles nearer the shore, beside a more frequented highway. The disparity with our night stop was positively alarming. Here were queues of RVs, a kiosk demanding money, fast food, litter and, above all, noise. Instead of being allowed to speak for themselves, the trees were being thoroughly exploited, and a cavity had been hacked in one so that a sizeable vehicle could be driven through its trunk. It cost a dollar fifty for a tripper to endorse this final insult, but because Roz had seen the tree in a childhood encyclopaedia she was determined to submit to the full experience.

While she waited her turn, I stood aside and talked to a grey-haired biker in a Breton sailor hat and an ex-Navy pea-jacket. He looked more like a New York tugboat skipper than a Hell's Angel. It was odd, I thought, that he too had just ridden through. He wasn't interested in the metaphysics of carving holes in eternal woodwork, but he told me that the best grass in the whole world was grown just down the road in Mendocino.

'Go there,' he urged me with faraway eyes, gripping my biceps like a vice, 'and score some.'

Then he reverently drew a roach out of his shirt pocket, lit it with a petrol-soaked zippo at serious risk to a fine moustache, kicked his ancient Harley into gear and rattled away through the tourists.

'How was it?' I asked Roz as she pulled out of the line of vehicles returning from the Big Tree Experience.

'I had the distinct impression that the tree was laughing at us,' she said. 'It's like the thing with Salisbury Cathedral; you drive up in your car, roof down, shades, cool hat; you feel you're quite something. Then it strikes you that the building was there 600 years before even the railway came to town. Motor vehicles have been around for less than an eighth of its life, and the place will still be standing long after we're all forgotten and our descendants have discovered a better way to get around. It makes you irrelevant.'

'Yes, but what about the butchery of the tree?' I was determined to extract a confession, or at minimum some sort of remorse.

'At least it hasn't been chopped down for house-building or pulped for cheap paper,' she responded. 'Ninety-five per cent of them were, you know. There's photos up there of heroic lumberjacks crowded on to the stumps, thirty of them or more. Now that really is disgusting. OK, so the management are screwing it for all they're worth, but in a sense the redwood has the last laugh, because if just one tourist out of ten thinks beyond the fact that they've just driven through a tree, it's done more for the cause of reason than all its felled brothers put together.'

As we descended the last few miles to the cliffs, huge, snorting log trucks began to proliferate, heading for the great cities of California. Was their cargo still plunder, or was it sustainable farming nowadays? I thought about the one-off 'harvesting' of the redwoods and began to consider all the unimaginable natural riches that America has ripped from her heartland over the past century and a half. Before the continent was settled, the Indians hadn't disturbed it in a millennium. They took exactly what they needed, wasted nothing and made sure there would always be enough for next time. Not so the European. Arriving from an already tired continent, the opportunities for short-term wealth offered by an untouched world would have been massive, and only a very few would even have considered resisting the opportunity. This ultimately finite abundance is the source of one well-established world image of the United States, ordering more food in the restaurant of life than it can possibly eat, then watching without remorse as the rejected excess is tossed into the garbage can. I have seen even thinking Americans do this. It is as much a part of the nation as England's soccer hooligans, or inhuman treatment of veal calves by the French.

With these gloomy thoughts filling my head, I almost forgot about the sea, so when it appeared, finally, azure blue, calm, with a distant fog bank obscuring the western horizon, I almost dropped my bike in amazement. We had just wound around a tight bend at the foot of a steep slope somewhere south of Cape Mendocino. The pines were crowding in as usual, when suddenly there were no more trunks to the right of us. Instead, there was a sheer drop and, fifty yards ahead, a pull-off.

Without needing a word or a signal we stopped, unzipped our leathers and scrambled down a rocky path to a tiny cove 100 feet below. The black, volcanic beach was deserted except for two sea-smoothed tree trunks very likely carried on the current from Kamchatka. Life existed beyond America, and the Pacific was ours.

Like a couple of kids, we stripped off the last of our clothes and ran through the gentle surf into the ocean. The water was seriously cold, but we shouted for pure joy as it shocked away our breath. I swam straight out for 100 yards then turned, treading water, to look back at California. The last ridges of the coast range rose steeply, covered in trees, the road was invisible and the noonday sun was slightly muted by atmospheric moisture that felt as if it might later turn to fog. Roz doesn't enjoy cold water and was already back on the beach, a great sight towelling off with the yellow T-shirt she often wore for riding. Raising her arms to tousle her hair, she gazed out to sea. Even from this range I could feel her satisfaction and I felt a wave of admiration for the courage that had driven her on this far.

As for me, I was surprised at my own elation. After all, I reasoned, swimming slowly back to revel in the undertow sucking the sand from around my feet, the true heroes were the bikes. They had come 6,000 winding miles through hot, hard conditions, often on the poorest of roads, and neither had missed a solitary beat of their iron pulses. You'd expect no less from a 1990s Japanese whizzer, but these were thorough-going motorcycles in the traditional sense. They were personal. They revved so slowly that you were aware of each of the interdependent moving parts and I marvelled that nothing had broken, that no weak link in the chain of metalwork let the rest down.

So far, so good, then. Nobody had expected Black Madonna to fail, but Betty had put a few ghosts to rest by cruising from sea to shining sea with no more maintenance than a couple of oil changes and a freshening of her drive belt tension. But it wasn't over yet, for me, at least. Not by a long, long way. I was already game for riding back to Annapolis, but I feared Roz must be considering abandoning Betty here on the coast, then flying home. The logical way back east lay across the great deserts of the South-West, the legendary lands of New Mexico and West Texas, then the Deep South. I was hungry for them all, especially the deserts, but San Francisco was crucial to a balanced journey. I had friends there, yet I knew that the thorniest obstacle in Roz's way was the California freeway system that was now unavoidable.

All that would keep until tomorrow, I decided as I walked, dripping and fresh, out of the sea, renewed by its familiar salt tang. Today would be lived for its own glorious sake and nothing more. We agreed to find a place we both liked, and stay there until the stress had eased off. Ten miles down the road we discovered the secret township of Westport and paradise on Earth.

Westport. My diary describes the community as a comfortably spread-out cluster of wooden houses strung along a low cliff fronting a rock-strewn shoreline, a small store with a post office and creative delicatessen, a pretty wooden motel right over the sea, and a whale's vertebra by the roadside. It is a fair description. There is also a black beach, a conspicuous lack of neon and a house at the end with a sign, 'One nice person and one old grouch live here'.

Outside the motel, two ladies of between sixty and seventy were taking lunch at a cleanly painted picnic table under a wild parasol. I stopped and wished them good day, still in my saddle.

'Is it too late to order?'

'You can't order,' responded the one who somehow looked like the owner. 'We don't serve meals. But if you wander over to the store, they'll fix you up. Bring your food over here to eat and I'll make you a pot of coffee.'

In the shady shop opposite, a woman about my own age who had watched us arrive from her beaded doorway made us up burritos from heaven. She wore a loose, psychedelic top and sold all manner of herbs. Flowers were everywhere and a tinkling wind chime picked up the young sea breeze. Back to the sixties.

'You go back over to Thelma to eat,' she said in a rich, unaffected voice that sounded as if it never wished anyone anything but the best of fortune. 'Enjoy your lunch, and stay awhile. You look like you could do with a rest.'

And so we signed up with Thelma and her husband Otto. 'Two nights to begin with, and see how we feel.'

Life in the Westport Inn turned out to be different from any other lodging house in our American experience. Perhaps it was because the large, airy rooms had no air-conditioning, no television and were stocked each day with fresh flowers, but it was notable for its lack of the urgent, must-get-on, today-is-just-the-prelude-to-tomorrow feeling that had pervaded everywhere else. The lack of air-conditioning was a plus so far as we were concerned, because the climate for once did not demand it. The cool breeze off the sea kept the day temperature in the high seventies and gave rise to nights when at last we slept snug beneath extra quilts as the land breeze settled in to blow offshore until soon after dawn. I missed my Weather Channel, but on the whole we were blessed by evenings without the futile search through trash-stacked stations for something decent to take our minds off the road.

The flowers went right along with Thelma's offer of coffee to two total strangers, and in the resulting quietness, we and the other guests were able to get to know her and her family.

Nobody seemed to stay at the Westport for one night, then move on. The total lack of anything inappropriate seemed to entice people in and keep them there. On one side, our neighbours were a tall blonde widow in her sixties, travelling slowly with her son in search of a new home. He was an ex-tennis professional, declared by Roz to be the 'Hunk of the Trip'; she, the complete artist. Willowy build, spaced-out manner, gauzy scarf, sun hat and eyes always on the next world. Her loving son had given up the courts to generate a modest income for them from his oil paintings. We stood together on the first evening, drinking champagne with Thelma under a particularly ancient tree on the cliff edge. As the sun slipped away to warm the beaches of Hawaii, Roz asked her what type of tree it was.

'This is the Westport Tree,' she responded. 'It's famous all down the coast.'

'Yes, but is it a cypress? A cedar? What is it, that it's lived so long?'

'You know, dear, I can't tell you. I could have once. But the person in charge in my brain won't open that file any more. It's just the Westport Tree now. Doesn't really matter if you can't put it in a category, does it?'

Just then, the people in the room on our other side arrived in a jacked-up pick-up. A young man jumped down with a distinctly sheepish glance at us, then he helped his girl from the passenger's side. He was bronzed and blond and could have been a student with a trust fund, she was surely straight from a bar in Mexico. She looked me up and down provocatively, then wiggled after him.

'Sweet couple,' Thelma said with only the shadow of a twinkle. 'On honeymoon, the boy said.'

I observed to Roz later that the girl had to be a hooker who had landed a week's contract. Whether the relationship was amateur or professional, however, the peace was shattered towards midnight by some of the noisiest honeymoon activity I'd heard since the enthusiast renting the room next to me in downtown Southampton years before had laid into a girlfriend with his belt, apparently enjoying her eager connivance. The difference was that while the Californian drove a pick-up, my sometime fellow-member of the tenants' association was a soft ice cream salesman whose van bore the improbable legend, 'Victor's Super Whip'. Remembering Victor, Roz and I chuckled at the sexual excesses and snuggled down companionably as the lace curtains blew gently inwards on the first of the night wind.

Creeping out of bed early, I gave the bikes a general fettle while Roz slept in. There were cables to oil, spark plugs to sharpen up, carburettor mixtures and dust-choked air filters to attend to. I was totally content working on those lovely machines, because I'm the sort of simpleton who needs to indulge in menial mechanics as much as my motorcycles like me to. Except that you do it alone, in its way it's as satisfying as singing a good Elizabethan madrigal. If I'd had a torque wrench I'd probably have lifted a cylinder head or two and cleaned up the valves, enjoying the spotless interior of a healthy internal combustion engine, but my tool kit didn't extend that far. Besides, Betty and Madonna had run so sweetly this far that I prudently held back my primeval urges. I replaced their gleaming tweakable parts carefully and took Roz a cup of herbal tea from over the road.

She sat up in bed, stretched and gazed out the window at the ocean.

'I feel as though I've just completed an ocean crossing,' she remarked, taking a sip in the morning sun. 'I can't really believe that a whole phase of my life is over. The ride wasn't like a car journey with a beginning, a quick middle and an end. It was a thick slice out of my life. It was far more than a hiatus between here and there . . .

'Do you remember when we thrashed down the Greenland Sea from Iceland to Canada?'

I recalled it only too well. It had been distilled misery. I thought it would never stop. Nineteen days in big square waves without more than three hours sleep at a time, wet, literally ice-cold and the boat in danger of breaking up.

'It was like that on the bike just now, but I think I finally understand what that churchwarden in Finland was trying to explain to us about the sailing ships hanging in the rafters of the nave.'

I looked blank.

'We met him on the trip to Russia. He said they were to remind people that life was like a long voyage. You have to take each day as it comes, because it's a vital part of the whole. The point was you can't climb off a boat on to the waves, so there's no way you can give up on life just because you don't like it. Remember what he said about jet aeroplanes?'

I had asked how his theories related to today's time scales. He had responded that air travel was not a journey in the full sense, it was the spiriting of a person from one place to the next. Within our inherited framework of time and distance, its brief span has no meaning. A sea voyage, on the other hand, especially one that is inevitably slow, forces its people to reflect and observe. They are obliged to accept the passing weeks as part of life, to be lived for better or worse.

'Travelling endless rough roads on a Harley-Davidson comes under the same heading . . . ' Roz concluded.

We did not mention motorcycles in the context of the vastness of the American continent again for several days.

Late in the afternoon, we were considering making the short trip south to the town of Mendocino itself, two-up on Madonna in search of a meal, when Otto knocked on our door and invited us to join him and Thelma.

'Our friend Rose is here. You'll enjoy meeting with her.'

We did.

As we sat back after dinner, Rose told us the tale of her family. She was sophisticated in a particularly European sort of way. Even her spectacles had style. She seemed more French than anything, yet her accent was local. Her story could have been any one of a million in America.

'In many ways, I'm exactly the person Joan Didion was thinking about when she wrote about this state,' Rose observed. 'I remember the essence of what she said because it always seems just right. "California is the last stop for all those who came from somewhere else, for all those who have drifted away from the cold and the past and the old ways."'

Rose's parents had arrived in Ellis Island, New York, from French-speaking Switzerland in 1914. Someone on the boat had taken a shine to them, or maybe it was a hustler looking to engage talented people in a factory in the Midwest. Whoever it was, however, he had done the young couple well when he advised them to hang back when steerage berths were being allocated. Finally, the cheap bunks were all taken and the Swiss were 'up-graded'. This benefactor also saw them through the difficulties of non-English speaking immigration in the dreadful, confusing queues, from where many were sent home again. Next he put them on a train to Indianapolis, advising them of work in a factory only three blocks from the railroad station. Then he disappeared.

Rose's father was immediately hired in the glass works, where he discovered a small community of French-speaking Swiss from near his home, some of whom he actually knew. He built his family a house with his own hands from cinder blocks he and his mates made from factory waste. It had a kitchen, two further rooms and no electricity. Inside water, outside toilet, and wine with every evening meal. Here, Rose was born, but hard times in the thirties brought further moves, and young Rose ended up in California.

Rose and our hosts seemed like living history when they mentioned the depression, remembering Steinbeck's families from *The Grapes of Wrath* arriving from the dustbowls of Oklahoma and Kansas. Such scenes had parallels with the Tyneside shipyard workers' march on Downing Street during the same period, but at least the Jarrow Lads had homes to return to. A migrant clan driven from their few dried-out sections by foreclosure, wandering this land of plenty without work or hope was the very stuff of tragedy.

Otto and Thelma told of a very different set of travellers who passed their place in the 'Summer of Love', when San Francisco was the centre of the world hippy movement of love and peace.

'There was always someone on the road in those days,' Otto smiled wistfully. 'I recall one girl, walked all the way from Mexico City with two Siamese cats. One feller came by bound for Canada on a skateboard, and another guy rode in on a donkey. Looked just like Jesus Christ. Probably smoked more grass than Our Lord, though.'

'What about that group who arrived at midnight in a hearse, coffin and all?' Thelma broke in. 'They crept into Room 5 and stayed the night. They looked so weird we didn't bother them. In the morning they'd gone, and they'd piled the sheets up all neat. Not a mark anywhere. Not like the two elderly schoolmarms from Colorado. They drove up in a nice car, sweet and charming. Booked in for one night, and nobody, but nobody ever trashed a room so totally as they did. They must've chopped pink grapefruit into halves, scooped them out then filled the husks with vodka. They went on drinking till they fell over, I reckon, from the number of quarts that they left empty. Then they had a pillow fight, pulled down the curtains, ripped up the mattresses and did some other stuff that wasn't so nice. You can't ever tell with people from how they appear on the outside.

'Do you remember Mad Marvin?' she turned to Otto.

'Jesus, that was some crazy,' her husband agreed. 'Tiny little guy in XXXL dungarees. They darn near smothered him. He kinda mooched around outside all day. Finally, he comes into the office and he says in a funny voice, "Gimme a room. Then you'd better call the cops 'cause I don't know what I'll do."

'We gave him food and treated him kind, then told him to sleep in the room you two're in. We didn't call no cops, but he locks himself in and doesn't come out again. He was in there three days, so finally we had to call the sheriff. Here comes the sheriff with his deputy and his squad car and they ask him nicely to come out, but he looses off a couple of rounds at them from something heavy and they dive behind the house. Then we have a siege. Goes on for another day. Finally, Marvin gives himself up. The sheriff takes him away in 'cuffs, and as he's leavin', he swears he'll have our lives, Thelma and me.'

'What was his problem?' I asked, fascinated that such people should be walking the streets.

'Marvin was one of those guys let loose from the loony house under Reagan's 'community care' deal. Turned out he was armed to the teeth, but by their lights he wasn't a criminal, he was just crazy, so they let him out again after three days and me and Thelma lived in fear he'd be back.'

'And was he?'

'No, thank Christ. We was jittery for months, but he never showed. Perhaps he'll come tonight,' Otto turned to Roz, his eyes all laughter. 'Might be wanting his room back, he liked it so much. Better put that chair behind the door.'

The following evening, after another welcome day of cliff walking and just breathing the clean sea air, we were all sitting around outside enjoying the moonrise. One of the guests, a cyclist from over the mountains, handed around a sweet-smelling joint which Otto and Thelma politely refused. Everyone around here seemed to smoke socially. Why not them?

'We tried it once,' said Thelma. 'A guy with no hair at all left a huge one with us one day. We thought it was a gift, so we put it in a drawer. A week or two later we smoked it while we were in bed. Just for the devil of it. I guess it was kind of good. We giggled all night anyways. Following morning the fellow came and asked for it back. I couldn't believe it. "Too late," I told him, and he went away. We haven't bothered since.'

It seemed common knowledge on this coast that marijuana was big business and that extensive fields of America's most profitable cash crop waved in the hills. We were advised more than once not to walk far east of the road, unless we knew where we were going. To happen upon a plantation, even innocently, could lead to incidents with armed guards. Occasionally intruders are shot and their bodies disposed of. There had been one pitched battle with the 'feds' in which at least one person had died.

Intimidation was also commonplace, such as the incident of the school teacher who had inadvertently messed with a grower's daughter and returned from an assignation to discover his car riddled by gunfire. He left without fuss. So did the suspected informer whose house was machine-gunned from under him while he cowered upstairs in bed. Both were considered lucky.

The general feeling was that somebody with serious power was turning a blind eye to the trade. The local sheriffs certainly didn't have the clout to ignore it on their own initiative and keep their jobs. An unknown official far higher up the pecking order was receiving the pay-off. Nobody we met knew or cared who this might be, because apart from the odd mistaken identity or occasional outsiders finding themselves in the wrong place, the farming had no effect on local life at all, other than to spin off some good grass and obliquely boost the economy. Many middle-of-the-road Americans I know are of the opinion that out of the generally available narcotics, marijuana at least should be legalised, at one stroke doing away with a major sector of crime while bringing joy to the world.

Three days after arriving at the Pacific, Roz turned to me as we sat on the beach below the Westport Inn. I had been deliberately avoiding the issue of what was to happen next. The question of whether Roz was going to tackle the eastbound leg or would be satisfied and give up now that she had fought her way to the West Coast was unresolved, in my mind at least.

'Do you think we should be moving on soon?' she asked.

Time to grasp the nettle.

'How do you feel about the trip home? Do you really want to make it?'

'Well,' she responded, 'I won't say I'm not still frightened by traffic, and to be truthful I wish there was some way we could miss out San Francisco, but I said I'd ride here and back, and that's what I'm going to do.'

Beginning to realise that I had lost Roz's plot somewhere, I put it to her carefully that she shouldn't do this for my sake, although I'd miss her if she went home without me.

'It'll be fine,' she replied almost indignantly. Then she made it clear that my doubts about her seeing it through were of my own making.

'I've never had any intention to quit half-way. I've developed my own little fantasy, actually, and I have to cross the deserts and all of Texas to live it. I want to ride through Baton Rouge past the Lakes of Pontchartrain and down into New Orleans. And if I've gone that far, I might as well run off the last 1,000 miles and sell the bike back to Gary at Annapolis. I can't wait to see their faces in the dealership when Betty rolls in through the door!'

She knocked hard on wood for her bike and grinned at me, confounding my dark suspicions.

'Just don't leave me behind on the eight-lane, that's all.'

My whole world lightened up, but I said no more. Never disturb the Bulldog Spirit.

And so we loaded up, said farewell to the people of Westport and rejoined Route 1. Our whole little community came out to bid us adieu. Even the Mexican tart showed a leg and waved her bandana. The rocky coast led us to a vegetarian lunch in Mendocino town, but the relaxation of that whole area, together with the dreamland vineyard country further south faded in a long afternoon as we filtered into the real-time horror show of the California freeway system.

We joined US Highway 101 around seventy miles north of San Francisco. This turbulent river of steel runs from Oregon to Los Angeles by way of the Golden Gate Bridge across the narrows at the entrance to San Francisco Bay. The pleasant, leafy city of Alameda where an old shipmate promised rest and recreation lies on the eastern side of the Bay in the shadow of highly urbanised Oakland and Berkeley. To reach it, one must cross the Gate, negotiate downtown San Francisco then hack all the way over the seven-mile bridge which crosses the enormous bay itself. Thousands of commuters make the same trip every working day, but for us, swinging into the automotive hurly-burly out of the space of central North America, it was a major trauma.

Even after living in the States, I can never come to terms with the semi-legal practice of overtaking on either side of a slower vehicle on a divided highway. Anyone who passes 'on the inside' in England is immediately branded as a lunatic, subject to public vilification and liable for prosecution, yet throughout the US, otherwise sane individuals make it their daily habit. And nobody seems to mind. Perhaps we avoid it because, knowing our nearside is safe, we can concentrate on our offside mirrors and so decrease the likelihood of anyone running into us from the back as we change lane. Anywhere in America, it is vital to check both mirrors, particularly the right one if you are moving into a 'slower' lane. The fact that overtaking is not subject to any lane discipline encourages lazy drivers to cruise along at sub-speed-limit velocities in what should be faster lanes. This in turn sends quicker drivers lurching into the inside streams of traffic, causing those already in them to brake, sometimes violently, sending shock waves back for hundreds of yards. Add to the whole dynamic mess a dense heat haze, one of the world's heaviest traffic loads, trucks the size of houses, ill-maintained cars that would not be allowed on any northern European road and the fact that many drivers simply do not bother to use their direction indicators; then you start to understand that this is the jungle. It is certainly no place for two motorbikes in convoy, especially if the leader is trying to find unknown exits and the follower is struggling to stay in touch.

The surest formula I know for staying alive on a motorcycle is to assume that every other being on the planet, human or animal, is making a well-planned effort to kill you. Once this is established in your craven mind, it takes only a modicum of skill and self-discipline on a busy highway to make sure that none of the bastards get close enough to hurt you. Out in the country the discipline bit is more difficult, because there you must presuppose that each gate in the hedge hides a tractor and trailer poised to trundle out just as your brakes are past the point of no return, or that the woodland you are belting through at ninety is full of moose, one of which is limbering up to leap at you, spelling a rapid departure from this life for all concerned. Working this principle on the California freeways would have been fine for me on my own. It was a nightmare for two.

The most effective control for making motorbike space in fast-moving traffic is the throttle. A good squirt and even a Harley can out-accelerate most cars up to legal motorway speeds, but you must have the confidence to give it some 'welly', and two bikes absolutely must stick closely together. Roz had always left a technically safe distance between us, and sometimes we were separated by half a mile or more. Now, the only chance of her keeping with me was to stick like glue within ten feet of my exhaust pipes, always to one side so as to have a better view and be clear of anything I might drop. She must maintain concentration and trust me not to brake suddenly. It wasn't easy, and each time we were split up by some chancer poking into the gap between us I was faced with my own problem of how to make enough room behind me to give Roz a slot. This meant I was spending more time looking in my mirrors than ahead. The stress levels spiralled. For an hour I thought they would go through the roof, but Roz hung on and we made it to the glorious Golden Gate where the whole dice with death was dragged to a standstill by a steaming, raging gridlock half-way across the bridge. The last words I had heard from Roz had been a loud oath hurled at a woman driver who had been hassling her. I dreaded what was coming as she wormed through the lanes and pulled in alongside me. The afternoon was warm and sultry as she checked ahead for traffic movement, saw none and removed her helmet. Shaking out her hair in the sunshine she ran her sleeve across her forehead and, to my deep relief, something was amusing her.

'What's that Harley slogan?' she asked, rhetorically because it was inscribed on Madonna's air cleaner alongside a golden eagle. "Live to Ride, Ride to Live?"'

'What about it?'

'The "riding to live" bit makes sense on this Highway from Hell,' she said, 'but as for "living to ride"! You get past caring what happens to you, don't you? I can't believe the way some of these idiots are driving, but I'm in some sort of limbo.'

'I'm sorry if I lost you a couple of times.'

'That's OK. You can't do more. That stupid bag who nearly had me would have tried to squeeze her rusty heap into a gap the size of our garden path. The only pleasure for me is knowing she won't live long.'

I sat back on Black Madonna a happy man. If Roz had survived the past hour emotionally intact, the traffic could do its worst from now on. Having been driven tens of thousands of miles by her in cars and respecting her basic road sense, I had always worried less about her being knocked off her bike than about her state of mind. From now on we could enjoy riding together. I could hardly believe the transformation, but I'd seen her make up her mind before and was glad for whatever had happened inside her head at Westport.

Looking beyond the angry faces in the cars, I watched a fog bank march strongly in from seawards below the bridge on the sea breeze. It hesitated for five minutes, during which the traffic remained stationary, then it drifted on almost as far as the one-time prison island of Alcatraz. Today's wind wasn't strong enough for it to inundate the whole bay and the low wall of mist held back just short. Up here we were in clear air under a cloudless sky. A ship sailed out of the damp blanket, radars spinning, and shaped up towards Oakland. To the right of it, I could see the corner of the isthmus of the city itself, the unusual skyscrapers of the business area gazing down on the redeveloped waterfront. Once, this area was Sailortown, where hundreds of clippers and lesser Cape Horners were laid up in 1850 while their crews jumped ship to dig for gold. Shutting my ears to the thrum of the overheating engines around me, I could almost hear the hard-voiced shantymen banging out the time as the hands sweated around the capstans.

Blow boys, Blow, for Californ-eye-o,
There's plenty of gold so I've been told,
On the banks of Sacramento.

So many ships were abandoned here that a number were given up by their owners and turned into warehouses. One even became a famous hotel.

The traffic started again and our local batch of the 100,000 vehicles said to cross the bridge in a single day jerked forward. To our discomfort, they did so too slowly for even first gear to run sweetly, so riding our clutches until our left arms ached, we negotiated the city itself and out on to the Bay Bridge. Eventually, we made it to Alameda where my mate was in charge of a major sea school. A management training day was just finishing with a group of smart executives coming ashore. In my sailing time I've handled a number of these sessions, but right now, thinking of my best lens sitting on a bullet-mashed fridge in Oregon, the Wounded Knee prayer rags fluttering in the prairie wind, the farmer whose crop was dashed by hail a day short of the harvest, and the moonshiners back in Virginia, I couldn't take the adult games seriously.

'Ever thought of just issuing the customers with motorbikes and sending them up 101?' I asked David. He looked at me oddly. He's a sailor through and through. I don't think he understood how throttle-happy you can get after two months in the saddle.

That night we telephoned around the bay and rounded up a few more salt-caked sailors. Everyone brought enough booze for a week and as we drank into the night, Ray stoked himself up and began to talk of the days when he worked 'The Free Store' at the centre of the hippie movement. I watched his familiar oval face in the lamplight, deep-tanned by many an ocean crossing. Long grey ponytail and moustache, big man, big spirit. I never knew whether he would be tough in a tight corner, or if he would just walk away from a confrontation in memory of the year-long love-in. I still don't. Sometimes it's better to keep people guessing.

'1967, I suppose it would be,' he said. 'We traded most things in that store down on Haight Street. Someone had spare food, they brought it in for the shelves. Clothes they didn't need, nails, mattresses, books; in they came. We could fill most needs. Whatever you had a requirement for, you just asked for it. And everything in the place was free. Even the money.'

'What money, if it was all free?'

'Every so often, one of the brothers or sisters would find they had cash. Maybe they did some job for a square, or perhaps they just arrived with some then found they'd no need of it. They'd pass that in as well.'

'Jesus!'

'You say so, but it worked. For a while. Folks was so straight, one guy came in and asked for twenty bucks. Of course we gave it to him. Never enquired why. Not our business. Our job was to hand it over. Next day, in he comes with a ten-dollar bill and presents it to me.

"'What's that for?' I ask him.

"'I needed it to pay for a neighbour's rent. He was broke. I thought it was twenty but it was only ten. Here's your change.'"

David swung back on his wooden chair.

'You can't imagine that happening today, can you?' he said.

Ray leaned forward, sadness and an ancient enthusiasm mixed in his eyes.

'No,' he said slowly, 'but that's how things were then. It couldn't last, I see now. Commercialism crept aboard, and where people are that plain good there's always some greedy asshole screws things up. But for a while, it was cool.'

Thinking of this generosity of soul, I contrasted my own experience in Santa Monica, Los Angeles in the same summer as a student. I'd travelled to LA looking for some imagined sun-and-sand 'Beach Boys' paradise. I'd taken a job washing up in a foreshore diner and met a couple of girls who showed up in a black Chevelle SS. The car was the business. Seven litres of all-American oomph, carburettors like tunnels and a 'four-on-the-floor' gearbox. Ci-ci, the owner, had some money and didn't need to work. She was also beautiful. Her friend Kay was literate, plain and fell in love with me while I, being young and foolish, yearned for the immaculately-presented Ci-ci.

I moved into the girls' apartment, about which I recall little except that it had two bedrooms, a kitchen and a peach tree outside the living-room window. Ci-ci's father paid the rent and it seemed like heaven on earth to a lad from the North of England. Kay read to me from W. B. Yeats. Ci-ci drove me nuts but wouldn't soften to my lewd advances. After three or four days, our trio arrived at an amicable equilibrium and Ci-ci was more than happy for me to stay on until I was ready to split for the East Coast in a few weeks. The days were golden as we cruised the Hollywood boulevards in the Chevelle. We swam, the girls shopped and I carried on with my washing-up. Not a stimulating lifestyle, but we liked it, and so it might have continued had not Ci-ci's official boyfriend returned.

Craig's code didn't run to his 'date' putting up long-haired foreign men in her apartment. In his check Bermuda shorts, white polo shirt, white socks and loafers, he was so clean he squeaked when he walked. He was as good-looking as Ci-ci in a 'Thunderbirds' sort of way, and just for a moment it occurred to me that maybe they deserved each other. But Ci-ci was still warm and human and she hated it when he had her throw me out. It never occurred to him that she'd argue, but backed up strongly by Kay, she made such a fuss that in the end Craig temporarily installed me in his local fraternity of the high-powered UCLA. There, he and his intelligent chums could keep an eye on my subversive activities.

The fraternity house was denominated by three letters of the ancient Greek alphabet. I don't remember what they were, but I recall asking Craig what they signified. 'Drink more beer and chase more tail!' he replied.

In this house of learning, I discovered all there ever was to know about old-fashioned male chauvinism. No 'peace and love' in this flop-house. It was shags chalked up on bed-ends with names and ratings, including my friend Ci-ci; there were vile jokes and a great deal of binge drinking. Of the serious conversation British and Irish students experimented with in those days there was no sign. Life was a giant kids' party with a table stacked with cream cakes. All you had to do was help yourself, and anyone fool enough to ask questions was laughed to scorn.

In the UK, my crowd rollicked into the typically profligate sex-lives of the period, but even at the time I couldn't recall such a lack of respect. From where I stand now, it is hard to believe that the denizens of that academic fraternity house were not all homosexual misogynists, so afraid were they of women, but at the age of twenty I was not equipped to draw any conclusions at all. I put up with the place for two nights, then I bought a bus ticket for Boston and left my new acquaintances to their training for running the world. If I'd originally wandered into San Francisco instead of Los Angeles thirty years earlier, I might have met Ray, not Craig. My life could have been very different.

Roz and I stayed a further three days in the city. Betty Boop was garaged at David's place and we cruised the hilly streets two-up on Black Madonna. As only a city can, San Francisco drained money out of us at an alarming rate, handing out a heavy beating to our budget. Sitting over lunch in 'The People's Café' on Haight, I did some rapid workings on my napkin.

'We're going to have to be back in Annapolis within a month,' I said, expecting Roz might feel pressed by this.

'How far is it?'

'Depends on the detours, but if we take in Death Valley, Las Vegas, Flagstaff and New Orleans, it'll be 4,000, maybe 4,500 miles.'

'How much is that each day?'

Maths was never Roz's strong point.

'Taken straight it's only 150, but we're bound to rest up every so often. We might have to make some 300s, or even more.'

'That's six fifty-mile hops. If we only choose roads that are good, we'll eat it. Perhaps,' she added as an afterthought, 'we ought to make a start?'

chapter eighteen

flat out to death valley

The urbanisation of the Bay area soon gave way to a modest coastal range of a different character to its counterpart behind Mendocino and points north. We crossed it on the scurrying freeway almost without noticing it. Next came a long haul across a wide expanse of flat farmland. As the sea receded behind us, normal service was resumed on the heat machine. By afternoon, the altitude had risen further, but so had the temperature, which now nudged 100 degrees at Copperopolis, a sometime one-horse mining settlement high in the Sierra Nevada foothills. The mineral-powered boom years were history and even the solitary nag had either trotted away or was taking an afternoon nap.

Back on the coast, we had lost some of our painfully developed resistance to living in an oven, so we poured ourselves into the local store to buy larger bottles for our water. One thing was sure. We might cool off over the 9,000-foot pass the following morning, but the climate was going to deteriorate considerably in a day or two as we rode into the wastelands of America, where the idea of rain was an empty hope. There was a great deal of zig-zagging coming up but, as the eagle flew, we were only 200 miles from the north end of Death Valley.

From Copperopolis we wound on up the mountains, increasing forestation growing in response to precipitation on these ocean-facing slopes. The long first day's leg ended at Sonora which we had innocently imagined to be far enough from Yosemite to furnish affordable lodgings for a pair of honest travellers. A major error. The accommodation was expensive and crowded. We found nowhere suitable to camp or sleep rough and in the end we dug deep in the communal wallet, annoyed to be paying for luxuries of which we had no need and to part with three days' budget in a single night. But we were tired, hot and our rip-off resistance was low, so we handed over the blood money and bedded down in clean sheets.

If there had remained a ghost of doubt, Yosemite was now definitely off the travel plan. We did not need discuss it. America has landscape in abundance and we craved solitude, or at least the company of people living in their own environment. We skirted the park on its north side at dawn, crossed the Sierra Nevada watershed at the Sonora Pass, ate snow by the side of the battered, winding road and began slowly to lose altitude towards breakfast.

Breakfast in America is every bit as comprehensive as those served in England or Ireland. No continental milk-sop junk for the full-blooded Yankee, Westerner, or Southerner. Across the continent and back again, we made breakfast a main meal whenever we could, tucking in to the most reliably cooked eggs in the world, crispy bacon, spicy sausage meat and glorious fried potatoes. Nothing touches it at nine o'clock after two hours on the road. The company is good at the bar of a truck stop or a small-town café, the multiple mugs of weak coffee grow on you once you've learned to take it black, and the whole experience gives the morning the boost it frequently needs. Plus, of course, for six or seven dollars you have fuelled your body for the day. After breakfast, lunch becomes a mere strategic stop to shelter from the heat with a light bite to make it seem worthwhile. Even dinner can be a carefully selected snack if nothing more substantial offers itself. This throttling back on appetite is something to do with never feeling chilly except perhaps first thing in the morning. A long ride in an American summer is a great way to lose weight.

Route 167 dropped several thousand feet in short order, then went straight as a gun barrel directly away from Yosemite towards Nevada. At one point I stopped the bike to stretch my shoulders and looked behind. The cracked tarmac with its worn yellow centre-line ran like a ruler until it climbed out of sight into the snow-capped Sierra fifteen miles away. Far ahead, still on the same direct bullet-flight, it disappeared into a cleft like a gun-sight into an impossibly distant ridge. As we cleared out of California, the last of the trees and brightly coloured flowers gave way to the browns and pinks of the dried-up Nevada mountains. Cruising down the straight, gently sloping valley floors into the heart of their country, the sierras became progressively more lunar in form, their deep folds unsoftened by even a hint of vegetation, the sharp desert light picking up every detail. Sparse clumps of dried-out sagebrush looked as though they hadn't seen rain in years, but the bikes loved it.

In full-on desert at last, the Harleys rose to their work like troopers. I calculated that the average altitude hereabouts must be between five and six thousand feet, the sun was high and the road stretched out, totally deserted until it faded out miles ahead. I glanced at the speedometer on my tank and discovered, rather to my surprise, that in the widened perspective I had been steadily speeding up without realising it. The needle was hovering around 90mph. It seemed rude not to give Madonna her head, so I opened her up and waited. At exactly 100 she topped out and would do no more.

As the sagebrush flashed by and the distant hills grew rapidly closer, I decided that this lack of top-end poke was probably accounted for by the altitude. The bike's set-up hadn't been materially altered since it was last tuned at sea level. Six thousand feet is a substantial drop in oxygen content, but even so, 'one ton' and no more from almost 1,400 cc of motorbike didn't seem like very good value.

The roads were so lonely that I'd given up looking in my mirrors. Indeed, where flashing blue lights are not an issue, travelling at a hundred or more renders mirrors as redundant as they are in New York City traffic. There, the only way to survive is to ignore everything except what is happening right in your sights. I was considering these paradoxes when a crackling roar over my shoulder gave me a serious fright. For a split second I had no idea what it was, then the yellow bike pulled alongside me, Roz leered across from behind her visor and twitched her right wrist. Betty Boop, the bike the lads back East had shaken their heads over, actually accelerated and left me standing.

I caught up with Roz ten miles further on when she stopped for water. She was laughing fit to bust and I knew she'd finally worked out what it was I like about motorbikes. She never overtook me like that again, but we kept up high speeds when it was safe and there were no representatives of the sheriff's office at hand. It helped move things along, nipped off any incipient boredom and I'm absolutely sure she grabbed a charge out of it. At that water stop I sat comfortably, side-saddle on the Heritage. My legs stretched out and my boot-heels in the deep dust. The sun was well past its height now, and the striations in the mountains were becoming dramatic in the early evening light. The valley floor was pancake-flat and there was no impression of altitude. I had to check the map to see that the naked crags rose to eight and nine thousand feet. The heat remained intense, but the air was bone dry and it was not difficult to bear so late in the afternoon. Not a breath of wind disturbed the stillness, and no flying bugs spoiled the peace. The sky was bluer than I had ever seen it and still not a car, a truck or a living soul appeared. It was incredible that the same morning we had left a wooded town so full of wealthy visitors we had struggled to find a bed.

Where were they all? Why weren't they here? The beauty of the place was awe-inspiring, but the people were crowded together somewhere else.

'Good luck to them,' said Roz, ever practical. 'If they're there, they can't be here, so we get it to ourselves. What do you say to pressing on to Tonopah for bed?'

'Why Tonopah?'

'Because anywhere with a name like that must have something going for it. Besides, it's only seventy-two miles. We'll be there in an hour if we don't run out of fuel . . . '

Back on the bikes, we revelled in the stunning splendour of our surroundings. We'd cross one enormous valley, rise up over a pass in the moon mountains and drop down into another dip, always with a flat bottom and a straight road. We flew by Pilot Peak and Emigrant Peak, and finally found ourselves in a series of desolate passes as Tonopah approached. A couple of pick-ups went the other way, then a shining truck from Albuquerque. With the town in sight several miles ahead we stopped again to decide what to do.

'Shall we save money and sleep rough?' I suggested. 'There's nothing out here to hurt us, and we're hardly going to be shot for trespassing.'

Roz kicked at a dead rattlesnake some vehicle had run over. It was still flexible and clearly wasn't long gone to its reward.

'What was it that guy back in Kansas said about rattlers cuddling up to you in the night to keep their body temperature up for an early start?' she asked. 'And what about the scorpions? You sleep out here if you like, but I think I'll squander resources, take a nice cold shower and watch TV in bed. You'll be able to see the Weather Channel . . . ' she added like a carrot to a dying donkey.

'There isn't going to be any weather until we reach New Mexico and Texas,' I responded. This was true. The only item of meteorological interest out here in high summer was the academic issue of exactly how hot each succeeding day would actually be, but I capitulated without much struggle. After the long day I didn't honestly fancy the hard ground and the plummeting night-time temperature either.

Tonopah was a classic Wild West mining town. It seemed to hang absurdly at the brow of a hill with an industrial complex at the apex. A hotch-potch of buildings lined the road and prices in general were back to normal. The lady at the Mexican restaurant told us to turn on the TV at nine.

'There's a show about women bikers,' she announced. 'It's really important. It's on the national channel and everyone will be watching it. Folks are dying to know about that stuff.'

And so we tucked ourselves up at the appointed hour, opened a pint of Jack Daniel's and watched agog as a troupe of five Barbie-doll women pranced through a very short motorcycle trip doing a lot of talking and acting like fashion models all the way. They were obviously getting off on the power symbols, the big bikes, but we noted that the ladies were never hot, there were no flies and, of course, none of them ever fell off. The last item was a mercy because if they had, they'd never have looked so pretty again, wearing only their flimsy gear. The exception to this frippery was one girl who favoured a very fast Kawasaki 'crotch rocket'. She was kitted out properly and, we thought, put up with the Harley babes with saintly patience. Every so often, boredom would overtake her and she'd open up her 'Kwacker', disappearing over the horizon in a thrilling 10,000rpm howl, blowing the rest into the weeds. She turned out to have ridden some major distances and Roz admired her attitude. As to the rest, Betty Boop's owner helped herself to ice from the machine outside and topped up her drink.

'More fantasy to feed the ill-informed,' she said, taking a long hit. 'Nell's still the only girl we've met riding her own bike outside Sturgis. She'd have had a good laugh at that shower. 'Death Valley in the morning, is it?'

We had already covered 100 miles when we rolled over a 4,000-foot pass up to the rim of Death Valley at ten in the morning. As we dropped down a wide gulch past a group of ruined mine workings, we strayed into a side canyon to marvel at its 'badland' pinnacles, buttes and crevasses. Even up here, nothing whatsoever grew. We shut off the bikes, scrambled 100 feet up on to a ridge overlooking the main valley and gaped.

The overriding impression was one of brooding silence. No life at all. No birds, no vehicles, no aircraft. Instead of rising, the hot air seemed to be sinking into a chasm so wide and deep that the towering, oven-red cliffs well over ten miles away on the far side were fuzzing out. Across the valley,

Telescope Peak stood 11,000 feet. Down there, the salt pan lay 300 below sea level. The lowest point in the United States.

The general height of Nevada seemed to us to maintain its desert at 100 degrees or a little more. Below us on the sun's anvil, there were no such restraints. The air temperature soared as we descended, inexorably becoming part of a landscape that dwarfed us as surely as Manhattan might subdue an ambitious ant. The valley runs north–south with a road which favours the eastern edge of its bottom. It is a national park, but there we saw no turnstiles. Even the ghost town of Rhyolite was not despoiled. This stood, generating weird shadows in the rising sun, under a cliff once rich in minerals. It came complete with bottle-walled houses for better insulation, creaking jailhouse doors, an abandoned railroad station and a burial ground for those who stayed behind when the others packed up to leave. Their headstones were enlightening. Some perished from unknown diseases, others died in gunfights or were 'overcome by the elements'. None was posted as having succumbed to the natural passage of the years.

We dismounted at the bottom of the hill at around zero feet and found the rocks already too hot to touch. To the north rose an undulating area of yellow sand dunes. Southwards, the road disappeared from the world of the tangible into a liquid haze. Somewhere in there, fuel for the bikes was reported for sale at the only settlement, Furnace Creek. Battling towards it at 60mph was like riding into a hair dryer, with the moisture being blown clean out of us. On our left, just out of shadow as the sun climbed towards its awesome zenith, were the towering, convoluted eastern rock walls, still bluish in the oblique light. To the right, the earth was baked, crazed like a seabed waiting for water to return.

Furnace Creek did indeed sell gasoline. It also purveyed ice-cold Cokes. Beside the freezer chest, well-sheltered by the welcome shade of the pump canopy, a large thermometer read 123 degrees. It was not yet noon. In back, a tiny stream materialised as if it had no business being there, watered a couple of palm trees, then apparently vaporised. A Coke was double price, and the premium on fuel was usury.

'It can't cost all that extra to truck the stuff down here?' I asked the man at the till, who had us and all other passers-by as firmly by the balls as any man on Earth.

'It's like this, Mister,' he replied unemotionally. 'It's a free country, and I've got the franchise. You either pay what I ask or take your chance out there.' He nodded south towards where the salt pan swam beneath impossible cliffs and a brazen heaven. 'Thirty people still turn into leather here every year. Most folks choose to pay . . . '

We stumped up, and we took double Cokes. They proved a prudent investment, but I swear they steamed inside us as they hit our throats. Since we were such good customers, the proprietor let us fill our water bottles for free.

Pressing on under the sun towards the salt pan, the heat became more intense than any we had yet experienced, including equinox on the Equator. Within half an hour it was virtually unbearable and we stopped to rest as the great plain of salt opened out across the valley. A nattily dressed group of tourists stepped out of their air-conditioned car, exclaiming excitedly about the temperature. They greeted us, hung about for a brief few moments, their activity level slowing down visibly by the minute, then they dived back into the power-assisted shade of the vehicle and drove off.

There was absolutely no shade of any description at midday, and the temperature must have been up around 130 degrees. It was August and if we had ever doubted before that the motorcycle was a favoured way of experiencing the truth about America, we certainly didn't now. The folks in the car were seeing almost as much of Death Valley as we were, but they weren't suffering the power of the sun, hour after hour. They might have thought about the miners from before the air-conditioning revolution, prospecting so desperately that even this God-forsaken wilderness held hope, but they can have had no clue as to how they might have felt. Occasionally, a family travelling to California would wander into this kiln either by mistake or in a madcap attempt to save time and distance. There is no record of how many did and which of them survived, although there are stories of groups pooling their water, setting up a rudimentary shelter up on the cliffs and sending one man for help. They must have imagined themselves already in the Inferno.

Carried away now in my desire to wallow in the raw beauty and murderous conditions, I decided to walk across the dry salt lake and see how things looked a mile from the road.

'You can go on your own,' said Roz with certainty, adding, 'you must be barking mad.'

So we parked the bikes a few feet apart and rigged an awning between them so Roz could lie in the shade, I drank a litre of precious water and marched out to the west. Two hundred yards from the road, I had lost fifty feet or more in height and was on the beginnings of the salt. I had never walked a salt flat before and had imagined it to be hard and smooth. What the others are like I cannot say, but Death Valley proved a surprise. I had kept on my heavy leather boots against the remote possibility of snakes, and soon was glad I had done so. The going was surprisingly soft under a crunchy surface covering of white salt that reminded me for all the world of thin ice setting off above tidal mud. For a few minutes I trod gingerly, in fear that I was crossing the floor of some diabolic cauldron which might at any moment cave in and send me to the Devil. I didn't fall through, however, and crunched forward with slowly increasing confidence.

I decided to walk for thirty minutes, heading straight for a distant cleft in the cliff wall so as to maintain a known course. I worked on the basis that at my slow rate of progress half an hour would take me a mile or more from the bikes, and I didn't look back. I had no fear of getting lost, because I had worked out a contingency plan in case I couldn't see Roz when I turned around. In fact, finding my way back proved the least of my problems. The enemy was, of course, the heat and the unbelievable dryness of the air.

When the bleeper of my watch told me my thirty minutes was up, I stopped. The opposite side of the valley towards which I had been hiking for maybe a mile and a half looked no closer than when I had begun.

The glare from the salt was so intense that the mind-numbing heat seemed to come from all angles, not just the sun. I suppose the Sunday joint feels similar as it sizzles in the oven. My body was desiccating. No sweat came or, if it did, it was instantly vaporised by the tumble-dryer air. I had noticed that wet clothes hung out on the bikes in this climate were ready to wear within a half-hour. Now, the same was happening to me.

I stood up and turned so that my datum cleft lay exactly behind me. The road had disappeared, so had the bikes, so had Roz. Whether they had blended into the fast-reddening cliff or sunk into the mass of shimmering air lower down I could not tell. By now I felt noticeably weaker. After quenching my thirst back at the bike, I had foolishly not carried more water with me. We packed only three litres in all. Normally this was plenty for a day, but here, drinking it was like pouring it on to the sand.

I squatted down on my haunches deciding whether to rest or to return as quickly as I could. As I scratched idly in the ground with my fingers, the salt broke away in quarter-inch crystals. I pulled out my knife and hacked out enough to fill a film cartridge I found in my pocket. We can season our fries with it, I though wryly. Then I stood up, overcame a dizzy spell and began the trudge back.

Keeping my landmark behind me for the first ten minutes, I watched for any improvement in the visibility. The mirage danced on. It occurred to me that I could have been there 100 years before with no road, no awning, no welcoming woman, no water and no magic carpet called a motorcycle to spirit me away to a cool motel. Perhaps then I'd have had only a stumbling mule for company, the pair of us dying by the hour.

After fifteen minutes I had floundered twice and was really feeling the pinch. Craving water, I reminded myself again that I'd drunk my fill less than an hour earlier. It helped a little, but I realised that although it meant extra distance, I was going to have to veer off to the south to cut my chances of failing to find the bikes to nil. If I'd struggled on straight ahead and not been able to spot Roz when I arrived at the road, I wouldn't know which side of me she was and which way to turn to reach her. If I made sure of missing her to one side or the other, there would be no question about what to do when I reached the tarmac. I might walk a little further, but in this basic sea-fog navigation policy lay certainty. If I took a chance and it didn't come off, I might stagger down the road for another hour hoping I was going the right way. If I'd guessed wrong, I would have to decide at some arbitrary stage that the bikes could not possibly have been this far north or south, then reverse my steps. By then Roz would assume I had broken a leg out on the salt and be facing a nasty dilemma.

Still with the cleft behind me, I now chose an unmistakable fold in the east wall that was around thirty degrees off my imagined direct track. Noting the time, I altered my heading, keeping my new landmark ahead as my legs steadily turned to jelly. As I clambered up to the track after a further quarter-hour, there was still no sign of Madonna and Betty Boop, but I took a left on to the melting blacktop, following it around a bend and through a pile of boulders 100 yards away. There, glinting in the distance, were the bikes.

I joined Roz under the awning and gulped down what she had left of the water. Pahrump Nevada was eighty miles away. This morning, such a distance had seemed insignificant. Now, I had a different perspective. There wasn't much traffic and it had struck me forcibly out on the pan that our air-cooled motorcycles had so far only had to run downhill or on the flat in Death Valley. To get out, they had to gain 3,000 feet, a very different task. Having seen what the place did to my body, I was concerned lest they overheat and perhaps seize up, leaving us in dire trouble if nobody happened by with bottles of sweet, cool water. I remembered the conversation with Red and the crowd back in Branson Missouri about the problems of air-cooling the back cylinder of a Harley-Davidson V-twin. The poor thing had to breathe red-hot wind blowing off its sister right in front of it. Well, we were about to find out the truth. A pity, I thought, that we wouldn't be seeing the boys and girls again to set the matter to rest, one way or the other.

Climbing out of the deep valley, we used the gearboxes carefully to maintain modest revs and kept our right wrists gentle on the throttles. As we gained height, we left behind the worst of the heat until the sun dipped and the temperature fell to what felt like the usual 105 degrees. The buzzards flew over us once more and the bikes had taken the whole experience without flinching. I never complained again when my Harley-Davidson service manuals told me to change the engine oil at 3,000-mile intervals. That lubricant worked harder for its living than any oil in my experience.

Back up on the Nevada valley floors with the stark mountains rising from them like islands in the sea, we bummed a fill of water from a lone trucker who had plenty, then found a dirt road and cooked our supper in the wilderness. We fried a clove of garlic and a few chopped chillies in the bottom of the pan, used a pint of precious water to activate a packet of excellent Mexican rice, lobbed in a can of black beans when the rice was cooked and finished the creation off with a sprinkling of Death Valley salt. The sun was setting by the time we had scraped our tin plates clean and were relaxing on our selected rocks to finish our well-warmed bottle of red wine. Jupiter was rising between two peaks, and the air was so clear I thought I could make out a couple of his moons with the naked eye.

Starlight took the edge off the blackness of the early night as once more I set out from the bikes to walk into the desert. The air was cooling nicely although the boulders were still hot, but I was thinking one more time about the people who passed this way 100 years before. As a seaman, I have often marvelled at the hardness of the men who carried out regular commerce from wooden ships under sail alone. You have to try it to understand how tough and heartbreaking it can be. Trekking on foot across such country with no clear idea of where one was going to end up required similar fortitude. Perhaps it was even worse for the landsman, because at least the sailors knew how life was going to be. Their fathers had been there before them and they grew up expecting no more and no less. They understood from childhood that what to us seem virtually impossible feats of endurance would be within their everyday capacity. There was no alternative, easier way to tempt them, and this was surely half the secret. For wanderers and even organised operators in the unknown parts of south-west USA, increasingly heavy, unpredictable demands on physical and moral resistance must have come on a regular basis. The survivors were a breed apart.

The last twenty miles to Pahrump by motorcycle were a romp through the blessed high altitude cool of the late evening. As we breasted the final rise, the town spread out beneath us. According to our information, its population had risen from a single ranch community providing beef and provisions for the mining camps in 1876, to 18,000 assorted inhabitants today. From our vantage point, the place looked enormous but, with one area of exception, ill-lit. We could discern a dim chequer-board street pattern at least five miles square; in the distance, Highway 160 was visible as a row of lights heading south towards Las Vegas, but it was all low wattage stuff except for a single focus of shining floodlights illuminating the grandest US flag I had ever seen.

This glory of the desert, the bunting equivalent of a Harley-Davidson, a Pontiac GTO or a Flying Fortress, undulated gracefully in the beginnings of a night breeze in the centre of town, fully three miles away. The bold, beautiful banner marked the town better than a lighthouse beacon. After our traumatic day in Death Valley, and surrounded as the symbol was by barren land and a town with no features, I was surprised to find myself positively moved to see this grand statement of American identity.

No nation on earth is so in love with its flag as America, and I have seen strong men weep as it is lowered to the strains of 'The Star-Spangled Banner'.

As we rode slowly down the long, dark and dismal streets towards the flag, all the buildings seemed low in contrast to the shining, modern edifice beneath it. This turned out to be the casino, heart of many a Nevada town, and beside it we found the first of a short series of casino hotels, the best rooms of the whole journey.

Lying on clean sheets in the cooling draught of an a/c system that for once whispered instead of rattling and roaring, I gazed out of my window at the mighty flag filling the frame against the night sky. Understanding this business of the sacred colours is a basic requirement for travellers in America, where unpatriotic behaviour in any form is despised, from stately government offices and leafy suburban streets all the way to San Quentin prison, where dead men walk as they await execution for first degree murder. These days, it is becoming acceptable to incorporate the national logos in garments and other diverse artefacts, but when Harold Wilson tried to crank up morale back in 1960s London with his 'I'm backing Britain' campaign, the Union Jack underpants that proliferated found no American equivalent. Any US male who allowed the sacred patterns anywhere near his personal tackle would have been deeply ashamed. The Peter Fonda 'Captain America' Harley in *Easy Rider* was further out of order for its time than most foreigners realised. It wasn't just Fonda's vagrant lifestyle and Dennis Hopper's caricature cowboy appearance that outraged the rednecks, it was the fact that they represented a different America, a movement that shook more than the trees with its slipstream.

Morning showed the truth about the temporary town of Pahrump. Apart from the casino, a couple of hotels and a few modern businesses strung out along the Vegas road, the community consisted almost completely of trailers parked on generous square lots delineated by grid-iron dirt streets. The place had gone on to mains electricity in 1963. Telephones did not arrive until 1965, even though the road in and out had been paved way back in 1954. What all these people did to fill their day was obscure, for we saw few of them. Our hotel had been more than half-empty and even the gambling house had seemed quiet. Perhaps the extreme weather kept folks indoors. It would hardly be surprising.

chapter nineteen

gamblers and good vibrations

After Death Valley, we were committed to press on for New Mexico via Flagstaff, Arizona and the great canyons, but we decided that it would be insane not to make a detour to experience at least one night in Las Vegas. We filled our tanks for the sixty blistering miles to the South-East, took a long guzzle from the water fountain and set course for the Crystal City. We pulled into the forecourt of the luxurious Palace Station Hotel a few hundred yards off The Strip, to be offered a full suite for the sort of money that would fill two motorcycle tanks. The girl on the desk seemed to be treating us like human beings, so I asked her what was the catch.

'There is no catch,' she replied straightforwardly. 'It's well-established that a man with his pockets full of money will ultimately lose more than one who has spent over what he really should on accommodation. The firm gives you a good deal on the price of a room so you feel richer and spend longer at the machines or the tables. We get your money one way or the other, unless,' she rounded off with a winning smile, 'you get lucky and win the jackpot!'

As if on cue, a machine in the foyer began noisily disgorging hundreds of dollars into a plastic tub held under its maw by an elderly lady clutching a large handbag.

'So, are we obliged to play here?' I asked.

'No Sir. You do as you please. But you'll find we have all you need for a sporting night out. Why look further?'

Our suite was on the ninth floor of the central tower of the complex. It offered the perfect retreat to sleep off a bad run of the cards. Huge bed, view of the Strip with the moon mountains beyond, the widest television screen I had yet seen, a beautiful bathroom and a small but tastefully appointed sitting-room in which to hatch a better strategy for the tables.

After a bath and a snooze, we inspected the various dining areas that fringed the casino floors. We opted for 'Tex-Mex' and were promptly and politely served with first-class food for practically nothing. Dining, like sleeping accommodation, clearly came under the philosophy of not tying up gambling money. The players were certainly making the most of the opportunity to feed in style and, for the first time since leaving California, the fat boys and girls were back. The desert doesn't encourage obesity and we'd seen plenty of lean cowboys and healthy, resilient women in the dusty towns. Here at the Palace Station, we were back in mainstream USA.

Despite the culinary largesse from the management, on balance the house must win on all games where the odds can be controlled, so the slot machines, roulette or blackjack will see you off in the end if you play for long enough. The punters, with notable exceptions performing excellent PR for the management by winning, mostly looked to be on the down side of even. I only saw one guy sitting with his head in his hands, however. The rest seemed to be bearing up stoically as they made their personal contributions to the 2 billion dollars worth of tourist gambling that pours though Nevada's casinos each year.

Over in one corner of the main floor was a small room housing three luxurious green baize tables. Poker. The gentleman's game. I'd learned the rudiments on the waterfront in Canada and I love a hand or two. For a while we watched the action to get a handle on things. The dealer noted I was there and courteously raised his eyes in query, implying that I might like to take a spare seat. I shook my head with equal civility.

'Later?'

He nodded.

The game was Texas Hold 'em, where each player receives two cards that he keeps to himself. A further five are dealt in stages face-up on to the table, with bets at each round. All players hold the five in common, making up their final competitive hand with the two 'in the hole' which are hidden from all but their own eyes. The climax arrives when those left in turn up their cards and show their hands to the world.

After observing for ten minutes I was impressed by the restrained good humour of this game. The atmosphere was so much more civilised than out there in the clattering, ringing hall where the best thing, by a very long chalk, was the standard of the cocktail waitresses. Needless to say, the drinks were free if you were playing. Depending on their individual aptitudes, the girls flitted, wiggled or floated around the floors with their little trays. Casino standing orders rendered them immune from propositions, at least officially.

Stakes on the poker table were affordable, with early players 'anteing up' one or two dollars and things following on from there. A good pot could go seventy dollars or more, but unless you were really going for broke, you'd be unlikely to lose more than twenty or thirty in a single hand. If you folded early, the losses would be small change.

In poker, a payment to the house can be charged to each hand, but the odds are not stacked. I reckoned that while some of the players looked good, one at least had less idea than me, so if I were prepared to hazard, say, 100 dollars, I might come out ahead. First, however, Roz wanted to see The Strip after dark.

A bus stopped outside the hotel every fifteen minutes to cart the faithful down to the slaughterhouse. Predictably, there was no fare to pay. We hopped aboard, climbed down at Caesar's Palace, then hiked from one end of The Strip to the other, popping into an occasional famous casino in its ludicrous fantasy building and popping out equally rapidly. The scenes on the main shop floors rapidly became boring. Rattling fruit machines, rows of blackjack tables and roulette wheels inexorably extracting their percentage. Touts on the seething street corners handed out leaflets advertising individual girls for sale, complete with inviting photographs.

Immediately opposite one of these centres of marketing enterprise we found a full-scale pirate ship raid with tiny lakes and actual wooden ships. The crowd was huge and the kiddies loved it. In an oddball sort of way, so did I. People visiting Vegas seemed on the whole to be having a good time. We saw a lot more smiles than suicides. Even the pictures of the whores had a charming, schoolboy ring to them. An ironic honesty was veneered on to the general tackiness and essential amorality that seemed to say, "What you see is what you get," or, "This place does exactly what it says on the can."

To us, Vegas compared favourably with the huge, factory-like casinos shooting up in Connecticut on Indian Reservation land, beyond the jurisdiction of the state 'no gambling' laws. These promise 'family entertainment' and employ all manner of subterfuge to hook the kids while Dad is fleeced of his last buck, his shirt and, in all too many cases, his home as well.

Punters are bussed in by the thousand from New York and Boston, and the house winnings are literally carted away in sackloads. These places have an ugly feel to them, the victims appear demoralised and humiliated, while the buildings themselves are a major eyesore in the lovely woodlands of New England. They may be the red man's only route to revenge, but a quiver of well-aimed arrows would be tidier.

As the pirates fired their last cannonball into the desert night, we realised that we were hot, sticky and our legs were giving way. We both needed another shower and I was ready to play. The Palace Station was only a few blocks away. In fact, it was visible in glimpses between the towers so we opted to promenade home. A bad mistake.

Our guard was down and we were tired. Peace and security was in sight at the Palace Station. The trouble was, we couldn't walk straight to it. Every road seemed to have reconstruction problems, while every wall stretched too far and across our path. We veered away to the right of our track until suddenly, the streets became dark, the buildings shabby and the music throbbing out of the casinos faded away. On our left, raised up ten feet, was the main drag into town with cars humming by. The only way of reaching our goal was through an underpass whose width was reduced to half by the cement-stained plywood boarding of yet more construction work. Gratefully, we turned into this dark alley not a quarter-mile from salvation. It was only when the highway was right above our heads that we came face to face with our stupidity. The subway had so far been deserted, but as we rounded a sort of chicane in the boarding, three men materialised out of the shadows thirty yards ahead. They were waiting there for something, and it certainly wasn't a meeting of the church organ committee.

I felt Roz falter, but I knew there was only one thing to do. 'Just keep going, and don't slow down,' I hissed.

I straightened my back and thanked my stars the light was behind us. I might be grey of hair but I do have extremely wide shoulders. We were also wearing jackets, jeans and nondescript leather boat sneakers, not fashionable trainers. At least we didn't look like tourists.

My insides felt like water, but I kept my eyes ahead, checking the men out as we approached them. Black; maybe eighteen or twenty years old. One, tallish, exhaled a cloud of smoke, threw down his cigarette and ground it out with his boot. The other two were smaller, but equally menacing. Maybe we could run through them if they challenged us, I thought, but what about arms? I put one hand inside my jacket as though I were handling something heavy and turned to them as we went by, close enough to have to twist sideways to squeeze through. I gave some general 'excuse me' greeting in an American accent, as though meeting them in there was like asking for space in a crowded elevator. Then we were past. I turned to Roz and whispered,

'For Chrissake, don't turn around. Keep walking steadily.'

We strode on, waiting with undiluted dread for the following footfalls, coming faster as the boys closed in. Worse was going to be the command to stop if they decided I was bluffing and one of them pulled a gun. But nothing happened. We had convinced them we were locals, maybe armed, and they had fallen into the elementary mistake of judging the book by its cover. Ten minutes later we were slugging back Wild Turkey in our padded suite nine floors up. Roz was physically shaking and I was still sweating. After a few minutes, half-way down a second drink, we settled down.

Everyone I speak to about travelling in America warns me about bandits, muggers and drug-powered street crime. Since my advisers are often Brits whose experience of the US is far less than my own, and culled mainly from television and violent movies, I refuse to spoil my day with it. During the long winter holed up in the Bronx with a disabled boat, I had picked up some basic street wisdom. Apart from never dressing like a tourist, or letting anyone think you don't know where you're going, the essence of this was twofold: don't be in the wrong place at the wrong time but, if you are, try to look like you're at home. For a lone, middle class white to appear as though he belongs in Harlem late on a Saturday night is a major challenge, but you learn if you live. That night, we knew we had come close to blowing it.

'I think you should grab a hundred bucks and go and play poker,' Roz announced as I finished my drink. 'If you could fool those creeps, you'll clean up with nothing more than a 'ten-high' – so long as you keep your face straight.'

And so I showered, tidied myself up, bought a hundred's worth of chips and found a table with the seventh chair empty. The company was as congenial as it had been earlier that evening, and watching the dealer was a lesson in professional card handling, but for half an hour I never found myself holding anything approaching a hand. I folded regularly and was thirty dollars down before I finally won a round. A pair of aces was face-up on the table and I had one more, backed up by a king and a jack. Three of a kind. There was one more ace out there somewhere, but it was better than evens it hadn't been dealt. Plus, I had 'king high'. Not a great hand, but a playable one. Besides, I was suddenly feeling extremely fatigued. There was a minor showdown with a charming gentleman from the South who reminded me of Colonel Sanders, the man on the Fried Chicken advertisements. He folded when I raised ten dollars and I ended up ahead, but not by much.

Three hands later I was back down to ninety dollars and the dealer had turned up the unusually high tally of two kings, a queen and a pair of jacks with no particular suit favoured to encourage a flush of any sort. I had a king and a queen in the hole which gave me a king-high full house, a tough hand to beat. The betting had been brisk as the dealer flopped out the cards, with me calling the shots as lightly as possible so as not to frighten off my victims. The Southern gent looked slightly hesitant. He was fiddling with a diamond ring, a nervous habit, but he stayed with me all the way, following like a lamb when I went 'all in'. This meant that I shoved my whole pile into the middle and stood to walk away with only my shirt in the unlikely event of my losing.

Without showing vulgar triumph, as is proper at a poker table, I quietly displayed my royal hand.

'Ah,' breathed the Colonel slowly. Very kindly, with the sort of sympathy normally reserved for funerals, he turned up a second pair of jacks. He had four of a kind, and I was busted out. It wasn't my night.

We slept late in the morning, revelling in the personal safety which came with the tower block package. At breakfast, we were planning our route through the Arizona and Utah canyon country of Bryce, Zion and the Grand Canyon itself, when I lamented the loss of my short lens. I'd been managing with my long zoom, and Roz had more than made up the slack with print films on her Olympus, but it was my job to furnish transparencies, and I was falling short.

'Look at all these punters,' Roz said, indicating a restaurant full of gamblers. 'Some of them must be desperate. They'll have done their money and don't dare go home until they've made some back. If you were in their shoes and your credit cards were empty, what'd you do?'

'I'd hock my camera! You're a genius. This town must be full of pawn shops.'

As we checked out, my friend the receptionist asked how we'd made out.

'I lost, you won.'

She smiled her brilliant smile.

'Why not stay another day? You look lucky to me.'

'I used up all my luck somewhere else.'

A great place to lose your shirt, the Palace Station.

The downside of staying in an uptown hotel was that we had to hump all our stuff from the bikes below ground in the lockup along to the elevators, up to the room, then back again in the morning. Even though we had only allowed ourselves the minimum of personal kit, there were also tools, redundant fleeces, leathers, cooking gear, tent, bedding rolls and the cameras; plus fifty other lesser items that somehow disappeared into a studded Heritage saddlebag but were worse than a pig to carry. It took several journeys. In a standard motel room we could just heave it all in through the door. Easy. Sleeping rough or in the tent, we didn't even unpack; a major benefit, as loading up the bikes took a half-hour every morning. The chore never grew any easier, and we never really believed it would all fit in until I heaved down the last meaty leather strap.

Ready for the road at last, we cruised the baking streets of downtown Vegas searching for pawn shops. We scored first time. The brisk, dark-suited man behind the counter had no Nikon zooms, but he was able to sell me a neat little 'straight-through' fifty. Under pressure, he threw in a twenty-eight and a lens bag for the ludicrous all-up price of forty dollars cash. The purchase more than made up for my 100 dollars handed over to the Southern gambler.

Ahead of the game again and fired up by this new possibility for bargains, we spent the morning checking out the trade some more. On sale were colourful examples of gamblers' watches with diamond-studded bezels, loud card faces and other horrible features. Many a wife or girlfriend had handed over her jewellery, and in one emporium, an evening suit was prominently displayed. I pitied this spectacular loser, who must have had little indeed to his name when he walked back out on to the street. But it was the personal firearms that really turned over the money. Nominally locked up in show cases behind one counter gleamed the widest possible selection, from shiny ladies' handguns to ugly-looking automatic weapons. The needs of all could be met here and, if the money accepted for my camera lens was anything to go by, at the right sort of price. Had the armouries been pledged by gangsters down on their luck at the tables, or did they represent a cross-section of what the middle American family packs in its travelling bag?

Three days after Vegas, we found ourselves cruising south down US Highway 89. Behind us spread the Painted Desert. Somewhere ahead lay Flagstaff, Arizona. In the past seventy-two hours we had clocked up 600 miles through some of the

314

world's most fantastic scenery and were pretty much dead beat. First had come Zion Canyon with its smooth road surface clear from the lower end to the tunnel out on to the plateau at the top. A great ride. On the two subsequent mornings we had turned up at Bryce and Grand so early that, as at Glacier, we had beaten the Rangers to their posts and entered free of charge. Both sunrises had been moments to hold on to. Bryce Canyon, with its miles of unique pinnacle rock formations flushed vibrant pink by the dawn light, a totally feminine experience; and Grand, enormous and masculine. It's easy to find oneself carried away with hyperbole when considering these geological phenomena, but for me the final word on them was reported from Mr Bryce himself. A century or more ago, this bold adventurer homesteaded the difficult land outside the Canyon that now bears his name.

'A hell of a place to lose a cow . . . '

The journey down to Flagstaff saw us dodging the first rain we had seen for weeks. The substantial town stands at almost 7,000 feet and even higher mountains guard the road in from the north. The wind was a gusty westerly, with bike-shaking squalls ripping down the hillsides and black thunderclouds gathering around the peaks. The land was wide and the mountains smoother-sloped than back in the full desert of Nevada. There was some evidence of cultivation here and there, but the overall effect was barren. Traffic was thickening up as we approached within thirty miles of town and a deep grey rain wall driving out of its windward edge was threatening to drench us. We crested the shoulder of a bare hill and although I had hoped to outrun the storm, I stopped to take in a totally new sight.

A long, dark market-stall set a short distance off the highway ran for twenty yards, surrounded by battered vehicles and colourfully dressed people. One or two smart cars stood slightly aloof fifty yards clear. Above the open-sided tent, in front of it and on both sides, small flags of all kinds snapped in the blustery airstream. US ensigns, confederate flags and international signal code flags competed with pennants of coloured bunting, while strips of cloth very like the ones at Wounded Knee gyrated at the top of willowy ten-foot poles whipping in the strong wind. The overall effect was of brave optimism. Close-up, the people running the show became recognisably Native American. I guessed that these would be Navajo. They were selling trinkets, beads, belts, and souvenirs to the passing tourists. Nothing they had for sale was any use to us, but they chatted in a friendly way about the bikes and the fact that we were going to be very wet shortly unless we made tracks.

The Indians were right. We passed the snowy San Francisco Mountains in a downpour and called Clark's friend Mara from the edge of town, so totally soaked that we might as well have jumped into the bath fully clothed.

Mara is a highly independent woman, someone who knows exactly who she is. When she left her last husband and the easy life of the East Coast, she travelled with her family straight to Flagstaff, a place that feels like a frontier town surrounded by desert and mountains despite its position of importance in Arizona. She was waitressing in a small café on Route 66 when an unusual-looking fellow came in for lunch. He had dark eyes, dark bushy hair tied back, a small beard and his casual gear failed to hide a fine physique. They looked at one another over the menu and not a word was exchanged, but they both knew that this was It.

Mara, Fred and the kids now lived in a tiny apartment in a one-storey block. The communal rear pathway was a sort of social centre where the plain people of America could air their views. There was a hint of greenery, vehicles approached with difficulty and the yard might have been a haven of peace if not for the neighbours' dogs. Several of these beasts lived a crazed half-life caged up next to Mara's patch. The animals were clearly not fed properly and were apparently never walked, so they howled and barked continually. I looked out of the window to analyse a particular crescendo of canine anguish and saw a small girl stretching out of a broken window tormenting the beasts with a stick.

Fred leaned back in a chair.

'I spend my life teaching martial arts,' he said to my surprise. 'Sure, a lot of it is high-contact physical stuff. Showing people how to react and take care of themselves. A few of my folks go on and make the grade in the sport. But a lot of what I do is about encouraging people to be at peace with themselves. You can't fight, even in a stylised way, until you have respect and have shed all bullshit. These guys here,' he angled his head, 'some of them are missing the point.'

The girls walked out to the supermarket and Fred and I stayed behind with Mara's twelve-year-old son. Small, like his mother, but equally well-formed, the lad was a model of what a boy should be. He was enthusiastic and joined in when he had something worth saying, otherwise he listened. The rain soon cleared and the three of us went outside to check over Betty Boop. She had been misfiring in the wet and I assumed she had moisture somewhere in her guts. As we worked, we talked, as men will at such times. Partly our minds were on the puzzle of the misfire, but we were also getting to know one another. For some reason I asked Fred if he kept a gun, as most people seemed to in these parts. Unlike many, he did not proudly reel off a list of his weaponry.

I told him about the 'Bubba Bill Clinton, Yellow Beret Commander in Chief' caricatures in Kansas, expecting the usual supportive reaction to the artist. Instead, Fred looked at me sadly.

'The president is an unusual man,' he said, 'but he wasn't dodging the draft while he was over the Atlantic. He spent a deal of time in Russia talking with the Communists, trying to foster the start of a greater understanding.'

'How do you know that?'

'Just as well as those rednecks seem to know he was ducking the draft. They want us to believe he's a coward and a treasonist, but I don't buy it. He might not be a saint, but he's the only president who's had the balls to stand up to the 'right to bear arms' lobby. In the end, his is the only sensible way, and the sooner people realise it, the better for America.'

I looked at his strong, competent hands as we wrestled Betty's carburettor out from between her mud-splashed cylinders and thought how safe Mara must feel living with this even-mannered, up-together man. He lifted off the float bowl and emptied it carefully into the dirt.

'No water in there,' he said, showing the tiny metal container to the boy as I upturned the body to hunt for the main jet. I blew that out and together the three of us tooth-combed the delicate mechanism for dirt. It looked as though it had been spotless all along. The induction seals, however, looked past their sell-by date.

'Common problem up here,' said Fred. 'They don't look too bad, but it might be the answer. The combination of altitude and poor-quality gasoline on the Indian reservations burns them out. You'll be able to get replacements at Harley-Davidson on Route 66 west.'

I'd never heard of such a thing, but I sped down the road on Madonna, made it to H-D just as they were closing, and returned to Betty with the goods.

'Maybe she'll be OK now,' said Fred as we tightened up the final bolt, 'you never know what you've fixed, sometimes.'

'Let's hope so,' I agreed. We flashed Betty up for good luck. She started with a will and ran sweetly on her short test run.

The bike was cleaned up and back on her stand by the time the girls returned, and we men were setting ourselves to building a barbecue fire. Something about Fred's presence even calmed the evil dogs in their cages. They piped down and we enjoyed sitting out, breathing in the damp ground scent we had missed for so long. The neighbours made an appearance and shared a beer, but I suspected that they would not agree with Fred's views on either the president or his hand-gun initiative. Much later, Roz and I went to bed in Mara and Fred's room which they lent to us, bunking themselves down on the sofa. Joss sticks burned, while candles shed a gentle light over Mara's tapestries and Indian dream feathers. As we settled down Roz whispered,

'It's great seeing Mara in her own place. She and I had such a time just now and − no offence − but it was lovely being with a woman for a change. We went and had a drink in the bar as well. She asked me about Sturgis, and I told her how the whole business was such a strong statement of style, much,

much more than any motorcycle or boat rally would have back home, she said something really interesting . . . '

Roz fell silent, as though turning over Mara's comment in her mind. Stopping in mid-sentence was a habit I had developed and at this time it was driving Roz crazy. Perhaps she was picking it up. I hoped not, but waited to see.

'Out here,' she finally continued, having marshalled her thoughts, 'culture is only paper-thin. It's because apart from the Indians and some Spanish, these lands have only been settled for two or three generations. The effect is a deep need for roots and something to hold on to. The bike thing is typical. It helps people belong.'

This was certainly a new angle. Right or wrong, like most broad-based statements that sound plausible it had a basis of justification, but when I considered the individual bikers we'd met, it didn't stack up all the way. Steve and Nell certainly weren't in search of an identity. On the other hand, the public image of the Western motorcycling world with its style, badges and clubs, fitted neatly into the theory. The conundrum was like that of individuals and nations. I thought how often I had caught the mean little Brit who lives in the back of my head thinking archetypally derogatory thoughts about the French as a whole, only to shame him by recalling some of the excellent French men and women I have known. There are too many exceptions to rules about human alignment to classify people into neat armies. I saw what she meant, nonetheless.

Silence for a while. The wind had gone down with the sun.

'How on Earth does Mara manage in winter?' Roz spoke again. 'It must get really cold this high up, and there's no sign of any heating in here at all. But Fred's the perfect dishy lover. I expect he'll keep her warm.'

I told her how Fred and I had enjoyed playing at 'guys' with Betty Boop and Mara's lad, then my gaze wandered to the moonlit window recess. I doubted the wall was more than three inches thick. The whole building was totally uninsulated and probably made of reinforced concrete. Imagining the blast of the February gales roaring down from North Dakota around the Alpine height of this outpost city, I shuddered for Mara and Fred. No doubt they had some way of coping, but as I went comfortably to sleep in the perfect night-time temperature of August, I couldn't see it.

'If you're going east to visit the Hopis up on the mesas, you're stuck with Interstate 40 or Highway 15,' Fred gazed into his morning coffee. 'The 15 is what they call an Indian Service Road. The surface'll be lousy but you'll see some magic country. It goes straight up through Navajo land. Or you could try the remains of Route 66,' he looked up. 'I don't know how far you'd get . . . '

We came out of town on Interstate 40, cutting off at the first interchange and heading east down the service road that runs into the historic trail. The fabled Route 66, migrant route west for so many dispossessed families in the 1930s and more recently the subject of a sixties Rolling Stones hit, did not feature on my map at all. Rendered redundant by the superhighway, it now runs only in sporadic bursts, left behind to provide access to businesses and the occasional homestead that would otherwise be out in the cold. Initially, we found it close alongside its successor; later, the four-lane disappeared from sight, and ultimately, the almost mythical road veered off into the wilderness.

We ricocheted along the steadily deteriorating surface into the desert with Roz listening for Betty's engine to start missing again. I don't think she really could believe the carb was fixed, and after the bad-mouthing the low-capacity Sportster had received from numerous H-D experts along the way, I could hardly blame her. Had Fred and I actually managed to sort her out? Was it really just the poor quality fuel sold on the Indian reservations coupled with fast running at low oxygen levels, or was it in truth the beginning of the end?

But Betty's strong steel heart never skipped a beat all day, and Roz hung on with increasing confidence. From the comparative security of Black Madonna's wide saddle, I watched with an affection that surprised me as the yellow machine bucked gamely down the remains of Route 66 towards a distant mesa. Choosing Betty was turning out to be one of our better decisions. Despite the prognosis of doom from the experts, the rattlesnakes couldn't catch her, the worse elements of the Sioux missed their one chance and the wire-snared tyre treads flying off sun-fried trucks at ballistic velocities had rocketed by on both sides. Against the odds, she had also turned out to be faster than my full-blown giant. Zipping up to a ton was no challenge for Betty. Any quicker than that on a Harley and you're in the wild woods. Riding this dusty strip of history, I felt deep down that she was going to be a winner all the way. A lucky bike.

Much of Arizona, ceded to the Indians by the government and uncultivable without major irrigation schemes, is a vast, stony plain burned by the sun with all its features in the far distance. The flat top of a mesa stood clear ahead, perhaps ten miles away. On our right, individual buttes of non-eroded rock wavered on the super-heated horizon. This at last was the scenery of a thousand Western movies.

The road seemed to be of cement construction rather than tarmac. It had not seen a maintenance gang in decades. Fractures of ever-increasing severity dogged progress until we were riding around them one after another at an average speed of 10mph. Soon, even the weather-shattered concrete gave up and we were lurching along an ungraded dirt track into nowhere. There hadn't been a signpost for miles, and not a single vehicle had passed in either direction since we left the hardware stores and motels behind us on the outskirts of Flagstaff. Route 66 had become a ghost highway. We picked our way down it for at least an hour and were burning up gas at a high rate in low gear when suddenly it gave out altogether. Ahead, only a vague depression in the plain offered any hint of where it might have been.

Roz took off her helmet. I had not worn mine all morning as the likelihood of an accident other than a minor low-speed tumble was zero. We turned off our ignition and listened to the wind, waiting for spectral migrants in Model 'T' Fords to come rattling and creaking out of the wild. In a way they did, because the place had a strong atmosphere, as though the people who once struggled this way to California had left some of their burden along the roadside. Perhaps an unmarked grave hid its low mound nearby, for many had not survived the terrible journey. Nothing tangible could be seen. The extremes of seventy summers and winters had reduced any human debris to powder, but it was impossible to miss the ambience.

Retracing our own very visible tracks almost to Flagstaff, we gave up the struggle against progress and filtered on to 'I-40' to make up some time.

Within five minutes I remembered why interstates are a lousy selection for a motorcyclist with any instinct for survival. Crashing over a four-inch drop that stretched clear across the road, I cursed the often-poor surfaces that provide a throughway for innumerable speeding trucks carrying the nation's commerce. Roads such as I-40 are also heavily populated by private cars with a seasoning of 'RVs', many of which run up to the size of a double-decker bus. Apart from the deadly crevasses, such highways are dangerous for motorbikes for two main reasons. First, intermittent turbulence from the colossal trucks buffets like a vindictive gale; secondly, the biker is at great risk from the bunching created by that most sinister of modern car features, the 'cruise control'.

In the frenzied conditions of the California Freeways, the survival principle that everyone was trying to do us in had proved eminently workable so long as we maintained 100 per cent concentration. Not a problem when surrounded by maniacs. Out in the country things were not so easy, because the boredom of riding a wide, featureless carriageway saps the mental strength. Everything goes fine while there is no traffic. Then, even on a motorcycle, the only problem is falling asleep. The ever-present danger comes with the gaggles of cars.

Particularly on quiet sections, automobiles find themselves bunching together at exactly the speed limit, creeping ever closer to one another with mind-boggling slowness because the drivers have all set their cruise controls to what they fancy to be 65mph. Most will not disengage these handy aids to dangerous driving for anybody, especially a silver-studded phantom running up behind them attempting to keep close enough to the speed limit to fool any lurking cops. As the driver swanning along in the outside lane studiously ignores him, the biker is working hard at maintaining clear blue water between the motorcycle and a comatose zombie closing up inches from his rear mudguard. Meanwhile, some drunk who has actually fallen asleep at the wheel boxes him on the inside lane.

This may not sound like a terrifying scenario, but after it has continued for minute after agonising minute while you concentrate on the road, surrounded by the same representatives of the un-dead nominally driving but actually eating hamburgers, drinking scalding coffee, arguing with their wives on the cell-phone, raising both hands to emphasise some point you don't care about at all, or tuning their radios to yet another moronic substation, you can carve through the stress with a blunt hacksaw.

It is possible to cross America in three days on Interstate 40 without so much as a single interruption from a traffic light, and as we cruised up it at snail's pace, I pondered on the achievements of the 'iron-ass' motorcycle brigade. These fine role models for the young biker annually roar from New York to San Francisco non-stop, presumably to reassure themselves that they still have no central nervous system. And the Best of British Luck to them, I thought.

We pulled off the main highway as soon as we could to ride in glorious sunshine through more Clint Eastwood country up to the heights of Second Mesa where, standing proud between First and Third Mesas, the Hopi Indians still lived. On the way we stopped at a trading post run by the Navajo for fuel and water. Like all the permanent Navajo buildings we had seen, this one gave the impression of being tidier than the Sioux equivalent so far away to the north. Neither the storekeepers nor the hangers-on were drunk, and the dogs were friendly although, like Mara, how they and their masters kept warm in winter behind the matchboard walls of their shacks remained a mystery.

Further north-east across the huge desert land of the Indian reservation, we passed a scrapyard with a group of full-sized automobiles lined up under a tall red butte. The 'scrappers' were unattended, but the barbed wire fence that would inevitably surround them in a city was absent. So was the black, serial-killing German Shepherd that goes with it.

On close inspection, many of these redundant heroes were punched through with bullet holes, and though past road use, it was going to be decades before they rusted beyond recognition in the dry climate. The fact that someone had bothered to collect up their remains added another piece of subliminal evidence to the impression that the local Indians took pride in their barren, impossibly beautiful country.

We covered the remaining twenty miles to Second Mesa in fifteen minutes and were rewarded from even half-way up by a vast desert panorama. Adobe houses clung all around the steep slopes and as we banked carefully on the cobbles up to the summit, we found ourselves in a tidy square, built around the rocky table-top. By now it was early afternoon. Another friendly little mongrel dragged himself up from his post-prandial snooze and trotted across for a pat and a scratch of its belly.

These Arizona mutts were way out of line with the rest of the canine world when it came to attitude. Motorbikes and dogs are traditional enemies. I was bitten on the calf by a foul example in the streets of Liverpool as a youngster, for no better reason than revving up my Matchless at Penny Lane traffic lights. The brute's fangs went clean through my leather boot and having taken a good look at the state of them, my next stop was the hospital for a tetanus jab. You live and learn. Since those days I have often been pursued by Man's Best Friends while riding slowly enough for them to keep up. It's no use kicking them; they just chew you harder. The only answer is a solid twist of the throttle and 'Goodbye to all That'.

The short-haired little charmer in question led us across the small plaza to the door of a house marked 'Pottery for Sale'. There was no other indication of a readiness to do business and not a soul was in sight. Now squarely under the influence of the Spanish settlements of nearby New Mexico, I decided everyone must be at siesta. This certainly made sense, but we knocked the door anyway. It was opened by a healthy-looking Indian woman of around Roz's age. We indicated the sign and were ushered in without hesitation.

Frances stood around five feet three inches, wore white and her broad, pleasant face looked at the world through round spectacles. We explained from the outset that we were not in the market for buying her wares, as there was nowhere to stow anything on the bikes, but her open demeanour did not falter. She led us through the front room to the back kitchen and made us coffee.

The house was dark, cool and had been around a long time. Its rooms were around fourteen-foot square with heavy rafters supporting the flat roof. Simple clothes hung under the beams to dry. The plaster walls betrayed no roof leaks and the atmosphere inside was fresh. The only ornaments, apart from colourful pottery, were the Indian-design rugs on the stone floor. A gas cooker stood in a corner and the furnishings were completed by a television, a table and a couple of hard chairs. The single window, with its staggering view across America, looked in need of a handyman.

Frances was a Pueblo Indian from Santa Clara in New Mexico, where she had lived until five years previously when she met her husband at her grandfather's wake. She had dated him as a teenager but had not seen him in twenty-seven years. He was an active member of the Hopi tribe and the house on the mesa belonged to his family. He was so heavily involved in Indian festivals and the work of the tribal council that they found it hard to achieve anything as a couple, so she had reverted to her former trade as a potter. Her vases were beautifully painted with symbolic figures, black for rain, white for earth, four directions and four winds.

We sipped coffee from heavy earthen mugs and swapped life stories. Frances was amazed at the motorcycles and the length of our journey, but unlike the men from the Last Chance Saloon who had never travelled anywhere, she was fully aware of world geography through her pottery exhibitions which had taken her as far as Washington. She was undoubtedly in closer touch with the mainstream activities of the nation than some of the Indians we had met further north. Even her features were more European, but whether this was due to ancient intermingling with the Spanish, or just because she was native to a different part of North America and from a very different tribe, was unknowable. Unlike the natives of the plains, the Pueblo Indians, so called by the in-comers because they lived in villages with permanent dwellings, were not nomads.

The sun had marched around into the early evening by the time Roz and Frances exchanged addresses and we walked out into the glare. Bucking down off the mesa in second gear, our chum the dog followed us, picking up a couple of his mates as he ran. Anywhere else on Earth we'd have been accelerating frantically to leave them behind before they took a nip out of us. We liked what we'd seen of the Hopi and the Pueblo peoples, and we loved their pets.

A day later we had crossed into New Mexico and the transformation from the USA to something more like rural Spain was complete. Small, pink adobe houses turned their flat roofs to a sun tempered by altitude. Ancient mission churches with twin towers open to single iron bells nestled in green valleys. At Chimayo, eighth generation Navajo weavers clicked away next door to a '*sanctuario*' which outdated everything we had seen in Nevada and Arizona by several centuries. Inside, its ageless shade was illuminated by the flickering light of a thousand candles burning for joy, for gratitude, for thankfulness, for grief, or just in hope of better times. They might have been shining for the diversity of the American people.

Winding our way onwards, we were still less than 100 miles due east of the wide spaces of the reservation when we parked outside the 'Cowgirls' bar in the old city of Santa Fe. Clumping across the scrubbed boards in my heavy boots, I ordered two Lone Star beers. We each took a pull and sank down gratefully on high stools beside a blond man in his late thirties who looked like a refugee from a Beach Boys' album sleeve. He was drinking with an Indian woman.

'Hi, I'm Billy,' said the surfer. 'This is Nez. You come from far?'

'From England via San Francisco.'

'Oh, Sweet Jeeesus! You hear that, Nez?'

Billy grabbed half a handful of what I hoped was salt from an ashtray, stuffed it in his mouth and washed it down from his Lone Star bottle. Then he started talking so fast his words couldn't keep up with his mouth, but there was no hot air in him. Within five minutes he seemed to have introduced us to the whole bar, many of whom were lesbians. Hence, I presumed, the 'Cowgirls'.

One of Billy's cronies was a dark-haired young man with a fine-cut profile whose grandfather had been, he assured us, the Earl of Shrewsbury.

'Coulda had the title for myself when he died, but I was born here in the United States and this is my country. We don't have no m'lords here, so I turned 'em down. You guys ever hear of some king called George?'

'Which one?'

'Jeez, I dunno. Third, would it be? My old man reckoned we were descended from him. Wrong side of the sheets, he said. Something to do with a girlfriend. Otherwise I might be King of England. Waddaya think of that?'

There was no denying he had the sort of fine-drawn features often seen on the British peerage, and George had certainly ennobled more than one illegitimate son. Graciously, the non-Earl bought us more beer and made way for another man it was impossible to ignore. The writer had grey hair, a small moustache, a black-and-white shirt with a psychedelic pattern and was, he said, a great friend of Jack Kerouac's daughter. I didn't even know that Kerouac, America's most famous beatnik, had a daughter, but before we could find out about this relationship the conversation was rudely interrupted by a bore from Florida. The writer melted away with a resigned expression while Billy, our sponsor, led Roz off to meet a tall, thin gent wearing the highest cowboy hat in the place. My eyes began to close as the man from Miami described the intricacies of his remarkable patio, but through half an ear I was listening to Roz's cowboy. He was bringing her up to date on how he once worked as a rodeo rider but had since gone straight and become a cattle auctioneer. She asked him what his patter sounded like and he called the price of calves over the top of his beer. His ear-splitting chant sounded straight from a Nebraska cow sale and it brought the house down. The uproar gave me a chance to give the house-proud Floridian the slip.

We drank too many more beers before Billy kissed Nez goodbye and led us out to his jeep. Roz and I mounted up. Struggling to ride in a straight line, we followed him into the foothills of the Santa Fe Mountains for twenty minutes. At the end of God knows where, he swung into a driveway and stopped at the warm, brown adobe house he rented with yet another well brought-up dog.

The views across the Santa Fe valley with its surrounding mountains were uplifting, and everything about the place spoke more of Latin America than the USA. The raised beds in the garden grew long red peppers and even the hills somehow had a look of Brazil or Venezuela about them. Billy organised us a shakedown beside a floor-to-ceiling window and, while the dog made friends with Roz, he rolled a joint of the sort of gravitas rarely seen nowadays. We smoked this with more beers on the side, both assuming that this was the evening winding down peacefully. Just as I was fully relaxed after an extremely long day, Billy clicked his empty beer bottle on to the kitchen counter with dramatic finality and announced that as it was

Friday night, we'd better go back to town and check out the action.

Resignedly, we clambered into the battered fourtrack and were whisked away to the fleshpots. We needn't have worried. Billy, who really had been a Californian surfer, knew all there was to know about a large night out. Now a builder of custom furniture, he was very much part of the arts and crafts community. He also liked to dance and he appreciated good music.

It was fiesta time, and although we drove into town too late for the coincidental annual burning of an effigy of 'Gloom' in the main square, we never did find out what it was all about. The tree-lined streets were still thronged with revellers of all ages and we elbowed our way around, with Billy running into a friend on every corner. Eventually we settled on a bar where I would be happy to spend every weekend until they nail me up in my box. We each should have paid a five dollars cover on the door, but Billy somehow 'blagged' us all in. Most of the Cowgirls' crowd were already there, mixing with a wide variety of drinkers. The ready, high quality conversation inside was more like being in Ireland than in the US, the wine was of an unusual standard for selling by the glass and the burritos, which arrived to quell what by now was a raging appetite, were the best ever served.

The lights dimmed and the band started. A mix of Latin and easy-going jazz, the music was pure class and shortly we were up on the floor bopping with Billy's pals. Nez was there, and the writer gave me a wave. No sign of the Bore. Next to us, a Navajo with a serene face and braided hair to his waist was dancing with a beautiful woman of fifty in a Stetson and a long skirt with a striking silver-buckled belt. One raven-haired girl wore a scarlet, off-the-shoulder, flouncy Catalan dress, while a much younger girl in a ra-ra skirt gyrated like a professional with a different partner for every number. The best technical performers were a cowboy in a white waistcoat and immaculate blue jeans over gold-trimmed high-heeled boots, paired up with an Indian girl in a black sheath that revealed her warm colouring.

As things livened up and the dancing grew wilder, I banged hard into something extremely solid behind me. Turning around I found myself face to face with a man with a huge moustache who was as tall as me and even wider. He wore a full motorcycling jacket and an expression that announced, 'Lookin' for trouble? Yuh come to the right place . . . '

For a moment he stared me down. I couldn't hear the music anymore and was preparing to try and parry a massive blow as he raised his right hand. Instead of targeting my front teeth, however, he opened it in the classic bikers' upside-down handshake.

'You those guys pitched up at the Cowgirls from England?'

'Sure are,' I said, with a cool I did not feel.

'I gotta buy you a beer,' he said, and abandoning the voluptuous lady at his side, dragged me off to the bar. Later in the evening, Roz whispered that she had dubbed him 'Buster the Biker' amazed that he could possibly survive the night-club atmosphere in his riding leather. 'Probably takes it off on the road . . . ' she said, moving out on to the floor to leap around with her chum the auctioneer.

For a few minutes I sat alone, then a young woman from out of state arrived at my table. I listened with a despair that soon changed to annoyance as she started to fill me in on what a great country America is. This obviously wasn't the right time for politics, and the phrase 'great country' gave me a bad turn. A few years earlier, Roz had been subjected to exactly the same words towards the end of a formal dinner. They came from a lawyer who ten minutes before had infuriated her by announcing that blacks were physically unsuited for professional careers. She had laid straight into him on how his country was responsible for giving the world the litigious society, then she moved on to the question of civil rights. Veins were standing out on his forehead and all other conversation had stopped. The rest of the diners were right behind her, but there was no future in the exchange of views so I had broken up the party and taken Roz home.

The tempo of the music stepped up a notch as I submitted to the girl's eulogy on a curious mixture of passport-free travel, national parks and the interstate system. I could handle that much, but she soon worked around to a solid view on freedom and justice for all that was either naïve or mischievous. Inner cities, foreign policy and the vital issue of the growing under-class didn't feature in her fantasy. I finally managed to ask her about the journeys she had made to form her opinion. She mentioned half a dozen states of the Union but nowhere else. She hadn't even visited Mexico or Canada.

It was late, I was full of drink and unfit for any sort of intelligent argument. All I could see was the unworthy face America so often turns to an outside world that imagines it to be typical. I was about to let rip and spoil a wonderful evening when Billy appeared out of the throng. His social antennae had picked up the waves of anger and he was having none of it. Taking the woman firmly by the arm, he removed her to Buster the Biker's table.

gamblers and good vibrations

'There you are, Honey,' I heard him say amiably, 'this here's a man who'll appreciate your opinion.'

I saw her look at Buster. It wasn't hard for her to realise that the mountainous biker's idea of a great country might not coincide with hers. She didn't stop long. Buster winked at me and I bought him a beer with a whiskey chaser.

Looking over to Billy from Buster's rip-roaring reminiscences of riding with the outlaw gangs of the sixties, I saw him listening intently to another life story. The booze was really biting now and he seemed more than human. He was a saint from heaven. Sensitive, strong and endowed with a superhuman ability to make things come right. Through the bar-room smoke, his face looked almost holy in a devilish sort of way. Billy, the misplaced beach boy, was serving up good vibrations with a large ladle.

chapter twenty

tickets in texas and love bugs in louisiana

Roz slept deeply by my side under Billy's window while I lay suspended between dreamtime and morning. First light silhouetted the sierra, the moon had long set and the seven stars of the dipper wheeled low above the deeper black of the mountains. Refracted by the atmosphere, the constellation was expanded far beyond any semblance of normality. It reflected the state of my mind as my thoughts wandered into the West Texas Panhandle, now so close.

This was Cactus Jack's country, the border lands of El Paso where the lonesome cowboy in a Marty Robbins' ballad fell in love with a Mexican saloon girl, lost his reason in the gunsmoke of jealousy and shot his rival dead. He ran to the Badlands but in the end was drawn back to his lover, only to be cut down by the posse. According to country music legend, even today, sad-faced barmaids refuse virile young cowboys, preferring instead to walk home with hard, grey-haired men from the rodeo. Such people are so far from Washington DC they might as well be on the moon.

North of West Texas lies the New Mexico Line; southwards, the Rio Grande. Now, comparing distances and motivation, the words of Hurricane John Pournaras, a Greek seaman, came back to me.

'You can't do everything in this life,' John said as we slumped together in a bar facing a multi-choice immediate future.

He'd been right then, and I was beginning to think he still might be.

For the first time, I realised that I was near saturation point with new experiences. Part of me yearned to see the Rio Grande, to drink in the West Texas dancehalls on pay night and follow my luck to the card tables. But the more I yearned for it, the clearer I saw how close I was approaching blow-out point. The big river wasn't about to dry up and there would be other trips. We'd ground through some long days in the saddle since Nevada and I doubted Roz would be sorry that something in my head had shifted gear. Without seeing it coming, I had contracted what sailors call 'Channel fever'. I knew the symptoms. It is the concentrated desire to drive the ship home as fast as the winds will blow her, the final phase of 'long voyage syndrome'.

After the sun rose, Roz and I sat at Billy's table with the morning light streaming in, sharing a simple breakfast with the dog. Billy had left for his workshop. It was a good time for a policy discussion.

'You mean, just go straight from here to Annapolis?' Roz asked, as I began to untangle my thoughts. 'That'll mean Oklahoma, then back through Arkansas and Tennessee again. I can't face any more prairie and I hated Tennessee.

'I don't mind riding less far, but I do want to see New Orleans. And what about the Deep South?'

'I thought we could still do most of that, but just step up the pace a bit. You know. Really get stuck in. We don't have to hit the interstates, but the roads south from here look fine, and Texas has a 70mph limit. I bet the highways are smooth. I can't imagine Texans creeping round on crummy tracks.'

'So what would that mean in terms of daily runs?'

She twirled her fork on the edge of her scrambled eggs and I knew what she was thinking.

'It'll be a major dogleg to hack all the way down to El Paso,' I said. 'If we miss that out, go south-east from here instead, then make a straight dive across Texas towards Baton Rouge, we'll be back East before we know it.'

'It would suit me fine to miss out West Texas,' she said slowly. Her fantasies and mine do not always coincide. 'But what's the new deal on daily distance?'

'Three-fifty, maybe 400, perhaps more some days. Take it in stages. We'll be running 60 or 70mph. It won't be so bad.'

I looked closely at her expression. It did not change. Just to make sure we were going to be of one mind I asked,

'How long since you had pain across the shoulders?'

She shrugged. The fact was that we had both hardened up beyond what would have seemed possible when we had worked our careful way across the tight civilisation of Maryland in another life two months before.

'But if you really want to go to West Texas,' Roz said with genuine sympathy. 'I won't stand in the way. Don't miss it for me.'

'I do,' I replied, 'but I've no interest in tearing through it like a man in a video game. I'll come back another day. You never know. Maybe I'll find an easier poker game and clean up. Nothing by chance!'

We spread out the map on the breakfast table. The state line was a short day away, then Texas stretched over the hump of the coffee pot and clear across to the toaster. The place looked huge, but the bikes were full of miles, so I changed their oil and set up their belts. Then we packed the saddlebags, left Billy a 'Thanks, Mate' note and let the Harleys rip.

Steadily losing altitude towards the Texas line, the impact of the country receded from the haunting beauties of northern New Mexico. The mountains fell away behind us and featureless seas of silver grass stretched ahead, but instead of the impression of vastness we experienced on the high plains, some odd feature of this country contracted the views to a minimalist scale. The land was the antithesis of Montana, where the traveller felt almost crushed by the sheer size of the vista. Here, the margins of the grassy world fell away to some unknown dimension beyond the edge so that although the road was as straight as a bullet's flight, nothing seemed to exist beyond the next few fields.

We paused at tiny wooden towns that could not have changed since the 1950s. Even the women serving in the stores were dressed like fashion plates from my mother's *Home-maker* magazines. Some grain had been harvested and cattle flashed by from time to time, flicking their tails in the afternoon. The road wasn't smooth, but it certainly wasn't the worst we'd seen, so although our backsides felt every bump we made good progress. All in all, it was country to pass through fast. Perfect for our new mood.

A few miles short of the border we crossed a bridge which I somehow knew would be my last contact with the railroad. In the distance a train was coming, so I dismounted, jumped the fence and scrambled down the bank to throw myself flat on the ground as I had when I was a schoolboy. Roz pottered slowly on. She knew what I was up to.

In those days it had been steam that was the prime fascination, the smoke belching from the funnel, the six-foot driving wheels pounding to the pumping of the pistons and the shining steel connecting rods, all blurred by speed. Steam has gone from America as it has from Britain, but in the United States, the railroad retains its essential spirit. Perhaps the alchemy stems from the sheer size of the diesel locos, maybe it is the impossible length of the freight trains, or the continental distances travelled. Probably they are all factors, but what grabbed me about this one was the name of the railroad company. In the days when I was having my school cap blown off by the London express, my train books showed images of massive American locomotives. Instead of a prosaic 'LMS' – 'London, Midland and Scottish' – they bore the lyrical 'Atchison, Topeka and Santa Fe'. This giant red locomotive had 'Santa Fe' emblazoned down its sides as it rumbled under my bridge, hustling its standard mile or so of what looked like cattle wagons. I had seen it with my own eyes and so, like Tennyson with his rainbow, the child became father to the man.

I walked back to my bike, ruminating on the unpleasantness of having to grow up, and caught Betty Boop at the Texas border. Roz was lounging on her beside a stark sign with an unequivocal message:

'Don't Mess with Texas!'

I could buy that.

'Drive friendly – the Texan way,' encouraged a second hoarding on the other side of the featureless road. That would suit us too.

Properly encouraged, we plunged ahead.

With the exception of Alaska, the Lone Star State is by far the largest of the Union. Its territory is greater in area than the combined mass of Connecticut, New Hampshire, Vermont, Maine, Massachusetts and the substantial area of New York. The population approaches 15 million humans and, at last count, 13 million head of cattle. We careered across its seven hundred or so miles in two days, stopping only to sleep and eat, with the usual half-hourly rests for rehydration. The roads were as good as we'd hoped, and since we saw almost no traffic we took liberties even with the 70mph limit. Setting off before breakfast, the sun would be a red ball in the low haze ahead of us, with the cotton crops and cattle ranges misty after the cool nights of early September. Countless small oil pumps clanked steadily in the dewy fields. The same deal as Kansas, only more of it.

The towns were generally well-maintained and the whole state presented an air of prosperity and self-confidence, yet it was here that Roz confronted the power of chance. We had just restarted after drinks in the country town of Hico, south-west of Dallas – wide, straight streets, farmers in ten-gallon hats carrying livestock in clean pick-ups, silhouette cowboy ten feet high over a bar door – when we slowed down for a cross-road. It was as well we did, because a truck came hurtling around the corner, shedding a rusty forty-five gallon oil drum as it rattled away. What followed had a horrible air of slow motion. The drum rolled across the street, directly under Roz's front wheel from my perspective. I waited for her to go down, praying that the thing was empty and therefore not weighing half a ton. For what seemed like seconds, drum and bike came together as if magnetised. Roz had frozen momentarily, but suddenly revitalised herself and heaved back hard on her brakes. Her rear wheel locked and blew dirt, but the front kept slowing under control. As the back-end came around to meet her she put her outside foot down. The bike seemed to slide sideways, then stopped as the drum missed her front tyre by a yard. It looked like spectacular riding. She had

341

followed her instincts and they had done exactly the right thing for her. There was nothing to be said, except that it obviously wasn't her time to get hit. Our luck was definitely in for the time being, so we wheeled back to the Coke machine and had another.

Roz recovered from this fright with sterling resilience as we tore along eastwards down the temptingly fast roads. Soon, the open cattle ranges and giant cotton fields gave way to smaller countryside with an almost eerily English feel to it.

'I can't believe I'm in Texas, of all places,' she remarked as we stopped to lean against the creosoted fence of a flowery meadow where uncannily British-looking cows chewed rich cud. Tall trees rustled gently in the summer breeze. All the atmosphere needed was the crack of a cricket ball on the willow bat. Even the morning temperature felt like an English summer's day. But it wasn't. As if ordered up by a script-writer to louse up a lovely scene, a straight-faced deputy pulled up beside us in his big, burbling Chevrolet. That would have been fine on its own. It was the flashing blue lights that spoiled the decor.

The policeman opened his door and climbed slowly to his considerable height. His shoes shone and he clinked gently under the weight of the usual array of homicidal hardware at his belt as he eyed the bikes neutrally. Then he straightened up and turned to me.

'Sir,' he began in a deep drawl, 'five minutes ago I clocked you and the lady at 83mph. I'm not saying it's antisocial, I'm just remindin' you it ain't legal, but before I give you a ticket, you can show me your licence and tell me what kinda plate that is on the black bike.'

'How did I manage to miss seeing him?' I was asking myself, feeling as I always do when busted by a traffic cop – like being hauled up before the headmaster. Even so, I liked the way he made no personal issue out of our speeding. We had been travelling perfectly safely above an arbitrary limit on a straight road with no side turnings and nothing in sight. His job was just to collect the money from anyone careless enough to get caught. I mutely cheered the man for not giving me the hypocritical lecture about the dangers of speed that I received from the last policeman to nail me in the UK. The circumstances had been similar. The difference in attitude worlds apart.

The second remarkable thing about this officer was that he was only the second stranger to comment on my yellow, reflective Dorset number plate during the whole trip. Maybe folks hadn't a clue what it could be and didn't want to appear stupid by asking, but not this clear-thinking policeman. He was about to issue a well-deserved, on-the-spot fine and needed to know what sort of game I was playing.

'It's, er, British, actually,' I stuttered lamely, groping for my driving licence. I knew from ancient experience that the paperwork was going to psyche him out, because unlike the equivalent document carried by an American, a British permit carries no photograph of the licence holder. For all he knew, mine could have belonged to King Kong.

To keep the social side of things moving while I scrabbled through my studded leather saddlebag, I began to explain myself.

'I shipped my own bike over here rather than buying locally. Easier, I suppose. Beats the waiting list for a new Hog. Impossible to re-register. The bureaucracy . . . '

'I could see you was from outta state, but I never heard of a plate like that. Where'd'ya land the bike? Galveston?'

'Baltimore.'

'Well, Goddamn! You ride all that way down here?'

'We came via San Francisco.'

The cop looked hard at me, but he didn't pick up the 'we'. Women who rode Harley-Davidsons 10,000 miles at a sitting were not part of his normal round of experience. He peered down at Roz's Maryland plate and pushed his hat back an inch or so.

'Did you meet this guy locally?' he asked her. 'I mean, you're a helluva long way from home too.'

'I came the same way. We're riding together,' answered Roz.

'What? All the way? With him? You crossed Nevada on that little bike?'

'I'm afraid I did.'

There was a pause and for a moment I thought the deputy was going to ask how a girl with Maryland plates came to have an accent like the Queen of England. Instead, he shook his head, smiled very slightly, and put away his ticket book.

'Welcome to Texas, Ma'am . . . Sir. You all have a good day, and keep it below seventy in this county until I've gone off for lunch.'

He touched his broad hat-brim, folded himself back into the Chevrolet and turned off the blue lights. As he drove off, I listened to the music of his car and was glad we'd behaved. The engine sounded like pure Wagner. Trying to outrun him in anything short of a fighter plane would have been plain foolishness.

We crossed the Sabine River into Louisiana with a thousand or so miles under our belts from Santa Fe. If there had been no signposts, it would still have been impossible to miss the change. All the way from that first vague surprise as we entered Virginia from Maryland, we had noted subtle differences between the various states, but there was nothing subtle here. This was something different altogether. Arriving in Logansport Louisiana on our back road from Texas was more like entering a different country than sampling a change of state. West of the river were ordered fields, neat farms and tightly run communities. Immediately over the bridge, the town huddled around a narrow main street criss-crossed haphazardly by the sort of heavy wires I recalled from newly electrified villages in 1970s South America. The sidewalks were crowded with people, almost all black. Shops were boarded up, and the smart, Texan vehicles were replaced by a diverse selection of boneyard bangers blowing blue smoke.

We stopped for much-needed fuel and were relieved of our cash by two hard-faced white women. When we walked out into the sunshine, the bikes were surrounded by young blacks. Anticipating at least verbal abuse or my gear being tampered with, I shouldered my way through to Black Madonna, gleaming and immaculate amongst the crowd. My unease must have surfaced from some deep-rooted and unexplored fear of finding myself at the wrong end of a colour bar. Whatever its origins, however, the apprehension proved groundless. Instead of grief, the bike was the subject only of admiration, while I was treated to a friendly barrage of good-humoured banter. I struggled to tune in to the sweet, Southern drawl while my own accent was being greeted with open incredulity, but as we mounted up, I suddenly felt totally safe. Freed from social anxieties, it dawned on me that the most startling difference between here and Texas had nothing to do with the human inhabitants; the bugs were back.

I had almost forgotten their impact on the early part of the trip. California had been reasonable in this respect, the deserts had been virtually bug-free, always excepting the scorpions who keep themselves to themselves unless thoroughly annoyed, and although Texas did feature a modest population of honest flies, we both felt that nothing more odious than a bluebottle would dare show its face west of the Sabine.

No sooner had we crossed the bridge than we ran into dense black clouds of what, from the biker's sensitive standpoint, are certainly the world's most disgusting bugs. Not content to burst singularly across your bike, your leathers, your teeth or your air filters, these bugs do it in pairs. Perhaps 'couples' would be a more appropriate description, because they spend their entire day engaged in the most athletic forms of sexual intercourse. After watching them for ten minutes I could imagine the courtship scenario.

'Fancy a bit, Babe?' asks Mr Bug, probably in an Australian accent, as he struts cockily though the dirt.

'Only if you're bug enough for a twelve-hour shag,' retorts Ms Bug, outlining a frighteningly demanding schedule.

'Twelve-hour shag? Nothing to it. Brace yourself, Sheila!'

And with that, he hops aboard. The pair take off, well and truly on the job, then spend their day flying around at low altitude, irretrievably coupled and no doubt having a rare time of it.

Because of this habit they have of public fornication, these essentially nasty creatures are universally known as 'love bugs'. The name is their only saving grace. They were introduced into the Southern states some years ago by a caring authority who had been led to believe they would eat the mosquitoes. A sound plan on the face of things. Unfortunately, the love bugs found something else even more nourishing and tasty than the mozzies, so the original adversary continues to thrive, the love bugs have gone forth and multiplied in the best traditions of Noah, and the human population has to put up with a brand-new pest.

When any normal bug commits hara-kiri on a speeding motorcycle or car windscreen, it makes a bit of a splat and expires, leaving its recognisable remains for the undertakers to remove at the end of the day. Not so the love bug. These little chaps and their mates do not seem to have an outer body casing at all. They spludge themselves into a filthy grey ooze that spreads across an unbelievable area of clean metalwork, windshield, helmet or face. And because of their inexhaustible sexual energy, the innocent biker invariably gets two for the price of one.

As we negotiated the broken road out of Logansport bound in the general direction of Baton Rouge, still 200 miles away, we began to pass cars and trucks coming towards us that were barely recognisable on account of the bugs plastered all over their leading edges. Faces peered through opaque windscreens only partly kept clear by overworked wipers and washers. Every gas station was overflowing with drivers filling their washer bottles and wiping off their lights and screens. What happened to our Harleys almost broke our hearts.

I am realistic when it comes to keeping machinery clean. It's a fine enough thing to maintain your motorcycle immaculately if you never take it anywhere other than the pub, but if you're making a thousand miles and more in an average week, you do your best and don't get too upset by the odd splash of mud. Either that, or your life is a misery. Most evenings I would go over the bikes and shine them up a bit. I enjoyed that. What man with a pair of pliers tucked away somewhere in his soul wouldn't have fun laying hands on two of the loveliest motorcycles he could ever own? And every night I left the windscreens covered with a damp cloth to soak off any bugs that had done themselves to death during the day. This policy paid off and as we roared across Texas, the bikes looked almost as smart as when they'd left Baltimore. Louisiana and the love bugs changed all that.

Within one hour at most from a standing start, my windshield was totally opaque; the forward curves of Madonna's sumptuously painted black tank, with its perfectly executed coach stripe, were spattered all over with grey, acid death; the leading faces of my boots were more bug than black and my chrome and steel engine was merrily baking the fornicating little swine deep into its perfect finish. If anything, Betty Boop was faring even worse because she only had a small windshield of the type ludicrously described in accessory catalogues as a 'fly-screen'. Roz's leather riding jacket was literally soaked in dead love bugs. Her visor was impenetrable to daylight and poor Betty, who surely deserved better, looked ready for the knacker's yard. It was small consolation that the whole population was suffering the same misery.

The imperfect solution was to fuel up every hour and to slosh down the bikes at the same time, giving ourselves a spray-off for good measure. Nobody minded, and we met some nice people in the queues for the water hoses.

'Ain't never seen nuthin' like this before in the way of bugs!'

'You sure have. They was here in early summer too!'

'Yeah? Well, last year they only came once. How come it's twice this time round?'

'Those little guys, they jus' love makin' babies. Perhaps next year they won't stop at all.'

'Step aside there, an' let the lady hose down her bike!'

'How do you stand it, Honey? You poor thing. Why doesn't your man buy a car?' This from a large lady, looking at me as though I were individually responsible for the whole vile show.

'Same way as I do, I suppose,' I butted in, picking a broken head out from between my top teeth.

'Well at leas' it'll teach you to keep your mouth shut!' The woman slapped her huge thigh and laughed. Her chum was even larger and blacker and was showing a magnificent amount of cleavage as she rinsed buckets of water over her ancient Pontiac's windscreen. She winked disgracefully at me and said loudly,

'At least they die happy!' I was so wretched I tried not to see the joke, but the rest of the people waiting about certainly did. The big, healthy-looking lady was quivering like a jelly and I saw that I was suffering from a sense of humour failure.

'Sort of like an airborne snuff movie,' I said, brightening up. The women screamed with mirth.

There was obviously no spare money here, nothing much in the food stores, the supermarkets in the country towns were ill-stocked and the bugs were a serious tribulation. Compared with most Americans we had met, these folks seemed to have plenty to complain about. At least, in theory, they were far more disadvantaged than the Sioux on their Dakota reservation, yet strangely the country people hereabouts seemed to have worked out how to make the best of a poor hand of cards.

We dodged on southwards down a selection of minor roads, but the surface was so bad and the bug cloud so dense that in the end we capitulated to the delights of Interstate 49. The trucks were as awesome as usual and the cars did themselves proud with bad behaviour, but the flying menace definitely backed off. Plenty of them still meandered lecherously around the lower atmosphere, but the turbulence of the traffic seemed to push their adventurous couplings a few feet higher. We could now manage two hours between bug-stops if we had a mind to.

By the time we rolled across the swamps and into Baton Rouge we were exhausted by the heat and humidity, once again growing in volume, and by the sheer nausea of the insect genocide. Now, cruising weightless in the private swimming pool of the excellent hotel I had splashed out on to make up for our grisly day, life began to look almost normal. Palm trees surrounded the blue water, the sun dipped into their green fronds, the love bugs had 'fucked' off and nobody else came for a swim.

'Why did you want to come to Baton Rouge?' I asked Roz, who was floating by sipping a stiff rum and grapefruit juice balanced in a goofy-looking inflatable fish with a tumbler-sized depression where its dorsal fin should have been.

'I can't believe you don't know.'

'Why would I? It's only another hour and a bit to New Orleans. We could have eaten another sixty minutes' worth of insects and made the trip in one. I think I'm getting so punch drunk I never thought to ask.'

'I'm picking up your trick of hanging on to some stupid irrelevance that happens to grab me.'

'So what is it?'

'*Busted flat in Baton Rouge, waiting for a train.*
Feelin' just as faded as my jeans,
Bobby thumbed a diesel down just before it rained . . . '
'*Took us all the way to New Orleans.*' I finished the snatch of song. Janis Joplin and 'Bobby Magee'. It showed how little I knew my wife. I thought it was only me that travelled with inner music rattling my brain. And Janis Joplin of all people. The final word in wild rockers . . .

Roz took a long pull at her rum and said, 'I'm going to hit that highway past Lake Ponchartrain tomorrow with Janis on my buddy seat all the way. She knew how to live, and she found out how to die.'

Alone in a sorry hotel room, I remembered, head full of God knew what. But what a woman! With her cracked-up, passionate voice calling from the bottom of the pit, she'd never taken her foot off life's gas pedal; just kept it hard down on the floorboards until her tanks ran dry.

Over dinner, we talked about how to get the best out of a short stay in New Orleans. The danger was going to be a concentrated attack of tourism because we knew nobody in town to steer us to the right places. Basin Street in the French Quarter, some say the birthplace of jazz, could hardly have survived the onslaught of quick money to be made on the back of its fame. Yet there was no way of knowing where else to head for, and so when the sun rose out of the pollution haze of Baton Rouge we crammed on our gear, made space for Janis, then booted the bikes into gear and disappeared towards Lake Ponchartrain.

The outskirts of the 'Big Easy' were pretty much like any other American city, but the French Quarter, which we found without difficulty, was all it was cracked up to be, at least in terms of its architecture. Although looking ahead to Georgia and Joe, an old friend whose home we had never yet visited, we resolved to treat ourselves to a good lunch, then find a music club much later before turning in for the night. No hurry the following morning. We'd be fresh and fit for the long hard bash through the Deep South.

By now, we had become so immured to extremes of heat that the ninety-five degrees of a September New Orleans noontime didn't hurt at all. In our grandly seedy room, we shook out our best kit and strolled into the sunshine and shadow of Basin Street. Entranced, we explored the chequerboard that was once the New Orleans of the jazz pioneers and the steamboat card sharps. The uniquely French–American streets with their wrought-iron balconies, pillars, shutters and carved barge-boards reminded us more of Martinique than the USA. A background smell of drains mingling with fruit past its prime was faint enough to give the place an exciting, tropical air. Bars on discreet, first-floor levels served exotic drinks while restaurants spilling spicy aromas out on to the sidewalks vied for our custom.

We seated ourselves at a table with a snowy, white-on-white cloth, chunky silverware and two groups of crystal glasses, carefully haphazard, that promised nothing but the best. Lunching around us were business people. Sharp-looking men and snappily dressed women, some bent on mutual seduction, others on a deal that might just beat working for a living. Mostly it looked like both.

Our meal was the best of the whole trip. Creole seafood and wine from the section of the list where I normally avert my eyes. You would have done well to beat the victuals in Paris or Dublin, and the service from our waiter, clad in smartly casual pale orange and blue, was from life's carefully understated top drawer.

Satisfied and slightly woozy, we wandered back to our room around the corner. There, we made love on the squeaky iron four-poster, mainly because we felt like it, but also in memory of the itinerant gamblers and saloon girls, sailors and whores, and perhaps the occasional pair of nervous newly-weds who must have been doing the same here for a century or more. The hotel was shaded by trees on the street edge and as we lay back on the crisp cotton sheets, totally relaxed for the first time since Billy's place, a jiggling wicker fan wafted cool air across our bodies. I took a cold shower, dabbed myself half-dry, then lay down again on my towel. The slow turning whirligig evaporating the last of the water was bliss – perhaps not so efficient or long lasting as air-conditioning, but twice as sensual, less noisy and virtually free. I gazed up at the mature cracks in the plastered, European style ceiling and deliberated on what wondrous patterns the room's army of ghosts might have made out of their meanderings.

Roz, who never sleeps in the daytime, had given up the struggle to stay awake, so I let go and joined her in the Land of Nod, thinking as I faded out that the siesta is the natural submission to the body's demands in a hot climate. For a minute or two, a fault in the ceiling reminded me of a trombone slide, then I was gone. Tonight, we would be ready for anything.

Sadly, but perhaps not surprisingly, our night on the town in New Orleans proved a wretched let-down after a perfect afternoon. So far, we had been impressed with the way New Orleans caters for its inevitable tourist trade without losing its essential integrity. People who served us in bars were pleasant, men who admired the bikes were straightforward, the guys hustling custom for the burro-drawn carriages were polite, even when we said no, and the quaint buildings themselves had not been desecrated by glitz. All in all, the daytime city had seemed a class act. Walking the late evening streets in search of music, however, we noticed immediately that the tourist factor had risen by several hundred per cent. Instead of black guys wearing two-coloured shoes and slouch hats hurrying from one gig to the next, a procession of undercooked white people trooped by like walking invitations to a communal mugging. We tried our luck for a tune in a number of likely-looking establishments, only to be served canned music and at last discovered our nemesis in the tragedy that is The Preservation Hall. Here, one barman assured us, we would discover the Real Thing. By this time, we had concluded that this had probably taken wings for some other part of town many years ago, but since it was his advice or nothing, and the name had the right ring to it, we gave it a go.

Our first impression of The Preservation Hall indicated that it was either not a large room or was massively oversubscribed, because a long queue of tourists was lined up outside the lobby. Loud brass instrument noises were emanating from inside as we teamed up with an Australian visitor to give some weight to our stance against a bossy German tour guide.

'It is proper you stand aside, please,' she ordered irrelevantly, attempting to shove the three of us out of her way.

'Why's that, Sweetheart?' asked the Aussie in a voice that reminded me of my imaginary love bug.

'What is this 'Sweetheart'? You must move because my group must be walking in to see the jazz.'

'But they're all behind me and this lady and gent here.'

'Ah, but we have come all the way from Germany,' she announced triumphantly and elbowed him aside. She had picked the wrong victim.

'You can take them back to the Rhine right now for all I care,' said the diplomat from Oz, lifting her firmly by the shoulders and replacing her behind us in the line. 'We're here first, and that's where we stay.' He then proved himself a thorough gentleman by ironically raising his hat, which was as 'cobber' as his accent.

Before we could get to know the man from the outback better, the racket from inside the hall petered out and there seemed to be some general inward movement of our group of hopefuls. Making sure the representatives of the Fatherland stayed in their proper place, we trooped into the lobby to be relieved of four dollars each. Only then were we allowed to enter the Holy of Holies.

Inside, we were offered a scene of human degradation unequalled throughout all my American travels. My heart sank as I noticed large signs prohibiting more or less everything other than breathing. The ban on video cameras and flash guns I could perhaps understand, but when I saw a prominent 'No Smoking' sign, I knew we had been had. Big time.

The hall itself was everything a jazz dive ought to be. Perhaps fifty feet square, it had clearly remained undecorated and even undusted for a very long time. The light was low and the colour of the walls just right, although how the nicotine patina had been achieved in this sterile atmosphere was obscure. Perhaps it had happened long ago in a glorious past. But it was the band that put the final cap on an awful experience. The only good thing about them was that their efforts must even have hurt the ears of the German guide.

The tourists stood in rows, bemused, as the band unimaginatively and tunelessly struck up 'Hello Dolly', the number with which I shall one day be played down to Hades. The trumpeter we had heard from outside was having major problems with his lip. The trombonist had talent but was hamming it up so much that he simply had to be taking the piss. The piano was not just pleasantly jangly, it was unforgivably out of tune, and the bassist looked as if he'd have been happier back home watching the ball-game on television.

After fifteen minutes of this mind-numbing mediocrity, our group of sufferers was ushered out into the street through a door opposite the entry lobby. As we filed out, having been given our glimpse of the True Cross, the band nipped out the back for a smoke while a fresh bunch of suckers were herded in at the other end.

Croc. Dundee shook his head in despair.

'What is it with this country?' he said to me, still side-stepping creatively to ensure that Brunhilde remained behind him. 'They've got the best jazz in the world somewhere here and they offer us this insult.'

'I suppose if we knew the right people we could find the right joints to drink in,' I suggested.

'That's going to be true anywhere,' he retorted, 'but I flew into Dallas a fortnight ago and I've been driving around looking at all the places I've heard about all my life. And the buggers do it every time. They stuff it up. Let me tell you about Dodge City . . . '

I glanced at Roz and saw her eyes look to Heaven. She knew I had found a soulmate and given half a chance would spend the night raving about the insult of tourism both to the gawper and the gawped at. Somehow, she manoeuvred the pair of us into a small bar and bought us a whiskey to take our minds off the wretched affair. We left Mr Dundee subsiding, but still swearing he'd knife the next cynic who tried to shove tourist trash between him and the reality of America.

As we sagged off down a near-deserted Royal Street we stopped to hear a busker in a shop doorway playing the blues on a flat-top guitar using a bottleneck on the frets. The guy had talent, technical ability and originality. I tipped him generously and we walked home to our four poster, sad in the end only because after an experience sick beyond the telling, Dundee had missed the Real Thing at 'last orders'.

chapter twenty-one

crazy and cool in the deep south-east

Some years ago, I had a sailing contract in San Francisco. Among a variety of seafaring professionals from all over the US, one of my shipmates was Joe, a thoroughly Americanised man of action from what were once the Soviet Baltic States. Joe runs a sailing school at Darien in the Georgia swamp country and it was towards him that we now turned as we throbbed across a steamy Mississippi State and on through the far south of Alabama. Here were none of the Third World features we had found so striking in up-state Louisiana except for the loathsome love bugs, which continued to make riding a filthy 'stop-go' business all the way to Charleston, South Carolina.

No doubt Alabama was hiding her down-market zones somewhere else, but as we flashed through at speed limit velocity, we seemed to be in romantic *Gone With the Wind* country, with colonnaded mansions peeping out from prosperous plantations and groves of live-oak trees deeply draped with Spanish moss. Plenty of all-American cars rumbled down our route in these latitudes, often in first-class order, driven by Southerners enjoying being exactly who they were. Patriotic ensigns flew bravely from homesteads, many of which supported the starred blue cross on a blood-red ground of the Confederacy. Several times, we parked beside bikes and cars with Confederate flags beautifully painted on their tanks and bonnets. A powerful gesture, but at this stage of the trip there was no time left to dig into the subtleties of what it means in the modern-day USA. One thing was sure, however. The good manners to strangers we had encountered, with few exceptions, throughout the mainstream of society came to the forefront here. The 'Southern gentleman', be he farmer, businessman, skipper or garage mechanic is alive and well from New Orleans up to the Chesapeake Bay.

Georgia, which specialises in such paragons, has a comparatively short coastline. The small town of Darien falls about dead centre. As we arrived out of the forest, we were still well short of the sea and it became obvious that, like many of the state's secondary ports, it has developed some distance up-river. A lightweight, tasteful commercial strip of small, wooden business buildings lined a road through tall, long-leaf pines as we searched for the turn-off to Joe's dock. His directions proved admirably seamanlike, and soon we were bouncing down a woodland track. After a mile or two it opened on to a broad panorama of low-lying, green islands and swamp that wavered in the distance as the midday sea breeze kicked in to stir the hot, stagnant air.

I had no idea what to expect from Joe's establishment because many American sailing academies, like David's in California, represent major investments. Others are 'hometown', specialising mainly in local customers. The off-lying islands provided plenty of shelter around Joe's place, which was well-sited for learners, but it clearly hadn't helped him much recently. The small school with its classroom building, boat stores and mooring pontoons looked as if it had just been hit by a hurricane. Which, in fact, it had been.

Even from the driveway it was obvious that Joe had seen to his priorities. Dangling fifteen feet up from the launching crane hung a large motorcycle. It was undamaged, as were one or two of the yachts that must have been hauled out before the storm surge arrived. The sheds and the rest of the floating stock had taken a severe beating.

Joe heard the clatter of the Harleys and came walking towards us, hand outstretched. Above middle height, dark hair thinning a little and grey at the outsides of his beard, still strongly built in his fifties, he wore working pants and, incongruously, a blue pinstriped business shirt open on to a tanned neck. I congratulated him on saving his motorcycle from the mayhem. He smiled ruefully, was introduced to Roz, then led us into a blown-out kitchen.

'Three hurricanes in two years, I've had,' he said, brewing up a pot of European-strength coffee. 'Each time I get sorted, the weather just blasts the shit out of me again. This one passed close offshore on its way up to Carolina ten days ago. Blew ninety knots. The surge lifted my pontoon clear up the bank.'

It was three years since we'd met, and I'd forgotten that any traces of his Eastern European origins had vanished from his Southern accent. I'd been fascinated to see his spread ever since he told me that things were so 'back to nature' that some mornings he had to chase the alligators off the docks before the customers arrived.

'Depresses the life out of the students to see those hungry motherfuckers sunning themselves beside the boats,' he'd said. I hadn't been able to work out if he was joking or not. Now I saw he wasn't. The place was as near as you could get to jungle in continental USA.

A combination of storm damage and the resultant temporary dip in the local economy meant that today Joe had no takers. After we had shared a sandwich and more coffee he suggested taking one of his remaining whole boats out for a sail around the rivers inside Blackbeard Island. This nature reserve was named for the most famous pirate of them all, Edward Teach, who had plied a lively trade here, terrorising his victims by boarding their ships with his huge inky whiskers apparently blazing from sticks of 'slow match'. I could imagine Joe as his first mate.

As we sailed the inlets in Joe's lively little day boat, I was struck by how alike, yet at the same time how totally dissimilar, the waterways were to the Norfolk Broads where I had learned to sail thirty-five years earlier. The swaying reed beds were pure East Anglia; the heat was tropical. A lone fisherman angling from a drifting punt could have been floating down from Norwich on a Sunday afternoon, but the occasional thrashings at the riverbank, as some monstrous reptile tucked in to its luncheon, were more like the upper Nile or darkest Queensland. The tang of the salt wind over the marshes was a memory of Horsey Mere, but the ever-increasing howl of the mosquito squadrons as the sun dipped towards golden evening could only have been North America again.

One more time, I found myself speculating on the extent of the horror of this low-flying hazard to the first English-speaking Georgians, arriving innocently from relatively bug-free Britain. Living precariously huddled together in a wooden fort, under siege from the insects, they also had to repel organised Spanish raids from across an ill-defined and disputed border with Florida. The death rate was high. A few succumbed to enemy action, but far more gave up the ghost in the face of the diseases rampaging before modern medicine and clean drinking water. Some of these were insect-carried and there is no shortage of evidence to confirm that flying bug activity was at least as great in previous centuries as it is now. When a late August hurricane drove a pair of pilot schooners far up into the marshes in 1881, even the hard-bitten local contractor hired to extricate them commented on the bloodthirsty clouds of bugs. Since the blow, he stated, their numbers and virulence had made it intolerable to live anywhere near the marshes and virtually impossible to survive out on the sedge. For some reason, the general disorganisation of nature caused by a storm and its associated tidal wave has always encouraged massive mosquito activity.

As the evening fell, the wind died earlier than expected. We were without engine power, so it was dark as we drifted home on the tide in a calm interrupted only by a zillion insects, a million frogs and the occasional splash of something more sinister deep in the reeds. A monstrous yellow moon rose through the live-oaks, giving the Spanish moss an ethereal look, but it was not yet high enough to illuminate the dock as Joe asked Roz to hop ashore with a line.

'What if there's an alligator drying his feet on the woodwork?' she asked.

'Take the spinnaker pole with you,' he advised, referring to a six-foot length of aluminium extrusion. 'If you see any shadows, give them a shove around about midships with the business end. They thrash around a bit, but generally they slither off. Works most times.'

'What happens when it doesn't?'

'Often wondered that myself. You stay put, Ma'am, and I'll step off.'

Like a knight of old, Joe picked up the gleaming lance and, as I steered the boat, he hopped nimbly on to the darkened jetty. A few seconds later we were secure with nothing heavier on the dock than a king-size cockroach taking a late evening *paseo*.

We locked up the bikes and drove to the house of Joe's girlfriend, Gwynne, in an ancient Cadillac hearse which Joe and his mates used to trail their boats to regattas. At the top of the windshield, where a less imaginative owner might have inscribed his name and that of his loved one – 'Sid and Joline' – Joe had contrived the legend, 'Stiff Competition'. I doubted whether many of his rivals had seen the joke.

Gwynne's house was a wooden antebellum classic in a shady square. Joe and Gwynne were half-way through the restoration, but they had begun as lovers should, with the front bedroom. Selflessly, they gave this treasure up to us and slept goodness knows where.

'How do you come to be in the US, Joe?' asked Roz over a barbecue dinner.

'I'm an American, that's how!' he answered without cracking a smile.

'I thought Tom said you were originally from Latvia or one of those Baltic States.'

'Lithuania was my home.'

'Were your family economic migrants?'

Joe smiled.

'I don't think you'd quite put it like that,' he said slowly. 'I came out of there in circumstances you might call awkward. It was in the early sixties and after I'd seen my uncle and cousins shot by the Communists for not toeing the political line, I decided that I had to get back at them somehow. So I escaped and came to the Land of the Free.

'I signed up for Vietnam as soon as I could. There were plenty of folks over here didn't like that war, but I had a different perspective. I knew what we were fighting for. I'd seen it and I'd felt it. They hadn't.

'I did OK out there, and when it was all over I found myself on a civilian plane back to California looking after a young officer in a wheelchair who'd gotten himself shot full of holes. We're in the immigration line with our uniforms and campaign medals and all, and I need to take a leak. So I leave him and go off. When I come back five minutes later, there's all these draft-dodging bastards slapping the poor guy around, calling him a 'baby-burner' and a 'rapist'. I couldn't take that. The boy had bled for his country, right or wrong, and these people weren't fit to wipe his nose, so I laid into them.'

'How many were there?' I asked.

'Maybe four or five, but I was combat-hardened. I'd been at war for years. I don't know where they'd been. I had three of them on the floor when the cops dragged me off and the next thing you know I'm in the cooler.'

'I can't believe that didn't put you off America,' said Roz.

'No, Ma'am. It didn't put me off. Every country's going to have bad apples, and I knew how little almost everyone understood about the Commie business. Anyhow, I left the military then and became a civilian. Land was cheap over here and I bought my place and set up my little business. It ain't flash but, Jesus, Georgia's a great place to settle. Low bullshit factor hereabouts.'

'How do you mean?'

'I'll show you tomorrow night at the restaurant.'

Far down by the deepest swamp in town was a rickety shack that had survived the storm against all the odds. Outside stretched the night-time marshes where the mysteries of life and death were unfolding in secret. Inside, it was heaving with people.

'Hiya, Joe! Howyah doin'?' the barman greeted our host, hustling us to a prime site from where Joe could hold court to as many fellow diners as possible.

'I like this place,' he said as we scrabbled our chairs up to the rough wooden table, 'but it ain't what it used to be.'

'Nowhere ever is,' said Gwynne, an interior designer, 'but anything would have been an improvement.'

'I'm not talking about the decor,' said Joe. 'The food's so good nobody cares about that anyway. What I'm saying is that folks miss the animals they used to have in cages round the outsides. They had lions and tigers and all sorts. The big ones could stare in at the people eatin'. There was a hairy gorilla too, but he escaped.'

'What, at dinnertime?' I blurted.

'It was getting on to closing-up time,' replied Joe in a matter-of-fact sort of way. 'The boss said he just smashed his way out of his cage, took one look at the menu and marched clear out into the woods. Nobody ever saw him again. But that was nothing to the pair of chimps they had. Used to dress 'em up in dinner jacket and black tie and sit 'em down at table in the corner. Regular customers used to buy them drinks.'

'I just don't believe half the stuff you come out with,' said Gwynne, 'but you did get it right when you told that journalist our ex-sheriff wasn't so bad as some folks made out.'

'That made me sick, the way they was missing the point,' Joe was saying as the waitress came to take our order. No endless list of 'specials' here. Just the best seafood money could buy, beer, water, and a short wine list for those of the avant-garde who really wanted it. We ordered oysters, flounder and Becks.

'What was it with the sheriff?' I asked, curious that Joe should side with law and order after his experience in San Francisco.

'Somebody wrote a book that concerned him,' interrupted a beefy, red-faced character on the next table. There was no protocol here about privacy of conversation, and Joe did have a rather loud voice. 'It was one of those modern piles of rubbish. Said he was a nigger-hater, and so on. I don't know about who he hated and who he didn't, but he sure kept order round here.'

'He was some mean-lookin' man, Chip,' began Joe, but he had met his match in our neighbour.

'Tall as a stick, he was, and twice as thin,' continued Chip, now holding centre stage. 'But he was a wiry sonofabitch. Nobody messed with him more 'n once. You remember that hole he had in his ear, Joe?'

'Guess he was more hole than ear on that side,' put in Mrs Chip.

'How'd he get that?' asked Gwynne.

'I tell you,' said Chip, almost choking on a giant shrimp in his excitement, 'that was some front-off. The sheriff was face to face with this massive Negro with a .38 special who was threatening to blow his brains round the bar-room. I don't know what the sheriff ever did to this guy but his face is all screwed up with hate and his eyes are standin' out. Sheriff tries to stare him down – he can't pull his own iron in case the guy really does spread him all over the sight glasses. They stay there like that for, God knows, it seemed like minutes but I guess it was mebbe ten seconds, then the sheriff says, "Go on then, let me have it if you're goin' to do it." 'Course, nobody expected him to fire, but that's what he did. The guy shot the sheriff, but his hand was shaking so much he almost missed. Didn't put a hole in his head, he blew his ear off it instead.'

'Why didn't he finish the job?' asked Gwynne. Roz and I were sitting open-mouthed at this tale, which was clearly true or, if apocryphal, at least generally accepted, because the folks on the other neighbouring tables were all turning around nodding, waving beer glasses and generally making 'I-was-there-too' noises.

'I think he was so shocked, he ran out of nerve,' Chip replied, 'but the sheriff didn't falter. There's blood pouring out, but his eyes never left that black guy's face. He walks up to him, he holds out his hand for the gun and the guy passes it to him.'

'An' that wasn't the end of it,' put in a middle-aged woman who had mooched over from the bar and was leaning on our table. 'After that, the blacks all thought he was a zombie and they was scared out of their lives every time he showed up. I guess the doc sewed up what was left of his ear,' she added, ''cause after a year or so it wasn't too awful. Always looked ugly to the end, but you didn't mind that, cause of how he was. A real man.'

'He ran this town for nearly fifty years,' said Joe, finally squeezing in a word to finish his own story. 'I guess people stood against him sometimes, but he always got re-elected. And when he finally died, 380 cars followed his funeral procession.'

'Good thing for you he wasn't here that night you showed up with the 'gator in your station wagon!' said the lady, anxious to keep a lively conversation going. I gulped down an iced oyster and asked myself what under heaven was coming next.

Joe hadn't touched his flounder, but he was having an even better time remembering grand old days. Gwynne looked at him with a mixture of despair and motherly love, which struck me as philosophical. She must have been a full twenty years his junior.

'I think folks imagined I was out to make mischief that night,' Joe said with a low chuckle. 'But the truth was that I ran over that alligator just down the track. He was lying across it right on the bend by the pond and I was going too fast to stop. I got down to see how things stood and the guy with me says, "He's good and dead, Joe. If we sling him inside, mebbe we can sell him for skin, or steaks, or something." We'd had a beer or two and that sounded fine to me, so we heave him up through the tailgate and drive on here. We have a beer or two, then we go out to the car. I'm backin' out and suddenly there's this noise like wet sandpaper. Then there's snapping and gnashing teeth, so I look over my shoulder. It's pretty dark, but I can see the sonofabitch grinning at me from the rear seat. He's no more dead than you or me.

'We were out of that wagon fast, I can tell you, because I hadn't got my gun and the only safe action was to shoot that sucker. So we shut him in and high-tailed it for the bar for some sort of heavy firearm. Peashooter wouldn't be any use, 'cause this was a full-grown beast.'

'I recall that night,' put in the barman. 'You come in here looking like you'd seen Blackbeard himself, shouting about needing a weapon. Not many folks had brought theirs with them into the restaurant and I was keeping mine where it stays, but there was this girl . . . '

'I'll never forget her,' cried Chip, clambering back into the action. 'She had blonde hair and a figure like Mae West. We never saw her before or since. Cool as you like, she opens up her pocketbook and pulls out this machine pistol. "Will this do?" she says, and Joe grabs it like it's a rope for a drowning sailor. Then you was out the bar. I'll never forget it. The 'gator's going berserk inside your car, but every time you open the door for him to step out and get shot, he goes quiet. Not stupid, I thought.

'In the end, he comes flopping out all of a sudden, crashes into you and you drop the gun. He takes a snap at you and you jump up on the roof of some fancy convertible and it caves in. The other guy grabs the gun and unloads it into the alligator. I guess everyone was satisfied 'cept the poor ol' beast and the owner of that convertible . . . '

Some hours after this riotous interchange, Joe and I were drinking a nightcap in the other restored room in Gwynne's house, the front parlour. The ladies had retired at least two whiskeys earlier, when Joe's black-and-white cat Hebe, the feline equivalent of the late sheriff, padded around the finely panelled door and hopped up on to his lap.

Quietly, Joe began to sing 'Old Man River' in a rich baritone. For a while, the tomcat sat purring peacefully, then, as Joe reached the climax of 'You and me, we sweat and strain . . . ' Hebe began to make a strange sound in his throat. When we arrived at 'some plant 'taters and some plants cotton, and them that plants 'em is soon forgotten . . . ' Hebe was crooning in tune and singing along with Joe. I couldn't take any more. The swamplands of Georgia were a world where it seemed absolutely anything was possible. As man and cat rounded into their final cadence of 'Ol' Man River, he jus' keeps rolling along,' I slugged back my Jack Daniel's, shook Joe's hand and staggered off to the sanity of dreamland.

Leaving Joe, Gwynne, Chip and the ghost of the sheriff to manage as best they could without us, the road to journey's end from Georgia carried an ever-increasing sense of return to civilisation as we knew it. The riding posed little problem except for the rising density of the traffic. I watched with satisfaction how Roz and Betty Boop were now loping through it.

In a sense, whether Roz was enjoying the bike or not didn't matter any more. Short of some bad accident, we were going to make it and she'd have achieved what she set herself. Ironically, something had triggered a latent biker instinct back there in the deserts, because she was at last revelling in the power of the Harley. Betty had done her stuff and so had her rider, despite all the doubts from others about the bike and from Roz about herself. Nobody ever queried Black Madonna. She had been born to the task, but I too was drawing a good deal of job satisfaction out of the eastern air as the love bugs thinned towards Charleston. They finally disappeared at Shem Creek, sometime home of the Hungry Neck Yacht Club, where Ambrosio had given me the Ozarks' music tape and Ricky once lived in his pink Cadillac.

As we crossed the bridge we remembered so well, I noted with relief that the storm seemed to have passed Charleston well offshore. We rode through the familiar streets of pretty clapboard homes and even recognised the mailbox through whose rusty lid I had kept my parents informed of a filtered version of our affairs before e-mail or fax were thought of. It was only when we swung down alongside what had once been the old boatyard that I realised things had changed. The sheds were gone, and so were the boat hoist and the slow-moving, happy-go-lucky black work-force. There were no shrimp-boats and instead of the pilings where the smart yachts had once rubbed shoulders with us and the no-hopers, we found smart lawns and a block of condominiums with a carved wooden sign picked out in gold, 'The Boatyard'.

We hadn't really expected things to remain as they were, assuming, probably correctly, that old Charlie the owner finally took a developer's offer for his prime chunk of waterfront property and retired. I allowed myself a laugh at the fantasy of Suzie acting for him, then tried to imagine where all the bums and the longshoremen and the hobos had gone when the construction gangs moved in to clean the place up. The yachts would have been OK. They'd have found a newer, slicker deal at the municipal marina over in Charleston. Perhaps a few of their owners missed the smell of the boiling shrimp and the ringing sound of the caulker's hammer, but most of them probably didn't. The hippies, the fishermen, the Robin Hoods and the itinerant engineers had been blown to the four winds by the marching armies of progress.

We didn't linger. Nothing lasts forever, and very little that man has touched stays the same for more than a few years, especially in the youthful land of America. After so long in the heat of the central continent, Charleston reminded us that we were starved of the sea, so although Annapolis still lay two days ahead, we booted the bikes into gear and opted to take a minor diversion from the osprey's flight, following the coast instead. We hugged as close as we could to the great Waccamaw River with its untouched cypress swamps running parallel with the ocean, then we skirted the shoreline to pass close to the big Capes of North Carolina; Cape Fear, Lookout and Hatteras. The last of these is the most famous. Mother of shoal waters, breeding ground for depressions and bowstring of the vicious summer fronts that sweep up the shoreline with sixty-knot squall lines, Hatteras floats at the top right-hand corner of the string of sandy islands known as the Outer Banks. Soon, we would take the ferry to the first of these with a usable road, but before we got there, we were obliged to pass inside Cape Fear with its ocean inlet, and the city of Wilmington.

Wilmington had taken the full hit of the hurricane that had bounced off Darien. It is also the home base of the American family who adopted Roz and I when we landed in 1976, two bronzed young kids three weeks out from the Virgin Islands. The boat was tired and so were we. Our engine had been defunct for twelve months and I had broken two ribs in a squall north of Cuba. We had almost no money when John and Thérèse Roberts took us under their wing. They scooped us up in their truck and gave us a five-day holiday into the Appalachians for no other reason than to share their country with us.

At that time, we were, in a sense, living their dream. Not wealthy people, they had bought a small boat to experiment with living aboard. John had made up his mind to retire early from his engineering job so that he and Thérèse could spend their late fifties cruising the Bahamas. It took some time, but one day they sold the home that had seen four children raised, and sailed away. It might seem odd to some that a couple from up-state North Carolina should want to go to sea, but John was the first to explain to me that America is a travelling nation.

Times had been tight as they brought up their family. No fancy RV for them, but he was burning to see the West, so he'd built a wooden house on the back of his pick-up and fitted it out so they could all find shelter.

'OK, Kids, Let's Go!' he roused the children one summer's morning, and away they went, christening the vehicle 'Lesgo' before they had reached the town limit.

Lesgo made many land voyages and John remembers them all. His boats have been called by the same name and when his sailing days were done and his boat money reinvested in a full-blown modern RV, that too sported the familiar 'handle'. John and Thérèse now live on the highways of the United States, but they can always be reached through their children. Stopping by a roadside payphone, I called up their elder daughter on the off-chance that the telephone lines were up again.

'Tom, you're in luck,' the Southern Belle voice came clear down the handset. 'John and Thérèse are right here in town. They're seeing to old friends who live out on the beach. Their home got flattened.'

'How about yourselves?'

'We've been lucky. Just lost a tree and a few shingles. Get yourselves down there and find the folks. Pop'll kill you if you don't. They got plenty of space for you to sleep.' I scratched directions on the back of an old parking ticket and we altered course for Devastation Alley.

Passing through storm-shattered Wilmington to find the RV parked up behind a ravaged cinema complex, it was impossible not to contrast the Roberts family with some of the crazy characters a few hundred miles down the coast. Full of wry humour, intelligently aware of the world situation, the

Roberts tribe tend to take mid-line careers, yet they would not know how to be boring. Politically far removed from the often alarming 'my country right-or-wrong' position so common in the US, they nevertheless represent the real strength of America.

After a loud reunion and the best sleep of the trip, Roz and Thérèse updated recent family history while John and I walked down to look at the beaches.

It seemed we had followed the hurricane up the coast and, just as in Georgia, it was ten days since it ran over the town. While trees were still down across roads, the emergency services had made good most of the utilities essential to life on US earth. Linemen were hanging off poles re-rigging power and phone systems, while the fire brigade were on overtime pumping out cellars. The general impression was one of returning order. It was only as we approached the ocean edge that we saw what a hurricane can really do.

East Coast beach villages are built on or immediately behind the first line of sand dunes. The dunes are often only a few feet high and the buildings are fearfully vulnerable, yet such is the optimism or, some might say, stupidity, of those who choose to live there, that hurricane statistics are essentially ignored from the Carolinas down to southern Florida.

The communities are largely leisure oriented, with second homes, gift shops, restaurants and all the paraphernalia of seaside vacations. To someone who has never visited an active war zone, the sight that presented itself as we drove into this neighbourhood was mind-bending. All the streets were choked with sand. Many were impassable. Police cordons were everywhere, but we managed to approach the front line. Here on the ocean, every house had been either flattened or appeared to have suffered the effects of some distant nuclear explosion. Windows had become ancient history. Whole roofs had simply disappeared. Others were draped over the ruins of homes or businesses across the street. Looking into the rubble, any still usable furniture or appliances had been removed already to frustrate looters. Cars were up-ended or lay with doors open, half-filled with sand.

The devastation was best summed up by a gas station, whose office had gone altogether, leaving only its foundation and a few ripped-out electric wires disappearing underground like frozen multicoloured snakes. One pump still stood, as though ready to dispense premium unleaded to the sports car that sat forlornly hoodless beside it. The rest were torn up and lying at crazy angles. The most impressive single item was the canopy which had once provided shade in summer and shelter from any normal storm. This hefty erection bearing the logo of a well-known oil company had been supported by two massive steel stanchions which now were bent over like sticks of liquorice so that the canopy itself was touching the ground at an angle of beyond ninety degrees.

'Kinda makes you think, don't it,' said John in his easy Southern drawl.

'The folks have all gone by the time the storm hits, of course, but once that wave's been through, she don't leave much for when they come home.'

He poured me coffee from a Thermos into a plastic cup.

'You have natural forces at work here that people in Britain can't begin to imagine,' I said to John. 'You build a city, you call it San Francisco, then an earthquake flattens it. So you build it again and another 'quake dumps half the Bay Bridge into the sea, complete with cars, trucks and people. This summer, Roz and I have seen rain like we never knew existed, and now this . . . '

'We're the most powerful nation the Earth has ever known,' John said, 'but this beach reminds you that the whole thing is just a house of cards. And even if it don't get blown away, the country's changin' at some rate these days. When me and Thérèse came back from a few years in the islands, we were so shocked at how the dollar was takin' over from family values that we almost turned right round and went back again.'

'It's not only here, John.'

'I ain't a world traveller, but I know my own country. Right now I'm not proud of it, but I'm proud of my family. We're not greedy, we don't go round lyin' to people and thank the Lord none of us has gotten involved in a serious lawsuit. But I guess that's just a matter of time.'

I couldn't argue with that. I'd only lived here for a total of perhaps three years, and I'd already managed it. Sipping my thin, black, American coffee, I told John about what we'd seen at Shem Creek.

'I've been trying to package up how it made me feel,' I said. 'All I could think was that, somehow, the youth of the growing country is buried under those condos they've built over the boatyard at Shem Creek. What's left is a confident middle age, but it's not what America ought to be about. Now I'm not so sure if it's America's youth or my own that's down there.'

'Only history will tell us that, and by the time any worthwhile perspective has come about, we'll both be long dead. So never mind trying to work stuff out. How's the trip been, buddy? How's it really been?'

I thought hard.

'John, it's the best thing I ever did in my whole life. It's been like a long ocean passage with all those kind of satisfactions, with the added factor of people to meet all the way.'

'And what do you think of the American people now?'

I recalled the rednecks, the muggers, the dope dealers, the bent cop, the 'great country' and the phantom desperadoes always lying in wait across the next state line but one. Then I remembered the essential fairness and straightforward kindness of the silent majority, as fresh this morning as it had been when first I flew into New York in 1967.

'John,' I replied, 'this country's so huge and complex that it's beyond anybody's power to give a simple answer to that question. But you once told me that a man should only speak as he finds. It's windy out there, but the roots are still well set.' I smiled. 'You haven't as much to worry about as you may think.'

epilogue

the last lap

The Harleys gave all they had on the last frenzied ride up the sandbar of the Outer Banks, inshore of the sugar-stick lighthouse of Hatteras. We roared by Kitty Hawk beach where the Wright Brothers had momentously defied gravity, across the giant bridge north of Albemarle Sound and on up to Newport News, then 'hard-assed' it into Maryland. The place still looked like a park.

Pulling up outside the plate glass front of Harley-Davidson of Annapolis was a major high for both of us, particularly Roz. Apart from a postcard from Sturgis, the crowd at the dealership had no idea how far Betty Boop, the 883 Sportster, had managed to go. We'd been out of their consciousness for three months, doing what many of their customers wished their lives away for, running the long highway on what I now had no doubt were the best bikes for the job. As we stepped off, our spines tingling with the massive vibration of a Harley after a fast run, Scott happened to notice us shrugging off our leathers. He did a classic double-take, then called the boys and girls.

The whole team was still there, doing the jobs they'd had on the day we set out for the West. All the weeks, hours and minutes we'd been away, grey-haired, handsome Tim had been dispensing his well-organised spares, the girl with the best eyes in America had been marketing the gear, Scott had been solving everyone's problems and Gary had been selling bikes. Life for them had carried on at normal speed in those three months.

We felt as though we had passed through a lifetime. As the impromptu party fell to bits late in the evening, I began to evaluate what had really been going on.

Roz and I had ridden 12,000 miles, sipping the honey of the US like humming birds darting from flower to flower. We tasted deep from each bloom as it passed beneath our spoked wings, but it was not always possible to step back and view the garden. This, though, is the traveller's lot. Like many journeys, ours had taught us something about the land but a good deal more about the people who lived in it.

The cost of gasoline is low in the US and the Harley-Davidson holds its value so well that this rite of passage financially set us back less than might be imagined. Gary was so impressed by Betty Boop's performance and general appearance that he bought her back, making a fair deduction for mileage. Roz was gutted to see her go. Despite having had clearance to sell Black Madonna from the local customs right at the outset, I was still considering shipping her back to the UK. She suited me, and a proven bike is something you do not take for granted. But Gary had customers lining up for a clean Heritage, especially one that had survived the desert highways without even a dent in the tank. He made me an offer that was too tempting and, like many a traitor before me, I sold her, walking out with nothing worse than a tear in my eye.

The postscript is that when I returned to England I bought myself a 'classic' British motorcycle, a Triumph Bonneville. It's been around long enough to be given the key of the door and it would blow my Harley away for acceleration, but it doesn't give me the confidence to plan a trip to Scotland, let alone California. As for Roz, she hasn't taken on another bike and she still won't travel on the back of mine. Instead, she drives a Citroen 2CV, almost always with the roof down.

acknowledgements

[1] From *I Feel Like I'm Fixin' to Die*: Country Joe and the Fish, 'The Acid Commercial' (Joyful Wisdom Music Co, 1967)

[2] From *I Feel Like I'm Fixin' to Die*: Country Joe and the Fish 'I Feel Like I'm Fixin' to Die Rag' (Alcatraz Corner Music Co, 1965)

[3] From *At Folsom Prison*: Johnny Cash 'Folsom Prison Blues' (Columbia Music)

[4] From *Ballads and Poems*: John Masefield 'Roadways' (Heinemann, 1923)

[5] From *Elite Hotel*: Emmylou Harris 'Satan's Jewel Crown' (Sony Tree Pub. Co., 1983)

[6] From *Pioneer Women*, Joanna L. Stratton (Simon and Schuster, 1981)

[7] *Ibid*

[8] From *Bury My Heart at Wounded Knee*, Dee Brown (Vintage, 1987)

[9] *Ibid*

[10] From *Skiffle Sensation*: Lonnie Donegan, 'Grand Coulee Dam' (Ludlow Music Inc/TRO Essex Music Limited)

[11] *Ibid*

[12] *Ibid*

Trans-Siberia
Inside the Grey Area

Paddy Linehan

'...*Mapmakers in general display a distinct prejudice. Europe is planted on the middle of the pages and coloured vibrantly; pinks, blues and duck-egg greens. But when you venture East, things turn spooky. Colours become muddy, borders doubtful and names rare...*'

It all started in the mind of a child with the desire to travel. Siberia was full of darkness, struggle, cold and desperation.

Years later, haunted by a shadowy image that he just can't shake off, Paddy Linehan decides to pursue his Siberian dream. He learns to think on his feet and travels 'like a Russian' in a culture struggling with post-Soviet, post-Communist flux.

Traditional post-bath beatings, bonding with a love-sick Siberian boy, bizarre occurrences on the 44A Trans-Siberian train: this is an extraordinary and very human journey.

'...*very cold and very far...*' You almost want to go there yourself. Almost.

Paperback

Espresso with the Headhunters
A Journey through the Jungles of Borneo

John Wassner

The indigenous people of Borneo use blowpipes and poisoned arrows. They wear 'pan handle' haircuts, live in communal dwellings and some tribes have mastered the art of making themselves 'invisible' in the jungle. But above all, they have a reputation as fearsome headhunters.

Having cast aside his Armani jeans and bought up all the jungle equipment he could find, John Wassner sets off to experience and explore the wilds of Borneo, one of the last relatively unknown places on earth. His only concern: whether he would be able to find a decent cup of espresso in the jungle. Life in the wilderness, however, turns out to be quite agreeable – with wonderful (if unusual) food, all-night longhouse parties, drunken natives and breathtaking surroundings.

Interspersed with lively descriptions of places and people are anecdotes, glimpses of history, local legends, occasional lies and healthy doses of humour.

Paperback

For a current publishing catalogue
and full listing of Summersdale travel books,
visit our website:

www.summersdale.com

Suffer from wanderlust? Interested in
adventure? Planning to take off?

Go travel or read travel.
We've got everything packed into

www.travel-bookshop.com